215
Days
in the Life of
an
American Ambassador

(Diary Notes from Sofia, Bulgaria)

Martin F. Herz

Foreword by Peter F. Krogh

**School of Foreign Service
Georgetown University
Washington, D.C.**

Library of Congress Cataloging in Publication Data

Herz, Martin Florian, 1917–
   215 day in the life of an American ambassador.

   Includes index.
   1. Herz, Martin Florian, 1917–   . 2. United
States—Foreign relations—Bulgaria. 3. Bulgaria—
Foreign relations—United States. 4. Ambassadors—
United States—Biography. 5. Ambassadors—Bulgaria—
Biography. I. Title. II. Title: Two hundred fifteen
days in the life of an American ambassador.
E840.8.H47A33   327.2′092′4   81–13346
ISBN 0–934742–12–X   AACR2

School of Foreign Service
Georgetown Universtiy
Washington, D.C. 20057

CONTENTS

iii

Foreword

Peter F. Krogh
Dean, School of Foreign Service

For the life of me, I cannot understand why Ambassador Herz insists on speaking of his assignment to Bulgaria as "unimportant." I tried several times, without avail, to persuade him to change this adjective, pointing out that he himself has written (in an article on ambassadorships in the *Foreign Service Journal*) that "nowadays there are no unimportant posts in which an incompetent ambassador can be tucked away, for even seemingly quiet, out-of-the-way countries can erupt suddenly into importance, perhaps in a regional context, and decisions may have to be made on the spot which an inexperienced incumbent will find very difficult."

Well, Martin Herz can be a stubborn man, as readers of this account of his tenure as ambassador in Sofia will soon learn. He is now the Director of Studies of our Institute for the Study of Diplomacy, and in that capacity has written and edited publications that deal with the qualifications and duties of ambassadors. He would probably be among the first to acknowledge that he himself is quite untypical. He is certainly not the silky-smooth, slightly bland, overly polished person who used to be the prototype. He loves controversy, and with this book he will no doubt contribute his share of it.

"Nothing important happens," he says about his post of assignment. But there are literally hundreds of interesting things, and a preponderant share of useful ones, that we can learn from his account of 215 days of his life in Sofia. Not all of his diary entries deal with things that happened there. In fact, as a member of our faculty remarked upon reading the book in draft: It isn't really about being an American ambassador in Bulgaria. It is about

ix

being a public servant of the United States, about problems encountered in a large organization, about the price paid by the inner man; and it gives us also quite a few insights into East-West relations and into the mind of someone devoted to the principle of professionalism in foreign affairs. He has things to say about many matters other than Bulgarian-American relations.

I think Martin Herz's conception of the role of an American diplomat is well expressed early in his book when he records the following:

> There is a mistaken idea in some people's minds that being a diplomat means that you have to make special efforts to be popular. Diplomacy is a profession, and its job is to get certain things done. If they are best accomplished by being nice, then it is best for a diplomat to be nice. But if they are best accomplished by being unpleasant, then it is best for a diplomat to be unpleasant. Not too often, of course. A diplomat can quickly wear out his welcome if he is petulant and unreasonable, if he is vain, overbearing or fatuous. But if he can't be tough, he won't be effective.

When he joined the faculty of Georgetown University, I had known him only by reputation—as someone who was reading widely and who had published several high-quality books on foreign affairs, a professional who had worked his way up in the Foreign Service from the very bottom, someone who combined the qualities of an intellectual with those of a professional diplomat. But my colleagues and I were in for some surprises.

He could be smooth as silk if he wanted to, but when he encountered the first obstacle in an assignment I had given him, he "rolled up the heavy artillery" (his words) and pulverized the opposition. He said it was necessary. Perhaps it was. He obviously doesn't suffer fools gladly. If he thinks something should be done, and if he encounters obstacles that cannot be circumvented, he flattens them. What surprised me, and keeps surprising me, is that a man with those characteristics can also be so sensitive to nuances in human relationships, so given to self-doubt himself on occasion, and so honest about his own emotions. One poignant moment in his account of 215 days in Sofia is when he receives a reprimand from the Secretary of State—and is surprised, and dismayed, that he really doesn't much care what the Secretary of State thinks of him: He is much more concerned about the good opinion of his

x

peers in the Foreign Service. And he is disconcerted by his own reaction.

The interesting and instructive features of this book can be described under three headings: Things that relate specifically to his tenure in Bulgaria; views about diplomacy in general and East-West relations in particular; and insights into the workings of American diplomacy—its strengths and weaknesses, usually illustrated by things that happened or failed to happen. About Bulgaria we learn much through anecdotes, historical sidelights, and events: The great differences among the Eastern European countries, the importance of history and how it is sometimes rewritten, the utility (to the Communists) of "front organizations," the poignant subject of divided families and how it is dealt with painstakingly by an embassy.

On the way, we encounter fascinating American visitors: Barbara Tuchman, the historian; Daniel Lerner, the sociologist; Daniel Boorstin, the Librarian of Congress; and Zubin Mehta, the conductor. The visit of the Los Angeles Philharmonic Orchestra (LAPO) provides a high point in the artistic field and a dubious "happening" politically—how the orchestra faced down the Sofia police is an interesting but troubling chapter in our cultural diplomacy. And again we find the author, honest to a fault, marveling how wrong he would have been if asked to predict the outcome of the "LAPO incident." He shows, in any case, how the damage from the incident was minimized in a case study of day-to-day diplomacy at work.

On a more general plane, we have case studies of the importance of precision in diplomacy—but also learn why, in policy statements, it may be equally important to leave some doubt about what we will *not* do. The author explains why in foreign affairs telling the whole truth may sometimes detract from, rather than add to, credibility—because the full truth will simply not be believed. He discusses the importance of confidentiality in internal policy disagreements, and why this results in better policy. We learn about the "Sonnenfeldt Doctrine" from someone who was present when it is supposed to have been enunciated, and are given food for thought about how governments best communicate with each other—whether through the ambassador of country X in Washington or through the American ambassador to country X. Am-

xi

bassador Herz also discusses two subjects on which he has subsequently written or edited separate books: The pessimism of George Kennan, and the problem of the interaction between the media and foreign policy.

With regard to the workings of American foreign policy machinery, we have a case study of difficult communication between an embassy and the USIA (now International Communication Agency); we learn how information is extracted from seemingly bland and unproductive exchanges with other diplomats; we read, on the basis of concrete examples, what makes people move up—and down—in a bureaucracy, about the agony of waiting for senior assignments which never come, and about the importance of what Herz calls "non-substantive diplomacy," an activity the U.S. seems to ignore and in which the Communist countries are past masters.

As so often, the whole is more than the sum of the parts: What emerges is a surprisingly rich tableau of life as ambassador to an "unimportant" country which we find entails difficult and important work for many people in a busy embassy. The casual mention of the agenda of a staff meeting gives an idea of the problems that need to be solved, the environment to which one must adapt, the kind of people that have to be dealt with. An offhand remark about the difficulties experienced by wives in a hardship post gives an indication of further problems that are far below the surface. All in all, we gain insights not only about the American Embassy in Bulgaria but about the life of a hard-working diplomat, his personal and professional frustrations, and how his life is a never-ending learning process.

Someone who has learned a lot can also teach a lot. We at Georgetown University are now the beneficiaries of the author's experiences during a lifetime in American diplomacy, of which the present volume affords a highly personal and instructive sampling.

1

Ready, Set, Go! Why this is not really a diary. What the author is not. Reflections on a trip to Gabrovo, where the President received a delirious welcome. A little bit of Bulgarian history: Why Bulgarians like Russians.

I've decided to keep a diary because I think that what I am doing here as Ambassador to Bulgaria is interesting, even though no earth-shaking events are taking place. It is the *job* that is interesting, and my purpose will be to show what my work consists of. (Horrors! A dangling preposition! What will readers think?) And since there is no better time to start than right now, I am starting it today, on July 17, 1976. I promise myself two things: I will record not only what is happening here but also what I think about happenings elsewhere that have relevance to my job as Ambassador to Bulgaria; and I promise to include things about myself that I'm not particularly proud about, if they happen during this period and have to do with my position or my work; and I will stop not with some gigantic climax but when I have about as many pages as it takes to make a small book. As it happens, a new administration will come into office about half a year from now. Whether it is a second Ford or a Carter administration, my time in Bulgaria will then be just about up, and I will probably leave a few weeks afterwards; so the title of the book is already chosen. It remains to discipline myself to set down periodically—and candidly—what is happening.

And already I can see that I'm off on the wrong foot, for my remark about leaving Sofia soon after the new administration comes into office may lead you to suppose that I am one of those moneybags or other amateur diplomats, a political appointee who owes his job to services of a non-diplomatic kind that he has performed for the incumbent administration. Nothing could be further from the truth, and I will no doubt have some things to say in my diary on the subject of political appointees. I am a career man

1

who worked his way up from the bottom, rung by painful rung, to his present position. I have nothing to do with American domestic politics—which does not, however, prevent me from expressing strong opinions also on that subject when it has something to do with my work as a diplomat. I am proud to be a career Foreign Service officer, and I owe my ambassadorial position, unimportant as it may be, to merit and not to any political connection. So here we go—my first entry.

—0—

July 17, 1976. Back from Gabrovo, and a desk piled high with papers. The memorandum about Professor Halpern has not been found, and our reply to Congressman Conte is overdue; no news from Damyanov about the cultural agreement; a mealy-mouthed letter from the State Department about the Thracian exhibit; and an inadequate first draft about the matter of overstaffing in the defense attache's office. I shall have to work late this afternoon. But first I want to set down some impressions of the Gabrovo trip.

The chief of state, Todor Zhivkov (First Secretary of the Communist Party and Chairman of the Council of State of the People's Republic ot Bulgaria) had invited all "chiefs of diplomatic missions accredited to Bulgaria" to what is called the "annual outing." Two years ago it took place on a ship in the Black Sea. Last year it was at Pravets, the native village of the country's number one, where we were entertained in a magnificent silk-lined pleasure dome erected on an artificial lake. This year it was in Gabrovo, an industrial town in the Balkan range.

A jet plane of Balkan Air took us from Sofia to what must normally be a military airfield at Gorna Oryakhovitsa. The field, completely modern, was bare of planes—except for a little flivver near where we landed. We were taken from there by bus via the old imperial Bulgarian capital of Veliki Turnovo, first to a charming reconstructed old Bulgarian village named Bozhentsi where we were greeted by Zhivkov and a group of party leaders and ministers of the government. The group included 51 ambassadors and wives, some only accredited to Sofia without residing there, such as the Cypriot ambassador, Mr. Kranidiotis, who resides in Athens, and the Mexican ambassador, Sr. Cantu Medina, who resides in Bucharest.

Each of us was greeted individually by Comrade Zhivkov and then we were taken on a tour through the village. The atmosphere at first was a bit stiff. The village is charming and would be even more so if there weren't phony exhibits of old craftsmen's shops; for Bozhentsi—in contrast to the "museum" village Etera, which we visited later that day—is inhabited by people and has a real life of its own. In fact, it is a highly desirable summer residence for privileged artists and intellectuals. The atmosphere, it was said, is especially conducive to artistic creation. As one of the visiting diplomats remarked, the thought of losing the privilege of living in such a delightful summer colony (free, of course) must indeed be conducive to artistic creation of the kind desired by the authorities.

After the tour, we returned to the village square to find local (or perhaps specially imported) youths and maidens dancing Bulgarian folk dances in their colorful costumes. Refreshments were served, and the atmosphere became more relaxed. We were encouraged to join the *khoro* line, a chain dance with a rhythmn of one-two-three, one-two-three, one-two. One moves to the right at the one-two movement, crossing the left foot over the right. Many pictures were taken by some of the diplomats and official photographers. Then Zhivkov himself joined the *khoro* line.

A slight drizzle failed to dampen the growing enthusiam. A few ambassadors joined the line, including myself, but none of the ladies could be persuaded. The foreign minister was surprisingly awkward in executing the steps of this popular dance. After a while the dancing broke up and the guests embarked in the four buses to which they had been individually assigned, finding that the party functionaries and ministers had distributed themselves among them, to improve the contact between hosts and guests. Zhivkov himself preceded us in his limousine. We noticed that the road had been cleared of all traffic for our cavalcade.

The streets of Gabrovo were lined with people, many of them waving flags and cheering; and on the main square a multitude awaited us. There were special spaces where uniformed children cheered under the supervision of their teachers. There were rhythmic shouts of "Beh-Kah-Peh" for BKP, the initials of the *Balgarska Kommunistichestka Partiya*, and also "KPSS" which stands for "Kommunistitchka Partiya Sovietsky Soyuz". The BKP and CP-USSR are, after all, closely united. A military band was playing, and the commanding officer of an honor guard shouted his report to Zhivkov, about-faced smartly, proceeded to front-and-center, and ordered the troops to present arms.

Elisabeth tugged at my sleeve. "Have you seen the children with the machine guns?" she asked. I had overlooked them. There they were, in front of the monument to fallen heroes of the resistance, guarding a sacred flame that flickered yellow between two marble slabs; one boy and one girl, clad in blue Komsomol uniforms with bright red neckerchiefs, each of them holding a sub-machine gun across the chest. "It turns my stomach every time I see this sort of thing," said my wife, referring no doubt to her experience in Vienna when she had resisted being recruited into the *Bund Deutscher Mädchen*.

After the obligatory lecture about the accomplishments of Gabrovo and the obligatory paeans of praise to the wise leadership of the party under the enlightened guidance of Todor Zhivkov, we embarked again; and as we moved through the streets of Gabrovo we had a better chance to look into the faces of the people cheering the buses. As it happened, Comrade Zhivkov was sitting in the front of our bus, and I was sitting on the same side. It seemed to me that while people could be ordered into the streets and could be ordered to cheer, they could hardly be ordered to look so enthusiastic.

As some of them, especially women, caught sight of number one, they not only cheered but grinned broadly and in some cases had excitedly enthusiastic or serenely beatific expressions on their faces. I remarked about this later to the ambassador of an Asian country whom I have always found to be very perceptive in his observations about Bulgaria. There is no doubt, he said, that Zhivkov and the BKP would "win the first free election" if one were held today.

Well, how about the second one? Ah, there's the rub. It is of course all highly hypothetical, for the very idea of free elections is totally outlandish and inconceivable in the present totalitarian environment in Bulgaria. But even if by some chance an opposition party were allowed to campaign, said my Asian colleague, he thought at first a majority of people would give their votes to Zhivkov as someone whom they basically trusted; and to the Communist Party as a known quantity and as a party that had undoubtedly done also many good things for the country. But if an opposition party were then allowed to sit in parliament and to criticize the government, and if it were able to get its views before the people through the public media, the initial majority of perhaps sixty percent would decline rather quickly, my colleague thought.

I tend to agree with him that Bulgaria is perhaps the only country in Eastern Europe where in free elections the Communist Party would have a good chance of maintaining itself in power—at least initially. There are reasons for this, and I will discuss them later. But, as I pointed out to my Asian colleague, when one speaks of free elections one has to assume also that the opposition would be allowed to organize itself and to call attention to all the injustices and mistakes and lies that have been perpetrated or committed in recent years.

When the pent-up truth and grievances are thus allowed to explode, when all the skeletons in the regime's closets are freely paraded all of a sudden, the reaction of the people may not be so predictable after all, I suggested. One would also have to assume that new leadership personalities would emerge; and, worst of all for the regime, that suddenly it would be permissible to ridicule many of the sacred cows that have been venerated, rather unwillingly, over the years. Still, I said to my colleague, he probably was right. Zhivkov is not seen as an oppressor by the mass of his people, nor as a foreign agent, even if he depends on the Soviet Union for his position. He has elements of a father figure. Even if he is not loved, he is accepted; and he and his party are probably given credit for the enormous economic development of the country since the Communists took it over thirty years ago.

Later, when I suggested this line of reasoning to another ambassador, drawing his attention especially to the smiling faces along the streets in Gabrovo, he dismissed this curtly: "Ever since Nuremberg in 1933, we know how those things are done," he said. Naturally, totalitarian regimes inspire enthusiasm and loyalty in *some* of their people, and the regimes arrange things in such a way that those enthusiasms and loyalties are made to seem representative of all the people. He thought that if the old Agrarian Union were allowed to run in a truly free election, it would win hands down.

—0—

I have shown what I have written so far to Elisabeth, and she thinks it will be boring to a reader who isn't specifically interested in Bulgaria. There would have to be more dialogue, she said, more life, more excitement, to make this a book of general interest. She is probably right, but my purpose is to write without dramatization about the life of an American ambassador, just for those people who may be interested in the kind of life an American ambassador actually leads; and most American ambassadors lead quite interesting lives, even when they are not assigned to the hot spots which capture headlines in the press at home.

Too often have we been annoyed and disappointed by novels, and even by purported diaries of ambassadors, which tried to present the ambassador in the worst, or in the best light. I shall not try to present myself in any particular light. I am neither the kind of cynical and worldly ambassador whom Morris West pictured in his novel "The Ambassador" which dealt with Vietnam (which I know very well), nor am I the kind of intellectual given to grand generalizations like John Kenneth Galbraith who is a person of great intelligence, conceit and wrong-headedness. There will be no exploits and no glittering epigrams, but some glimpses that give an idea of what an ambassador actually does and thinks about his work. If there is anything I shall try to prove, it will just be that being an American ambassador is *not* particularly glamorous but is hard work, worthwhile and very *interesting*, even in a "dull" post.

Why is this so? Because most of us career officers sit somewhere way out in some godforsaken country and see a corner of the world from several points of view—from the point of view of American security and American economic and other interests; from the point of view of the local government and the local people; and from the point of view of our competitors in the world. Here in Bulgaria we have a ring-side seat with an unobstructed view of the Soviet Union. Sofia is an excellent vantage point from which to observe the workings of CEMA (the economic union of the Eastern European countries), of the Warsaw Pact (their military organization), and of orthodox communist ideology.

It is said, quite wrongly, that Bulgaria is for all intents and purposes part of the Soviet Union. True, there isn't an issue in the United Nations on which Bulgaria doesn't vote exactly as the USSR. Over fifty percent of its trade is with the Soviet Union. Certainly its ideological inspiration comes from there. So do its most vital raw materials and notably its energy and fuels—oil, gas and electricity, the latter two conveyed from Russia across Romania.

But the country has a personality of its own, which is not de-emphasized by the regime, despite the slogan of "ever-closer integration with the Soviet Union." Occasionally a visiting journalist, or one who writes about Bulgaria from the vantage point of Vienna or Belgrade, picks out a quotation of Zhivkov which would make it appear that Bulgaria really wants to become an integral part of the Soviet Union. There are also high officials in the State Department who believe that the country doesn't *want* to be independent. This is not my opinion. I think one has to understand Bulgaria, as one has to understand other countries, in terms of its national history and its national interests.

National history ties the country more closely to Russia than does the national history of any other European country. It was a Russian army, in 1877, which liberated Bulgaria and restored its independence after five hundred years of Turkish domination. Undoubtedly the Russians pursued imperial interests in their fight against the dying Ottoman Empire, the "sick man of Europe" at that time; but it is also true that Bulgarian freedom fighters fought shoulder to shoulder with the Russian armies and that the latter left many dead in Bulgaria—it is said that they lost 200,000 dead in the campaign.

At any rate, there is nothing in the history of Bulgarian-Russian relations to compare with the centuries-old rivalry, division and domination experienced for instance by the Poles; or the clash between nationalism and Communist allegiance experienced by the Yugoslavs after World War II; or the amputations suffered by Romania after it was "liberated" by the Russians; let alone the invasions and occupations suffered by Hungary in 1956 and Czechoslovakia in 1968. Sofia is the only communist capital in Europe which has the statue of a Russian czar in the center of the city—in this case Alexander II who sent his armies to eject the Turks from Bulgaria.

And there are no Russian troops here in Bulgaria, as there are in Poland, East Germany, Czechoslovakia and Hungary. True, there are also no Russian troops in Romania, but that is because the Romanian government had wanted to keep them out. Here in Bulgaria, if the Russians wished to station troops in some crisis situation, they would probably be welcomed or at least well tolerated. There is no memory here of the depredations that took place in other countries "liberated" by the Red Army at the end of World War II.

And economically, the country has had many benefits from its close association with the Soviet Union. Most of its industry, inefficient as it may be, has been built with Soviet help. Oil, electricity and gas come from the USSR, as do both iron ore and coking coal for its steel industry, and a host of other raw materials. As Zhivkov once remarked with his characteristic jocularity, "You might say that Russia is a Bulgarian colony. We export to the USSR all the manufactured goods that we cannot sell for hard currency in the West; and the Soviet Union delivers to us cheap raw materials."

A small incident that may show how the Russians are looked upon here: This story was told by the foreign-born wife of one of our officers. She was shopping in a food store one day, wearing a kerchief over her head (perhaps concealing her American curlers). When she asked for a certain item that was in short supply, the saleswoman asked her if she was Russian. Our lady didn't speak Bulgarian very well, so she just made an ambiguous motion with her head which the saleswoman must have understood as affirmative. (In Bulgaria, as in the Middle East, a shaking of the head can denote assent.) Then the saleswoman, obviously thinking that our lady was Russian, took her to the back of the store and gave her the pick of the things available there. The story itself may not be important, but surely no Russian woman is apt to receive preferential treatment in a food store in Prague or Budapest. . .

So I think that while the government here is a hard one and far from democratic, while it is so closely integrated with the Soviet Union that it is hard to see the country liberating itself economically from that connection in the foreseeable future, Bulgaria does have a national culture and a national consciousness of its own— even while it is far more pro-Russian than any other country in Europe, and for reasons both historical and economic.

Yes, but how about the Communist ideology? It is very much present here, but it is in my opinion not the principal determinant of Bulgarian policy. Experts are arguing constantly about how important ideology is in the Communist countries. My friend

Sidney Hook has written with great perceptiveness: "Because ideology is not everything, it is not nothing, a proposition that holds for almost all societies. But for Communist countries ideology is far from nothing. It is often a decisive factor, neglect of which by those whom Communist nations oppose may result in disaster—to those who neglect it."

I would agree with everything in that passage, except the word decisive. Under certain circumstances ideology may be decisive, but usually the Communist regimes are pragmatists first. They don't like to take risks. But when there are low-risk opportunities to push ahead on the ideological front, they can be counted upon to do just that. What do I mean by "pushing ahead on the ideological front"? Such things as supporting the MPLA in Angola, or supporting the Arabs against "imperialist" Israel, or supporting the "developing countries" against the United States. And supporting the Communist party in Portugal, supporting Castro in Latin America, or in Angola and Mozambique against South Africa. Or supporting North Korea against South Korea— all in the name of the battle against "imperialism," by which they understand first and foremost the United States of America.

—0—

Another glimpse of our visit to Gabrovo with the President. In the afternoon we were taken, in buses again of course, to a raspberry plantation. The weather was threatening, but it did not yet rain when we alighted from the buses. We walked up a country road, and in the distance one could hear young men and women singing lovely Bulgarian songs.

These traditional songs, which have a tendency to get on one's nerves when one has heard them very often, always make an excellent first impression. The voices, especially those of the girls, are pressed artificially so that they come out with deliberate shrillness. This is a convention, and some people say it goes back to the Turkish occupation. At any rate according to the standard of beauty of that particular form of singing, a deliberate cutting edge to the voice makes it lovelier. From a distance the mingled male and female voices, perhaps muted a little, were delightful.

The party approached the raspberry plantation, and one could see masses of raspberries piled in baskets on the right side of our little road. One could also see in the distance that the singers had concealed themselves behind branches and boughs, and obviously would cast these aside and come dancing toward us, or arrange themselves on each side of the road, as our party advanced.

President Zhivkov was walking with party officials and with some diplomats, preceded by photographers who were looking for action shots that would show the leader in his jovial mood mingling with the people, or with diplomats, or in serious discourse with the local officials. Then we saw the workers in the plantation. They were all youngsters clad in light blue uniforms, with light blue berets, somewhat like those of the United Nations peacekeeping forces that I had seen in Cyprus. Some of them were lining the road, and others came running. There was exultation on their faces, or mischievousness.

Suddenly the singing ahead stopped, and all the uniformed young people on the side of the road started shouting in unison, Beh Kah Peh (B.K.P.), the initials of the Bulgarian Communist Party. Again and again, they shouted B.K.P., and the lovely atmosphere of folkloric color was broken by a party demonstration. And it started to rain. (The Protocol office had fifty umbrellas ready at the place where Zhivkov and his entourage were greeted with the customary speech, plus raspberries and wine.)

Beh Kah Peh, B.K.P., whenever I hear voices in unison shouting those initials I shall now think of a slow drizzling rain and raspberry fields and umbrellas and buses.

The Bulgarians, who have a sense of humor, have their own interpretation of the letters B.K.P. They say they stand for Brezhnev, Kosygin and Podgorny.

My wife claims that even in the raspberry fields the youngsters (who were on "brigade" duty, working almost without pay to bring in the harvest) were shouting not only B.K.P. but also K.P.S.S. In Bulgaria one often sees graffiti on the walls extolling both parties equally—of course, "graffiti" are put on walls by the authorities and not by enemies of the establishment. They are very carefully painted. Many of the slogans also appear in the form of streamers or placards or billboards. Of course "Long Live the K.P.S.S." doesn't look that way in Cyrillic letters. It looks like this: СЛАВА КПСС!

2

First political jokes. The Fourth of July opportunity, how it was almost muffed, and how an ambassador makes himself unpopular in Washington. About the "difference between a diplomat and a lady"—and what they have in common.

July 23. At one of many boring diplomatic dinner parties we have to attend, a high Bulgarian official was in a story-telling mood the other evening and told these stories. By way of explaining the kinds of stories they were, he said to another Bulgarian that he "had heard them over radio Yerevan"—that mythical radio station in the Caucasus to which Russians attribute jokes about their regime. Both stories, he said, are circulating in the Soviet Union.

Will there be money under communism when that final stage is reached? Yes, say the opportunists. No, say the dogmatists. And the dialecticians say very simply, "some will have money, others not." Shouts of laughter from the Bulgarians—all of whom were trusted members of the regime. They know that communism hasn't ended inequality, and that it isn't apt to even when its more "perfect" stage is reached.

The other story is about the five greatest thinkers of the world. Moses, the story goes, said that everything comes from the Word, i.e., from the mind—and the story-teller pointed to his forehead. Jesus said that everything comes from the heart (with hand pointing to the heart). Marx has said everything is decided by the stomach (pointing again). Freud said it all comes from an area further down. But Einstein, he concluded this story, has taught us that "everything is relative."

While there was smirking when this story was told—and a rather prim reluctance to point to the area of the body which according to Freud determines most of our actions, the interesting thing was the reaction to the idea that everything is relative. Marx may have preached a materialist interpretation of history and of our present-

11

day lives, but those who laughed at the story seemed, at least to me, to recognize that there is more wisdom in a view that distributes the motivations among head, heart, stomach and genitals. But who could say this in public in this country?

—0—

On July 5, just before our Bicentennial reception (which we did not hold July 4 because that was a Sunday), Foreign Minister Mladenov urgently called me to the Ministry and told me three things: that the Bulgarian government had decided to have a number of high-ranking party and government officials attend our reception; that it wished me to transmit a "special" greeting to the U.S. government and people on the occasion of our bicentennial; and, most important, that it had been decided to do something special for us.

That special thing, he went on to say, was the offer of "five to ten minutes" of prime time on Bulgarian television to allow me to speak directly to the Bulgarian people. He said BTV was standing by and would be glad to record my address either at the residence, in their studios, or elsewhere, and they would also be available if desired to work with me in preparing the remarks. He noted that the provision of prime time, just after the evening news broadcast, was something that had up to then been accorded only to the Soviet ambassador. I expressed deep appreciation and made a counter-proposal.

I said there really wasn't enough time to prepare something really excellent for broadcast that same day, and that in any event the Bulgarian audience would perhaps not find it terribly interesting to see the face of the American ambassador on their television screens during ten minutes. However, I could make some brief remarks in Bulgarian which might be followed by footage taken from available films, showing how people live and work and play in America, and perhaps some scenes of our bicentennial celebrations. The minister agreed to this and said he would notify BTV immediately to cooperate with us on such a brief program, to be introduced by myself. I said we on our part could doubtless obtain some film footage from Washington; and since July 4 had already passed, a brief delay would not be fatal. After all, the whole of 1976 is our bicentennial year.

Thereby began a hassle between the embassy and Washington which is typical of the worst of the musclebound bureaucracy in the U.S. Information Agency (now International Communication Agency.) I am aware that in writing this I am expressing no more than the usual frustration of America's representatives in foreign countries—indeed, of diplomats everywhere—about the seeming insensitivity or lack of understanding of their home offices. Doubtless the matter looks different from the Washington perspective; but I can give only our side of the matter since Washington has been not only singularly obtuse in its reactions, but also in explaining the reasons for that obtuseness.

But before going into the story of the diplomatic hassle I should give a bit of background to the generous sentiments expressed by the foreign minister. First, I had on more than one occasion expressed my disappointment that Bulgarian television had during our bicentennial year showed only the most tendentious views of the United States. It had shown a broadcast, for instance, that began with the dictum attributed (falsely, I believe) to De Gaulle that "America is the only country in the history of the world that went from barbarism to decadence without having passed through the stage of civilization." And from that point it went downward, showing pictures of bums on skid row, sex shows (of course only the marquees) on Broadway, blacks being clubbed by the police, breadlines (of the early thirties, no doubt, but what Bulgarian would understand that?), and by contrast the pleasure domes of the idle rich and the soulless concrete buildings and concrete highways symbolizing the aridity and hypertrophy of our national life. I had talked about this even with the chief of state when I had called on him a few months ago before going on leave. Perhaps, I thought, my complaints were bearing some fruit at last.

When we received the *International Herald Tribune* a few days later from Paris, however, we noted that the Soviet Government on July 4 had offered time on Moscow TV to my colleague there, and he had given a sober speech about the state of American-Soviet relations (including the astute statement that despite differences between the two countries they were the only two major powers that had never in their entire history been at war with each other). When I mentioned to a Bulgarian the apparent coincidence that the offer of TV time to me on July 5 had come just after the American ambassador in Moscow had addressed a Soviet audience, that friend remarked dryly: "We here often open our umbrellas when it rains in Moscow." (I did not fail, of course, to point silently to the walls of the residence to recall to that friend that our conversation was probably being picked up by hidden microphones.)

Another aspect of the situation was that Zhivkov's son-in-law, Ivan Slavkov, had been invited by us to come to the United States two years ago in his capacity of Deputy head of Bulgarian radio and TV; and he and a Bulgarian technician had taken film footage there which they displayed on Bulgarian TV in several broadcasts. These had consisted largely of unfavorable views of the U.S., interviews with Americans in and out of government who were critical of our system or of our policies, all this accompanied by talk about the domination of the military-industrial complex, the plight of the minorities, the problems of inflation and unemployment, and the atrocities committed by our aggressive imperialism in Vietnam and elsewhere.

However one may think about those things, I had pointed out, and some of them are at least partly true, they do not constitute even a faintly informative picture of the United States. One may like America or dislike it, but there is no doubt that it is an important country; and so it should be of interest to the Bulgarian government to see its people given at least a modicum of objectivity in *describing* it, even if it is to be denounced afterward. The stultification of public opinion by such propaganda was not only unfriendly but unwise and probably also ineffective. Would it not be better, especially during our bicentennial year. to give a moderately rounded picture of our country—even while, if it has to be, describing our political and economic system in terms required by the communist ideology?

So I cabled Washington that the provision of ten minutes of prime time to show something about America was in the nature of a minor breakthrough, and we should move quickly to exploit it. The first message from USIA was full of gung-ho spirit. They had already started to research their files for scenes that could be used in accordance with our suggestions. When did we think the film was needed? They invited us to set a deadline.

It was at that point that Harvey Feldman, my deputy, remarked that he didn't really think that USIA could produce a film that would do us credit. He knew their bureaucracy. True, they had turned out some excellent films in the past (for instance, "Years of Lightning, Day of Drums" about the presidency and death of John F. Kennedy), but their most talented people had left and we should not put too much hope in their abilities. I thought Harvey was exaggerating. In any case, we did have an opportunity and it was now up to us to try our best to see that something proper came out of Washington to take advantage of it. Thinking that putting together ten minutes' worth of movie footage from available films would not take very long if USIA gave the project priority, I suggested a deadline of ten days.

The first sign of trouble was Washington's gleeful response that under the conditions of such a tight deadline, the project had had to be abandoned. They were sending us instead a film called "Morning, Noon and Night" which they thought would fill our needs adequately. Naturally I went back immediately and said in another telegram that if ten days were not enough, and since the Information Agency had already expended so much time in "researching their files" we would appreciate their pursuing the project even if it took a little longer. Meanwhile we would be glad to look at "Morning, Noon and Night" but it didn't seem to be what we had requested. One never knows with whom one is actually dealing in exchanging such telegrams, but from our perspective in Sofia we thought that if the recipients of our message were men or women of good faith, and if they understood the political importance of our project, they would now go to work and let us know when it could be finished. But we were wrong.

"Upon receipt of reftel A," the next USIA message informed us, "further extensive review of footage and discussion with acquisitions, production, planning and program divisions convinced us it would not be possible to consolidate in short film a credible story from available existing footage. There is not enough compatible material to develop a film that would not look like patchwork." They urged us to let them know about "Morning, Noon and

Night". We screened it immediately upon its arrival here and found it to be corn meal mush, nothing even remotely resembling what we had in mind and what would do us credit in what might be a one-time opportunity to show millions of Bulgarians something about the United States as it really is.

It is always good in diplomacy to claim that there is a "misunderstanding" even when one strongly suspects that one understands only too well the intentions of the other side; for by spelling out those intentions as one understands them one is apt to harden them. It is better to offer a line of retreat in case the position of the other side has not yet hardened too much. So we went back and said with pretended cheerfulness that we hadn't really meant to call for a coherent "story"; and since we could clear up that misunderstanding and would in fact be quite pleased to receive discontinuous material (showing perhaps the "tall ships" in New York, some scenes of American cities, and pictures of how people live and work etc.), we trusted they could get on with the job without worrying too much about perfectionism; for in comparison with what Bulgarians had seen of America in previous TV shows our film would no doubt be constructive even if it might look like patchwork to the professionals.

"A woman convinced against her will/Is of the same opinion still." That adage seemed to apply to the bureaucrats who received our message, for they came back saying they were sure we were making a mistake in not using the turkey they had sent us. And so I made a final appeal, "Personal from the Ambassador to Director Keogh," in which I laid out briefly the facts about the problem, the opportunity, the initially gung-ho attitude of his people, and their increasingly negative attitude toward the project, and enlisted his personal cooperation. Director Keogh didn't see my message since he was away on leave; but I got a dusty answer from his deputy, Mr. Kopp, saying they were sure they had given us the best they could. One can imagine a meeting in his office with all the people who had frustrated our efforts here, each of them giving an additional reason why they had been reasonable and we had not. I've attended meetings of that kind in Washington.

It is the ambassador's duty when he thinks he is right not to give in but to raise the issue to still higher authority; but to whom does the Director of USIA report? Not to the Secretary of State, except in matters of foreign policy, and our issue would be regarded as one of operations. But because we don't like to give up when we see an opportunity to tell the American story to an audience which is consistently misinformed about our country, we sent not one but two telegrams a few days later: One, written by Harvey Feldman, sketched out the scenario for a film made up only of film clips from footage he knew to be available, and even suggesting the kinds of shots that might be selected; and the other from me to the Assistant Secretary for European Affairs in the State Department asking him if he would take up the cudgels on our behalf. As of this writing we do not know if there was a higher-level review between Hartman in State and Kopp in USIA; but we did get a message from the latter bureaucracy stating that they were working on our new proposal. How they must hate us there!

There is a mistaken idea in some people's minds that being a diplomat means that you have to make special efforts to be popular. Diplomacy is a profession, and its job is to get certain things done. If they are best accomplished by being nice, then it is best for a diplomat to be nice. But if they are best accomplished by being unpleasant, then it is best for a diplomat to be unpleasant. Not too often, of course. A diplomat can quickly wear out his welcome if he is petulant or unreasonable, if he is vain, overbearing or fatuous. But if he can't be tough, he won't be effective. Nothing is more misplaced than the cliché of the striped-pants "cookie-pusher," the Caspar Milquetoast type of diplomat whom the movies love to depict. American diplomacy has all types of people, but they all know that popularity is not the way by which their effectiveness will be measured.

Once upon a time, when I was little, there was a joke about the difference between a diplomat and a lady. It went like this: "If a diplomat says yes he means maybe, if he says maybe then he means no, and if he says no then he isn't a diplomat. But if a lady says no she means maybe, if she says maybe she means yes, and if she says yes then she isn't a lady." Well, times have changed. Today a woman can say yes and still be a lady, and a Foreign Service officer can say no and still be a diplomat. Only, if you say yes too often as a lady, or no too often as a diplomat, some questions may arise whether you are really what you pretend to be.

About a week after I wrote the above, we got a message to the effect that USIA had scheduled our ten-minute film for production, that they had assigned people to procuring the footage, and that they would have it ready by a certain date. Immediately I sent effusive thanks to Keogh (who knows, perhaps upon returning from leave he did read my telegram?) and to Hartman (who may or may not have been involved on our side). It would have been nice to receive a letter from our desk about what actually happened, but the Bulgaria desk is manned by someone who doesn't know how to say yes, no, or maybe. For the most part he says nothing at all. And because Bulgaria ranks low in the priorities of the Bureau, he gets away with it.

(Yes, we got the film eventually. See future diary entries.)

3

First doubts about a future President. Introduction to the mysteries of the Bulgarian press. Ideological mumbo-jumbo? They're telling us what they think about the U.S. and about what "majority rule" means to Communists.

July 27. At yet another one of the endless dinner parties which people outside the diplomatic corps think of as "glittering"— twenty people along the table, with candles and gleaming crystal, and butlers silently serving, but often deadly in the quality of conversation—I heard one good story, among dreadfully boring exchanges of nullities; and it came from one of the more jaded participants at the affair, who must have told it many times before. But it was new to me.

There are two types of diplomats, he said, optimists and pessimists. And there are two types of people, active ones and passive ones. Consequently there are four basic types of diplomats: The active pessimists are the best; the passive optimists are the next best; and passive pessimists come next—but beware of the last category, for they are surely the worst: the active optimists!

Does my finding this story funny mean that I myself am a pessimist, and that I distrust the active optimists? In diplomacy, yes. But I am writing this under the impression of the criticisms that have been leveled at Henry Kissinger for having made pessimistic remarks about the future of our society if it doesn't pull itself together; and for having, in particular, once given Spengler's hoary "Decline of the West" to Nixon to read. Much is being made of this now, during the election campaign.

(Upon re-reading this two months later, I find that a Duke University political scientist named Barber has classified presidents and presidential candidates in a similar manner, categorizing Ford as "passive positive" and Carter as an "active positive" who narrowly misses being active negative—but here the idea seems to be

19

that any President of the United States has to be forward-looking, with the gift of initiative and the ability to inspire the bureaucracy. I do not believe that the qualifications of the ideal diplomat neces· sarily correspond to those of the ideal president.)

Americans somehow don't seem to be able to conceive that our country could decline and fall, that real catastrophe could overtake us. Somehow the environmentalists and the conservation lobby seem to be able to conceive this better than the politicians—it is the idea of *political* downfall that seems to be inconceivable to most of us. Only in the sense that the possibility of disaster should be constantly in the mind of an accomplished diplomat, do I share the belief that an "active pessimist" is basically the best type for the diplomatic profession.

I am profoundly convinced that the days of "Damn the tor-pedoes, full steam ahead!" went out with the realization that mistakes in foreign policy can affect the very existence of the United States. The times when, as Kissinger put it, "the United States could simply overwhelm its problems with resources" are over. The possibility of failure must always be taken into account, for the price of failure is going up constantly. The gung-ho diplomat, who still on occasion can dazzle his superiors in Washington, has become more of a liability than an asset. And the often-reviled Foreign Service officer ("cookie-pusher") who asks the unwelcome question, "Sir, have you considered all the implica-tions of what you are proposing to do?" has become even more of an asset, though an inconvenient one, than before.

But being an "active pessimist" also implies, at least to me, the kind of foresight that takes into account the consequences of a failure of nerve. It is not enough to eschew adventure; it is also essential to deter the kind of gradual encroachment upon one's own interests that can result in disaster sometime in the future. For this reason I am worried by Mr. Carter's campaign statement that he would "never again get militarily involved in the internal affairs of another country unless our security was directly threatened." Who is to determine when such a threat is direct? In public opinion, such a phrase is probably taken as meaning that we would not fight except where it is *evident* that we ourselves are being threatened. Such an attitude, if translated into policy, could mean opening the door to gradual encroachments.

—0—

This is probably as good a time as any to give you a "newsreel" of the Bulgarian press. In a country where foreigners don't have many opportunities to talk with ordinary citizens, reading the press often provides more questions than answers, but it is good to have the questions.

Here are, first, a few items from Bulgarian correspondents in the United States, and from commentators interpreting what is going on there: "The presidential elections," writes *Pogled*, "are a spectacle that is repeated every fourth year. With its euphoria, its clowning, it is a show of democracy (every American may become President) which is put on for the mass consumer. Actually the nomination of the candidates is according to a strict system of rules and subserviences, which precludes any surprises."

"An ostensible impression of surprise was created in political circles by the success of the Democratic candidate Jimmy Carter," the commentary continues. "But now, when the curtain is being raised, it becomes clear that his disarming smile, his admonitory style, his manifested devotion to the virtues of the 'average' American, conceal not only the features of an ambitious politician, unquestionably gifted with a keen sense of strategy, but also the support of influential representatives of the military-industrial complex, the big oil and gas companies, main groupings of Wall Street and pro-Zionist circles."

In other words, no matter who may be nominated by the Democrats or the Republicans, it is "capital" that is in the driver's seat in America. The people are being fooled by the capitalists into believing that they have a choice. But the powers behind the candidates on both sides are the same.

The newspaper *Trud*, which is read by (or at least issued to) the trade unions in Bulgaria, featured an article about the cooperation between the Mafia and American labor unions. "The interest of the gentlemen from 'cosa nostra' in the labor union organizations is determined by the money and influence which they are in a position to ensure, and these two things in the USA always go hand in hand, the one guarantees the other, and the two together are the dream and ideal not only for the Mafiosi, but also for the so-called average American."

Rabotnichesko Delo, the organ of the BKP, carried an article by Ulyana Popova, in reply to a question (allegedly sent in by a reader) about the status of the Indian population in the USA. "Land of the free, home of the brave," says Ms. Popova, is what the Indians used to call their land. Today, it is said in the article, this land is offering the Indians wretched shacks, poverty, hunger, diseases, and the status of second-class citizens.

The same paper featured prominently the congratulatory telegram sent by President Zhivkov to the conference of non-aligned countries in Colombo. It is worth examining in some detail. Sample passage: "As a result of the change in the correlation of forces to the advantage of peace, democracy, national liberation and socialism, of the principled and consistent policy of the USSR and the other countries of the socialist community, of the efforts of the peoples and all progressive and peace-loving forces, the process of relaxation of international tension has gained ever broader and stronger positions. Peaceful coexistence and cooperation among the countries becomes a prevalent trend in international life."

So far, so good. The progressive and peace-loving forces, which are those of Communism, are advancing everywhere as a result of the "change in the correlation of the forces", i.e. because "the USSR and other countries of the socialist community" are now stronger than the West. The process of détente, called here "relaxation of international tension," allows those Communist countries to gain "ever broader and stronger positions." This is about the same as what Zhivkov said at the Berlin conference of Communist parties just before I started this diary. Then he goes on:

"Along with the constructive changes in the international situation we must not underrate the activity of the aggressive and reactionary imperialist forces which are trying to impede the further easing of tensions, to undermine the results of the Helsinki Conference, encourage the continuation of the arms race, favor the existence of centers of tension and conflict, and support the racist regimes in South Africa."

The "aggressive and reactionary imperialist forces" means the United States, of course.

Or take a commentary by Professor Nikolai Iribadjakov, one of the ideological high priests of the regime, under the headline "General Rules and National Particularities of the Socialist Revolution." This was written with an eye to the current differences of opinion between the Communist Party of the USSR (and Bulgaria, etc.) on the one hand, and certain Communist Parties of the West who claim to be confronting special circumstances requiring special tactics. "Purely national models of socialist revolution and socialist society are impossible from both the logical and the practical point of view," he says, "for if they are different in their essence and if there is no common essence, then how can they be called socialist models?" This is of course circular reasoning, but it is preceded and followed by such a panoply of citations from history and from the founding fathers of Marxism that the reader may think that the professor has demonstrated something scientifically.

Then Prof. Iribadjakov turns to the Paris Commune of 1871 as a concrete example, "as it has been revealed by Marx, Engels and Lenin." He cites a letter of Marx to a Mr. L. Kugelmann in which he said that when it comes to the next attempt at revolution in France, "the bureaucratic and military machinery must not be passed from one hand to another, *but must be broken*, and this is the precondition for any truly popular revolution on the Continent." This, of course, is what the Communists think should have happened after the revolutions in Chile and Portugal. (In Portugal they originally thought that the military machine would deliver the country into their hands, but it turned out that they were mistaken.)

I think the key sentence of the professor's article is the one which says: "Whatever may be the force of the dictatorship of the proletariat in a given country, it is not able alone to resist the pressures of bourgeois reaction from within and without. That is why proletarian internationalism is necessary." Translated from jargon into plain English this means that Communist regimes will always be unpopular and therefore need the power of the Soviet Union to protect them.

How, then, is Communism to be expanded in the world? Here we can learn something from an article entitled "Words and Actions" by Mr. Dimitar Dimitrov, dealing with the social democratic parties of the West. The fact that some of those parties proclaim their adherence to some principles of Marxism, the writer says, is a "positive phenomenon," but it does not change the "reformist" character of those parties (which is of course condemned). The social democrats, Mr. Dimitrov says, "exaggerate" the parliamentary forms of the struggle for socialism, consider Communism the principal enemy of social democracy, enter into alliances with the bourgeoisie, etc.

There follows a quotation from Lenin in which he said scathingly that the social democrats will sign any agreement to preserve their position as leaders of the working class. "They pay lip service to the class struggle only in order to forget it at the most decisive moments, that is to say, after the taking of power by the proletariat when the class struggle must continue until the liquidation of classes." This of course means that after a "revolution" is won by the "working class", whether socialist or Communist, i.e., whether by the ballot box or by force of arms, the real work has only begun; for in Lenin's opinion, and that of the Bulgarian writer, the revolution must be followed immediately by the destruction of the class enemy.

The wisdom of Lenin has once more been wholly confirmed by history, the author concludes. The social democrats pay lip service to the concept of the dictatorship of the proletariat—claims Mr. Dimitrov ignorantly—but they also say that the "authentic" dictatorship of the proletariat must base itself on the approval of the majority, expressed in elections to be organized under the conditions of the social democracy. But "the dictatorship of the proletariat, as Lenin has written in response to such affirmations, would be impossible if the majority of the population isn't constituted by proletarians and semi-proletarians. Kautsky and company tried to falsify this truth, saying that a 'vote of the majority' was required in order that the dictatorship of the proletariat be recognized as fair and equitable."

The Portuguese Communist leader, Alvaro Cunhal, has said the same thing even more clearly—although he didn't say it to the Portuguese but to a foreign journalist, Oriana Fallaci. In an interview published in the *New York Times Magazine* of July 13, 1975, Fallaci asked him whether he could ignore the Socialist Party, which had obtained the largest number of votes in the Portuguese elections. Cunhal's response was:

"But we Communists don't accept the rules of the election game! You err in taking this concept as your starting point. No, no, no: I care nothing for elections. Nothing! Ha, ha! If you believe it's all a question of the percentage of votes obtained by one party or the other, you're laboring under a gross delusion! If you think the Socialist Party with its 40 per cent and the Popular Party with its 27 per cent constitute the majority, you're the victim of a misunderstanding! They aren't the majority."

To which Fallaci asked, with incredulity: "Is arithmetic nothing more than opinion? Are you joking?"

"I'm telling you," Cunhal replied, "that elections have nothing, or very little, to do with the dynamics of revolution. Whether you like it or not, whether the Socialists like it or not, I'm telling you that the election process is but a marginal complement of said dynamics. . .."

Cunhal would be perfectly at home in Bulgaria (and the Soviet Union). The only thing that is unusual about that western Communist leader is that he is so honest about his contempt for majority rule.

The same thought as Cunhal's in somewhat more authoritative fashion, though a bit less candidly, was expressed by Professor Zaradov in *Pravda* in August, 1975 when he condemned the concept of "arithmetical majorities" in a thinly-veiled reference to the situation in Portugal. For that Soviet ideologue, the true majority is the one in which the Communists find themselves, even if it is not "arithmetical." It's a little bit like saying that the head of the table is wherever the Communist Party is going to be sitting even if it should be below the salt.

And as a final exhibit, a recent article in "Narodna Armiya", the organ of the Bulgarian armed forces, written by Wilfred Burchett, the well-known Australian Communist journalist. (Whenever I read his name, I think of a former American prisoner-of-war in Hanoi who told me after his release that he and his colleagues, who had to undergo long interrogatories by this man, used to call him "Willie Birdshit".) Taking off from the recent incident in the Demilitarized Zones between North and South Korea in which two American officers were beaten to death by North Koreans, he writes:

"For the first time in 35 years, the Pentagon is not waging war. To the officers who fritter away their time in the Pentagon's labyrinth, not to mention their bosses of the military-industrial fraternity, the lack of war is an unfortunate situation. The only 'bright' spot, the only steaming battleground on the horizon is South Korea. The fanatics of the Pentagon, who keep their finger on the trigger, argue that after the unexpected insistence of the government of Thailand on an almost complete withdrawal of the American troops from that country, South Korea is the only remaining military bastion of the USA in Asia, the only possible place for a leap to new military adventures on that continent. Due to the flagrant military maneuvers of the United States of America and the South Korean authorities, the threat of a new war in Korea is growing incessantly. In their effort to conceal their plans for precipitating a new war, and in order to divert the world's attention, the US continues to advance the thesis of a 'threat of an invasion of the South.' But realities indicate that the real danger of war in Korea comes from the threat of an invasion of the North. . ."

The papers here have not printed the entire North Korean communique in which it is claimed, among other things, that it was South Korea that invaded North Korea in 1950. Anyone who knows anything about recent history knows that this isn't so, that the war in 1950 was started by North Korea's surprise attack on the South. But who, today, knows much about recent history? When the North Koreans attacked South Korea, an American (or Bulgarian) who today is 40 years old was fourteen. Even in our own country, the history of the post-World War II period is not widely taught in schools and not readily accessible to young people; and the older ones tend to forget.

4

Funny business about microphones. Is the regime paranoid? Are we? Why telling political jokes in public can be bad for your health in Bulgaria. Zhivkov's remark that "there are no political prisoners" in his country.

August 12. I have written earlier that when a Bulgarian friend made a remark about the Communist authorities here, I silently pointed to the wall to remind him that there are listening devices here. Some readers may think this an exaggerated precaution, but we know that microphones are in the strangest places here in Sofia.

For one thing, because of a malfunction of the microphone, we learned that *while the telephone was still ringing*, someone who called our Army Attaché could hear him and his wife talking in their apartment. One could hear the music they were playing on their hi-fi, the wife saying "I'll get it, Tom", etc. The telephone resting on its cradle is one favorite way of recording conversations in a room where every other plausible or implausible place has been checked for microphones.

The embassy "chancery", i.e. the office building, is under tight security protection by a small detachment of the United States Marines. It is checked professionally by security officers from time to time, with electronic gear that could detect most, if not all, electronic surveillance measures. But even so there are certain rooms of the chancery that are regarded as non-secure, simply because we know that the Soviets possess a microphone which can record conversations that take place beyond two walls—in other words, not in the room behind the next wall but in the room beyond that. And since some of our offices are on the sides of the building, which abut neighboring buildings in which Bulgarian listening devices could be operating, we have to resort to special measures to escape detection when there is something we don't want the Bulgarians to know, which isn't very often.

I myself have tried to communicate to the microphones, with one rather startling result—comparable to the remark that was made by a member of Churchill's delegation when he was inspecting his quarters in Yalta during the conference there in 1945. Churchill reports in the volume "Triumph and Tragedy" of his war memoirs that Lord Portal noted privately to his adjutant that the only thing missing in a large glass tank in his villa were some fish. "Two days later a consignment of goldfish arrived."

A friend of ours, the wife of another Western diplomat, was talking on the telephone with her sister in Paris one day, when the connection broke. Having waited for a long time to get her call, and having just gotten to the main point of the conversation, she was frustrated and angry, and instead of hanging up she cussed into the phone about the inefficiency of the Bulgarian telephone service, the urgency of the matter she had wanted to discuss, and shouted that she would make a complaint to the authorities. She was still holding the dead telephone in her hand when she heard a small voice, which said: "You must excuse us, madam, we had to interrupt because we had to change the reel."

Then there is the story of the foreign journalist (not an American) who attended a conference here and was put up, together with other foreign journalists, in neighboring rooms in the Grand Hotel Sofia. After the conference ended and everyone had checked out of the hotel, the man suddenly thought that he had forgotten something in his hotel room. Without checking at the desk, he took the elevator up to his floor and walked down the hall to his former room. All the doors were open, and all the light fixtures in the center of the rooms were lowered to the floor, and each of them was being manipulated by a technician. He never got to his former room, for he was hurriedly ushered back to the elevator. I was given this account by the journalist's ambassador.

Of course, foreign diplomats and journalists are not the only ones who are spied upon. Here is a Bulgarian joke which illustrates the matter. It was told me by one of the rare Bulgarians who dare talk with an American ambassador—during a chance encounter on one of our walks in the countryside.

It seems that in Sofia a man went to a café and ordered a cup of coffee. Because all cafés are very crowded, another man took a seat at his table and also ordered coffee. The two men started to talk, and before long one of them started to tell a political joke, a very mild one. The second man smiled and topped that story with another political joke which was a trifle less mild. Whereupon the first man, emboldened, topped that one with a really rather funny and cutting political joke. Then there was a silence.

Then the second man said to the first one: "Do you know what the difference is between all the other people in this cafe and you?" "No," said the first man, "do tell me." "Well," said the second man, "when all those people have finished their coffee or whatever they are having, they are going home. But you are going with me."

"Is that so?" asked the first man. "Do you want to know what is the difference between you and me? *There isn't any.*"

Usually there is a second or two before those hearing this story understand its humor. It resides in the fact that one *agent provocateur* of the secret police had encountered another. Each had tried to trap the other.

That people get arrested for telling political jokes against the regime was confirmed to me by a colleague who had had a young national of his country in jail in Sofia for some trivial offense. For some reason that foreigner was put in the same cell with some Bulgarian young people. He didn't stay long, but long enough to find out that most of his Bulgarian cellmates were there for telling political jokes.

As I said above, it's a hard regime. The fact that it puts people in jail for telling political jokes doesn't necessarily mean that the regime is unpopular. But it does show that it is very, very careful.

President Zhivkov recently had a long interview with the respected French foreign policy commentator André Fontaine. In that interview he flatly asserted that there are no political prisoners in Bulgaria. He said, according to *Le Monde*: "Once peace is assured one can discuss whether or not to apply the concept of the dictatorship of the proletariat. We have chosen popular democracy. That is the dictatorship of the proletariat. But at present there are no political prisoners in our country."

Perhaps *Le Monde* does not keep files on Bulgaria, and one can understand that Andre Fontaine, who lives in Paris, doesn't spend much time thinking about this faraway Balkan country. But it is too bad that no one reminded him that his own newspaper had carried a report a year ago of the conviction of Boris Arsov Iliev, the alleged leader of an emigre political group opposing the Bulgarian communist regime, who received a sentence of 15 years. At that time *Rabotnichesko Delo* had exulted: "Another enemy of communism dared to raise his hand against the socialist order in our country, and was thrown onto the political garbage heap." Perhaps Mr. Iliev has since then been secretly released—or has passed away? At any rate he is hardly the only political prisoner.

There were questions in the Western press after Iliev's conviction last year how he could have been brought to justice in Bulgaria for acts he had committed abroad, and indeed how he had come into the hands of the Bulgarian authorities. He had last been seen in Copenhagen. The suspicion was voiced, but not pursued, that he might have been kidnapped from Copenhagen and brought to Sofia in one of the 25-ton trailer trucks of the Bulgarian trucking monopoly which does business all over Western Europe and the Middle East, delivering Bulgarian produce and sometimes returning empty to Bulgaria. Those trucks are usually sealed by the customs authorities and not checked as they cross international borders.

5

Some day-by-day activities of an ambassador (among which the case of the abandoned children is first mentioned). Why our tiny embassy has had two full colonels as service attachés. A tug-of-war about that situation.

August 27. What does an American ambassador in a country like Bulgaria do? Here are a few examples of recent activities: We just finished negotiation of a new agreement on cultural, technical and scientific cooperation.—I called on two ministers and the heads of three government offices to publicize the American pavilion at the Plovdiv International Fair at which a number of leading American firms in the fields of chemicals and construction will be exhibiting what they can do.—Received a visit of an American businessman representing a firm that is about to conclude an agreement on construction of a soy bean processing plant, including the importation of soy beans from America and the repurchase of some of the products of the factory.—Held a reception for Bulgarian officials interested in our pavilion at Plovdiv.— Learned that one display area for that pavilion, which had been shipped here from Rome, arrived minus the pictures of America that it was supposed to display, and tried (unsuccessfully) to get pictures for it in time for the opening.—Alerted the Commerce Department to the fact that two American firms had signed contracts for the same piece of equipment for the same Bulgarian purchaser, and made a recommendation regarding the granting of an export license.—Called on a high official of the Bulgarian Foreign Ministry in connection with a very contentious question— Puerto Rico—that was about to be discussed in a committee of the United Nations.—Made a recommendation to Washington in connection with the case of an American of Bulgarian descent who had demonstrated in front of the State Department, pleading for assistance in bringing his children (whom he had to abandon nine

31

years ago when fleeing Bulgaria) to the United States.—Helped to arrange a concert by an American harpsichord player who is willing to visit Sofia in November.—Consulted by telegram with my colleague accredited to NATO about an aspect of implementation of the Final Act of last year's Helsinki conference.—Assisted in a matter involving trafficking in drugs (an area in which the Bulgarian authorities are co-operating in exemplary fashion with our own authorities).—And got myself into a bit of a fight with the Pentagon about a seemingly minor matter. This last story may be of interest because it illustrates how an American ambassador can be steamrollered if he doesn't watch out.

The United States Embassy in Bulgaria, which is surely one of the smallest embassies we have in Europe, nevertheless has two full colonels in its defense attaché office, in addition to one warrant officer and one non-commissioned officer with a working wife. What do all these people do, who make up about one-fifth of our total American complement (which includes five Marines)? Well, they engage in perfectly legal intelligence-gathering of the kind that military attachés engage in everywhere. It is a polite business with much protocol and entertaining but also a lot of traveling, and it requires a peculiar combination of keen observation, a filing-cabinet mind for significant details, a willingness to utilize all the leeway (but not one inch more) given by the local authorities, i.e. a willingness to be on the road very frequently and sometimes at unbelievable hours, plus an ability to stand a lot of cocktail parties and similar inanities. I have great admiration for our attachés. They have a tough job, and they are doing it very well.

But they are over-ranked. Two years ago, when a change was being made in the staffing, I told Washington that I thought two colonels were too much and that one of the two officers could and indeed should be of lesser rank. This produced no reaction, except that it took a certain amount of prodding to find out, one year later, that yet another colonel was being assigned here and had already been placed in language training. At that time I reiterated .my belief that two colonels were too many, that the situation created unnecessary problems in the office and excessive prominence of the American presence, and reminded Washington that every ambassador has a right to demand that assignments to his embassy receive his personal clearance. I thought that that had ended the problem, but it actually was only the beginning.

The Army and the Air Force have a problem because here in Sofia they have rotated the senior position, and since the two attachés should have staggered periods of service the situation could arise when it was time for the Air Force to have the senior position (called "Defense Attaché") while they actually still had a junior man on the job; and so both the services had come to the conclusion that the only way out of their dilemma was to have a rule that in places like Sofia they would have officers of the same rank. But they could not admit this, so they pretended not to have heard me and put yet another colonel into training without notifying the Embassy. This was too much, and I told our Defense Attaché that there was still time for his superiors to rectify the mistake but that, if they persisted, I would "non-concur", i.e. veto the assignment.

For a while the Pentagon tried to deal with me through the attaché, but when this didn't work I received a lengthy telegram from a Lieutenant General which made the following points: The assignment of the new colonel had been approved by the Joint Chiefs of Staff. It accorded with the rules established for military attachés. The Air Force needed a colonel here to be its direct representative to the Bulgarian Air Force and in order to advise me in matters having to do with military aviation. Assigning a man of lesser rank would "downgrade" the U.S. Air Force in the eyes of its Bulgarian counterpart. Besides, the colonel in question was a fine man who had suffered as prisoner-of-war, had already sold his household effects in expectation of being assigned here, was already in language training, and would suffer if I did not relent and give the necessary clearance.

These are really bureaucratic games, and I am almost ashamed to record them here; but bureaucratic games are also part of the everyday life of an ambassador, and I have undertaken to picture the reality just as it is. Anyway, having ascertained that the policy was by no means invariable and that the Department of State shared my view that three *faits accomplis* are one too many, I first decided to cool it, for I was much too angry to react immediately. The implication that I would be responsible for the inconvenience to a fine officer when it was they who had ignored my repeated warnings not to assign yet another colonel to the position, really got my dander up. Even after three days I produced a first draft which Harvey (my deputy chief of mission) had to tone down so that it was firm without being abrasive.

I told the Lieutenant General, first, that he must have been misinformed about the background of this case, otherwise he could surely not have put it to me in the way he had. I recalled that I had given my opinion on the excessiveness of two colonels in one small attaché office twice before, and the last time with a warning that I wished to be "consulted for concurrence" before the next attaché was put into language training. I then pointed out that there is no such thing as a "direct representative" of the U.S. Air Force in a foreign country. According to the Presidential directive of December 9, 1969 and Public Law 93-475 (1974), Section 16(1), it is the ambassador who represents the United States and all the elements of its government in a foreign country. Furthermore, it was my judgment that one full colonel in the Defense Attaché's office was enough and that the functions of the other service could be adequately performed if he had a rank of less than colonel. Then I came to the point that gave me the greatest pleasure.

Contrary to the general's expressed belief that assigning an officer of lesser rank would "downgrade" the U.S. Air Force in the eyes of the Bulgarian Air Force, I could assure him that the regard in which the U.S. Air Force was held by the Bulgarian Air Force depended on a number of other factors, notably the esteem in which the U.S. Air Force was held by the Soviet Air Force, and certainly not on the rank of the air attaché here. On the other hand it was true, I said, that the rank of the air attaché could be taken to indicate the esteem in which the U.S. Air Force holds the Bulgarian Air Force; but for the life of me I could not see any reason why such special esteem should be expressed for that air force by assigning an attaché of higher rank than necessary. But that was not all.

"If" what he had telegraphed me about the hardships faced by the designee implied that I would be in some way responsible for them if he was not assigned here, I said, "I would bitterly resent such an implication," for if that colonel now found himself in a predicament it was because his superiors had repeatedly ignored warnings that I had sent them about the assignment process. I ended the message with a seemingly conciliatory proposal that if it would help I would be quite willing to recommend that we do for a time with only one attaché here—"although," I concluded, "I realize that perhaps that solution would not make matters easier for you." That was, of course, an understatement. The very idea that only one of the two services might be represented here must have seemed so unpalatable to the Pentagon, also as a precedent for other attaché offices elsewhere, that the final "suggestion" must have been understood as a threat. At any rate, I have not heard anything further about the matter since the message went off ten days ago. On the other hand, considering how badly we are served here by the State Department, it is entirely possible that they have capitulated without telling me. But in that case they will be surprised.

I am not the ambassador of the State Department but the representative of the President and of the entire United States Government, and if the State Department should recommend that I give in and accept yet another colonel, I have the authority to say no. They would be very surprised at this and it would not exactly help my career, but I am in the enviable position of owing nothing to anybody for my job, and not caring very much whether they like what I am doing here, for I can retire at any time. Certainly I'm not going to do anything else than what my best judgment dictates. What a marvelous position in which to be, even if it concerns a relatively unimportant matter.

A somewhat more important matter has to do with an aspect of our policy toward Bulgaria which I criticized in a recent telegram to the State Department which we "repeated" to the embassies in Moscow, Prague, Budapest, Belgrade, Warsaw, Bucharest and Brussels (our mission to NATO). In that message, which cannot have pleased the drafters of a report on a meeting that I had attended in Washington in the spring, I pointed out the faulty logic behind a certain decision. I put my position entirely in terms of "clarifying what the position really was," to make clear that I would accept orders if there was evidence that my position had been understood and considered and *then* rejected by policy officers. Since that time there has been silence. It is a little odd not to know whether my telegram was received with yawns or with rage, but I will just have to wait to find out.

I have vowed, when I started to write this diary, that I wouldn't play games with the reader but really let him in on what is happening here, except if there are overriding considerations of security. There are no such overriding considerations in the dispute that I have described above; so I promise to return to it and offer a full explanation as soon as I know more about the State Department's reaction to my telegram.

6

Why few Bulgarians come (voluntarily) to the residence of the American Ambassador. Film showings for the "diplomatic corps." Some reflections on the offerings. Historical deaf-mutes on both sides of the Iron Curtain.

From time to time we show motion pictures here in our ambassadorial residence. We don't have much room, for our residence is not very large, but with a bit of squeezing we can accommodate 40 people in the main living room. The films that come through here must be shipped on within two weeks, so a decision must be made soon after their arrival whether we want to attempt to collect an audience. In this respect we have been disappointed so often that we only very rarely invite Bulgarians to these showings. When we made "maximum efforts" two years ago, and again a year ago, and again about six months ago, we got only a corporal's guard of officials who had to come because of their position dealing with America and with cultural relations, none of those artists and intellectuals and "interesting Bulgarians" whom we had on our list. Even now, in 1976, it is still just a bit too dangerous to come to the residence of the American Ambassador without a good reason for going there. For instance, when I give a reception or a dinner for a visiting dignitary from Washington, all the right Bulgarians will come because it is an "official" occasion. But if it is only a "social" activity it is safer to stay away. And in no case do we get acceptances until several days have passed by, which is a good indication that someone somewhere controls the attendance at any such functions in foreign embassies.

In fact, we know that this is so. One of my colleagues, who was expecting guests for an official lunch but had received the acceptances only that morning, was surprised to see a Bulgarian functionary arrive at the very last moment, after the table had been set in the expectation that he wasn't coming. In his embarrassment the late guest blurted out the truth. Taking the host aside, he said: "I apologize for coming so late, and for not having told you before that I was coming; but you see, I only was *told that I was to come* half an hour ago." That social activities can be ulcer-producing for the hostess under such circumstances can be imagined. Except in a few cases when the protocol department of the Foreign Ministry takes care of seeing to it that everyone comes—because it is a high-level function—one never knows whether Bulgarian guests will actually come, whether they will bring their wives, and consequently how one is to set the table.

I was going to write about movie showings at our residence, but since I am on the general subject of invitations and setting foot on American soil in the middle of Sofia, here is another story which can be told with full attribution of the name because the Bulgarian gentleman has in the meantime, regrettably, passed away. Sometime ago we made the acquaintance of a Bulgarian psychiatrist, Professor Shipkovenski, and we gave a dinner party to which he was invited and to which he came. Elisabeth is a doctor, and we had an animated conversation around the dinner table, together with other doctors who had also come—having accepted the invitation after the usual number of days. We thought we had hit it off quite well with the doctors, but later contacts proved a little more difficult. However, one day, to her surprise, my wife received a telephone call from Professor Shipkovenski that he wished to pay her a visit. Delighted, she invited him to come over that day.

The professor was urbane and charming as usual, and after some general conversation (in German) it turned out that he wanted to have some books or other materials on American literature for an article that his daughter was writing. His daughter, he said, was embarking on a career in journalism and was specializing in American affairs. How delightful, said my wife. She would certainly ask me to send Professor Shipkovenski some materials on American literature that he could give to his daughter. She had not known that his daughter specialized in American affairs. We would be delighted to have her come, perhaps, to some of the American films that we were showing from time to time at our residence. The professor recoiled from this suggestion.

No, no, he said, you don't understand. I can come here and nobody will bother about it because I am an old man and I have international contacts with other doctors and travel to congresses and, besides, I no longer hold an official position. But my daughter—no, no, she would never come to the residence of the American ambassador.

But back to our movie showings. You will understand, after this introduction, that they are attended largely by members of the Sofia diplomatic community. Although this makes those evenings a rather sterile affair, it has its advantages, for in the closed atmosphere of Sofia it pays to offer some extra hospitality to one's diplomatic colleagues. Also we make it a practice to leaven the lump by inviting some of the younger members of the community, and try, not always successfully, to have a little discussion after the film showings. Since we show American films, we also hope that something about America will rub off on the guests. And this is where the problem is. For all, or almost all the films that we have shown since we are here are critical of some aspects of American society. The question is whether our society is really as bad as these pictures make it seem to be—and whether the criticisms are seen to be dramatic exaggerations, in which case we might get credit for America's freedom to criticize itself.

Not until we had come here to Sofia and had begun to show these films to foreigners in our home, did we come to realize that there is a problem in the perception of America that is provided by those films. We showed *Serpico*, for instance, with its unrelieved picture of corruption in the New York police force. The film claims to be documentary, and although it ends with the Congressional investigation in which Serpico testifies publicly to the corruption he has witnessed, it then tells the audience that this single courageous man in the New York police force, fearing for his life, had to take up residence abroad. Our guests left with polite protestations that they had found the film well-acted and most informative. We ourselves were left with some doubts whether it really could have been that not a single honest cop existed in New York except Serpico.

On another occasion we showed *Godfather II*. Our guests were delighted with this insight into American society, and when we remarked that not everything—for instance the way the Mafia was pictured as thumbing its nose at the U.S. Congress—needed to be taken as gospel truth, our guests thought that we were trying to soften the impression of an "honest" film; and of course they were partly right. On another occasion we showed *Nashville*, an excellent film but one which, in my opinion, is as much social criticism as it is entertainment—there is not one relationship between people shown in that film which isn't either insincere or exploitative or both. Our guests murmured that they thought it a remarkably honest slice of American life. More recently we showed *Three Days of the Condor*. Rather lamely, in the discussion that followed the film, I tried to point out that the investigation by the Church committee had established that while the CIA had planned assassinations, none had actually taken place.

The film begins with the wholesale assassination of workers in a CIA "cover" office in New York—by the CIA; and its drama lies in the continued flight of one of the operatives, played brilliantly by Robert Redford, as he tries to find out why he is being pursued by members of his own organization. It turns out in the end that he has stumbled on a plan to "destabilize" some Arab oil-producing countries, and that an organization within the organization had overstepped its authority—for which the head of that sub-organization is made to pay by being assassinated in turn, presumably on orders from the top of the CIA. And all this, not unlike the Pentagon Papers, was allegedly to be publicized by the *New York Times* to which Robert Redford had given the true story. Since there is enough in this story that vaguely recalls what came out in the Senate investigation, though it is ludicrously exaggerated, our guests—sophisticated foreign diplomats—apparently left our residence thinking, once more, that they had been treated to a fictionalized form of a documentary about the iniquities of our government. Another film in this category that we showed was *The Day of the Dolphin*. If our dumbfounded audience understood it right, in that film the CIA seemed to want to use trained dolphins to blow up something that looked like the yacht of the President of the United States.

Elisabeth and I are agreed that in the kind of country in which we are serving, and considering the reactions of our more sophisticated audience, it is just as well that no Bulgarians have come to attend our film showings. Not all of my colleagues in the Embassy agree. They think the films are taken as entertainment, that our guests are sensible enough to understand that they are not being given a true picture of the United States, and that in the end they will realize that a society that is so free to criticize itself is quintessentially self-regenerating and therefore healthy. I am not so sure. And the reason I am not so sure is that so many of our guests remark about the "refreshing honesty" of what they have been shown, as if these indictments of American life were true reflections of the reality of our political and social scene.

Early last week we had another interesting experience in connection with these film showings. Harvey Feldman, my deputy, made me aware that in our film library we had a documentary made by the USIA about Czechoslovakia 1968, and my wife and I decided to screen it privately on a Saturday to see if it would be suitable for showing in connection with our showing of *Three Days of the Condor*. Since I don't trust myself to operate our projection machine, and since one of our Marines had volunteered to do the projecting on Sunday, we invited him the previous evening to look at the film on Czechoslovakia with us. Sergeant Wilson is a bright, personable and highly motivated Marine. He started the film for us, and we all sat down to watch it. We saw some shots of the early Czechoslovakia in the twenties, then the rise of Hitler, then Munich and the Nazi march into Czechoslovakia, then the war, and then the liberation by the Red Army which was shown being greeted by the Czechoslovak population.

Then the picture of Dubcek flashed on the screen, and Elisabeth exclaimed, "That is Dubcek." He was shown moving among his people after some meeting, then he was shown with Brezhnev and Kosygin, and while these scenes were being shown my wife turned to the Sergeant and asked him if he knew who Dubcek was. He did not. Then there were scenes of the Russian tanks rolling into Prague, and of people shaking their fists and yelling at the Russian soldiers. Then shots were fired and one saw people running and blood on the streets. The whole film, made some eight years ago, had no narrative, everything was documentary. One saw Czech civilians climbing on Russian tanks and being pushed off, one saw Russian soldiers moving through the streets firing rifles into the air, and then victims being carried to their graves.

After the film we chatted about what had happened in Czechoslovakia, and it turned out that our sergeant had only the vaguest ideas about it. Not only had he never heard of Dubcek but he did not know what the Czechs had tried to do, why the Russians had sent in their troops, and that the crisis in 1968 came after the similar beating-down of a communist government in Hungary in 1956 that had tried to show some independence from the Soviet Union and its form of Communism. Sergeant Wilson is unusually bright and generally well informed about what is happening in the world today; but nobody had taught him anything about the postwar history of Eastern Europe. Remembering the recent North Korean communique in which it had been claimed that South Korea had attacked the North in 1950, we asked Sergeant Wilson what he knew about the Korean war. He had been taught nothing about it in school; and in 1950 he had not yet been born.

There is a distressing parallel here to what Hedrick Smith, in his excellent book *The Russians*, calls the "historical deafness" of the younger generation in the Soviet Union which tends to idealize Stalin because it has never been told about the iniquities of his regime. It is difficult for Westerners, he writes, and especially for Americans who have passed through their moral anguish over civil rights, the Vietnam war, and the Watergate scandal, to appreciate what it means to grow up in a "historically deaf-mute environment." For the greatest moral issue in Soviet history, Stalinism, has been suppressed and, from all outward signs, the Russian youth generation of the seventies is growing up with a severely stunted historical memory of that time.

But they are not the only historical deaf-mutes. Our own generation of the seventies, in addition to hearing about recent American misdeeds (real or alleged), has also been treated to a new historical revisionism which claims that it was America that started the Cold War—but our young people know nothing, or almost nothing, about the events that determined the present rivalry and antagonism between East and West, about the imposition of Communist regimes on Eastern Europe, the Korean war, the Berlin crises, the beating-down of the Hungarians and Czechoslovaks, the Cuban missile crisis, in short about any of the events that either gave rise to or legitimated the policy known as containment of communism. Considering that our generation of the seventies has been so amply exposed to events in our country which called into question the actions of our own government, I would think it even more disarmed and morally rudderless and defenseless than the corresponding generation in the Soviet Union.

7

Celebrating the revolution that never was. How Bulgaria became Communist in 1944, and what happened to the Agrarian Union—its death and resurrection. And how its "corpse" is being put to excellent use today.

September 9, the anniversary of the 1944 revolution, is the biggest holiday in Bulgaria, and in Sofia it was as usual observed by a huge parade in front of the monument of Georgi Dimitrov who for eight years was Secretary General of the Comintern, the erstwhile organization controlling the international Communist movement, before he became Bulgaria's first Communist president. The diplomatic corps was invited to the parade, which was very impressive.

Facing the monument, on the other side of a large square, were huge blow-ups of Zhivkov and Brezhnev. To the right of Zhivkov's portrait were those of the members of Bulgaria's Politburo; and to the left of Brezhnev were 14 portraits of the members of the Soviet Politburo. One oddity was that among the 9 portraits flanking that of Zhivkov was also that of Petur Tanchev, who is not a member of the BCP Politburo but the head of Bulgaria's Agrarian Union. I will have something to say about that oddity later.

Very much like in Moscow, where the Soviet leaders stand behind a balustrade halfway up the Lenin Mausoleum, the Bulgarian leaders—plus the Soviet ambassador—reviewed the parade from an equivalent position on the Dimitrov tomb. Facing them, on the square, were at first about 200 men holding large red flags; and behind them on bleachers about 300 children with colored panels that they held up to provide either a huge field of red, or the Bulgarian colors, white, green and red.

Massed flags are always very impressive, and in this case the "choreography" made them even more so. On a small stand in front of the mausoleum stood a man with two small flags, like semaphores, who directed the initial ceremony: First, upon his command, all the flags were raised. Then they were unfurled to the left, then to the right. Most of the watchers, and the television audience, of course didn't see how the stage-managing worked. Martial music (there were three brass bands in the square) blared from loudspeakers all around, and the waving sea of red flags had a precision that would have done credit to a ballet. Next, several hundred girls in blue uniforms slipped into places between the flag-waving men, and upon command from the semaphore-wielding conductor proceeded to wave green veils rhythmically, while the children behind them shouted Beh-Kah-Peh and other slogans. This was then taken up by the young men and women. With suitable amplification, it seemed that thousands were shouting in unison.

Even while this was going on, huge red floats began to move into the square, as a path was made for them—again with complete precision upon command of the flag-waving conductor. The first float had an enormous picture of Zhivkov and Brezhnev holding hands. More cheers went up from the assembled multitude; the men with the flags and the girls with the veils marched off, and the parade itself began. It lasted, as usual, two hours, and the placards and floats featured such slogans as LONG LIVE THE REVOLUTION, ETERNAL FRIENDSHIP BKP-KPCCCP (Communist Party of the USSR), etc.

All this is about what one would expect in a totalitarian country which goes in for mass displays of regimented manifestations of loyalty. But there are two oddities that deserve to be remarked upon. One was the picture of Mr. Tanchev. The other oddity is that there never was a Communist revolution on September 9, 1944. There was a Communist attempt at revolution in 1923, but the takeover in 1944 was bloodless and the result of a *putsch* during which the armed forces, by prearrangement, did not intervene.

What happened in 1944 is that after the Soviet army came into Bulgaria a coalition of political forces, which called itself the Fatherland Front, decided to overthrow the fascist regime which of course was ready to be overthrown since it had sided with Nazi Germany. The coalition included a number of political parties and groups, among which the Communists were a distinct minority.

The first government after the putsch was headed by a member of the right-wing nationalist but anti-fascist Zveno group. It included members of the Bulgarian Agrarian Union—by far the largest party during Bulgaria's earlier period of democracy—plus Social Democrats, Communists and others.

In that coalition government the Communists held four ministries out of a total of sixteen, which was about right since they had done most of the earlier partisan fighting against the government. But their four cabinet positions included the Ministry of Interior, which controlled the so-called "people's militia," and the Ministry of Justice, which organized the purge trials. By systematically terrorizing the anti-Communists and non-Communists by means of the people's militia, and by mass purge trials of "facists" among whom were included other opponents of the Communists, and by splitting those who opposed them, the Communists gradually took over the government. What happened is interesting and instructive, and it will also explain why Mr. Tanchev's picture was displayed with those of the members of the Politburo.

The first target in 1944/45 was the Agrarian Union, whose leader (who happened to have the same name, Georgi Dimitrov, as the leader of the Communists) was ousted as a result of an ultimatum of General Biriuzov, the Soviet proconsul in Bulgaria. Dimitrov was succeeded by Nikolai Petkov as leader of the Agrarians. Next an Agrarian by the name of Obbov was found who was willing to cooperate with the Communists; and by packing the congress of the Agrarian Union with Obbovites and their own supporters, the Communists succeeded in ousting Petkov from control of the party.

However, even though he had been ousted as Secretary General of the Agrarians, Petkov refused to give up his position in the government and in the Fatherland Front. Then his private secretary was arrested and shortly thereafter reported to have committed suicide in prison. As other arrests continued, Petkov and the Agrarians loyal to him finally resigned from the government and the Fatherland Front, to be immediately replaced by Obbovites. But Petkov still refused to give up his seat in the Parliament, where Dimitrov openly threatened him when he complained against Communist "threats, arrests, intimidation, beatings, killings and concentration camps." The regime did not yet dare to move directly against him as long as the Western powers had not signed a peace treaty with Bulgaria. (Patience, I will come to Tanchev presently.)

Meanwhile analogous tactics were pursued with the Social Democrats, where the role of Obbov was played by one Dimiter Neikov. His followers took over first the party newspaper and later the entire organization. Since it had been decided that the Fatherland Front would put up joint coalition lists of all the parties in the elections, the Communists and their agents were now assured a majority. Zveno was cut down a little later, first by attacks on its leader, General Damian Velchev, then by arrest of his aide who also died while in custody, and in the end by his forced resignation and exile as minister in Switzerland.

The Western powers were in a difficult position in Bulgaria. The armistice agreement, concluded by the USSR on behalf of all the United Nations (then the name of the powers fighting against Nazi Germany), recognized that the Soviet army would act in the name of the others in controlling execution of the armistice. This was analogous to the situation in Romania, but also corresponded to the situation earlier in Italy where the USSR had been in fact excluded from a role in political supervision. (It is ironical that when the Western allies protested in Romania in 1945 that they were excluded from a political role, they were correctly told by Soviet Vice Foreign Minister Vyshinsky that they had the same role in Romania that the Soviets had been assigned in Italy two years before.)

For a while the Western allies were able to obtain postponement of the phony elections in Bulgaria by threatening that they would not conclude a peace treaty; and a factfinding mission came from Washington to look into political conditions in Bulgaria. Washington tried to gain leverage from the threat to publish the mission's damaging report; but the elections did take place in November 1945, and the conditions surrounding them were so bad that the non-communist opposition recommended that their followers stay away from the polls. As a result, 86% of the votes went to the Communist-dominated government. But by that time most people had come to realize that there was no hope of outside support and that the democratic parties in Bulgaria were doomed.

Even so, Petkov and a handful of courageous Agrarians continued to fight for democracy until 1947 when the Peace Treaty was signed. Shortly thereafter the Communists had the printers' union refuse to print Petkov's Agrarian newspaper; trumped up allegations of "conspiracies" by the Petkov Agrarians; and arrested some who were tortured into implicating Petkov. On June 6, 1947, Petkov was arrested on the floor of the Parliament. He was tried before a "People's Court," convicted, and hanged despite protests by the British and American governments.

Why am I telling this gruesome story in connection with the September 9 celebrations? Because most people here, including most of the Bulgarians who attended the celebrations or saw them on TV, probably really believe that the Communists staged a "revolution" whose anniversary they can celebrate; and because the lineal descendant of Mr. Obbov, former Lieutenant General Petur Tanchev, stood on the reviewing platform of Dimitrov's mausoleum and looked across the square on his own portrait flanked by members of the BKP Politburo, to give the present regime the appearance of being a coalition between Communists and Agrarians.

For the Bulgarian Communist Party has found it convenient to keep the Agrarian Union in existence until today, just as it still pretends that the Fatherland Front is a roof organization spread over the Communists and various other political tendencies. In fact, of course, the Agrarians are an empty shell. Nothing angers Mr. Tanchev more than the question whether there is even a scintilla of difference in the policies advocated by the Agrarians and those advocated by the Communists.

Absolutely not, he replies in stentorian tones. The two parties march shoulder to shoulder into the future. In what respect, then, are the Agrarians independent from the Communists? They are absolutely and completely independent, he insists. It just so happens that they find that the program of the BKP corresponds in every detail to the aspirations of the Bulgarian people. Anyone who wishes, or even suggests by such questions, that the Agrarians should differ from the Communists, must wish to divide the Bulgarian people. Never, ever will the Agrarians allow themselves to be separated from their brothers, the Communists. To people unfamiliar with the history of the Agrarian Union, Mr. (for he no longer uses his title of Lieutenant General) Tanchev even insists that the Agrarians and the Communists "have always cooperated."

But the story doesn't end here. One would think that political organizations in the democratic West would shun the Bulgarian Agrarian Union as a disreputable puppet of the Communists, but just the opposite is happening. The Agrarians hold congresses to which they assiduously invite non-Communist parties of the left or even of the center (and sometimes even of the right), and those organizations actually send representatives, and often they even sign agreements or sponsor meetings jointly with the Agrarians.

Thus the Finnish Center Party, which would not dream of sponsoring any event jointly with Finnish or other Communists, sponsored jointly with the Bulgarian Agrarians a conference of "parties of the center" to review implementation of the decisions of the Helsinki Conference. The Greek United Center Party, the Turkish Justice Party, the Austrian Peasant Union, the Association of Cypriot Peasants, Morocco's Independence Party, the Bangladesh National Awami League, none of these decent and well-intentioned organizations seems to find it odd to team up with this corpse of a once-vital organization which died almost thirty years ago. Altogether about 60 foreign non-Communist organizations have regular contacts with Tanchev's Agrarians.

One is used to Communist front organizations in countries where there is freedom of speech and freedom of organization; but it comes as a bit of a shock to see that front organizations flourish also in Communist countries; and even more as a shock to see that political groups and parties who wouldn't treat with Communists in their own countries, will treat with great respect an organization in a Communist country which is no less a puppet, in fact even more so. Of course, the Agrarians in Bulgaria have the facilities of a state available for them, which allows them to issue invitations right and left, to receive visitors quite lavishly, and to send their people to any international gatherings where they can make friends for the Communist regime of Bulgaria.

I have mentioned earlier that the Western allies were treated by the Russians in Bulgaria (and in Romania) in the same way in which they themselves had treated the Russians earlier in Italy, and that is true—up to a point. There is no doubt that the Western allies in Italy in 1944/45 favored the non-Communist parties and notably the Christian Democrats. But Communists were not persecuted there. In other words, while I think it was a mistake to exclude our allies of the time, the Soviet Union, from any role in the occupation of Italy, the situation there cannot by any stretch of the imagination be compared with that in Bulgaria in 1944/45. The Western allies encouraged the spreading of democratic liberties in Italy. In Bulgaria the Russians presided over the destruction of a nascent democracy.

Having written this much, I do not think that one can leave it there, for history is never simple. We, the Western countries, had no right to expect that Bulgaria would become a western-style democracy, and indeed we didn't expect it. When Churchill met with Stalin in the fall of 1944 he proposed a division of influence in the countries which were falling away from Hitler's control. As the price for acknowledging that the Russians should have 90% of the influence in Romania, Churchill obtained Stalin's agreement that the British would have 90% of the influence in Greece. There was some haggling between Eden and Molotov about the precise percentages in Bulgaria, but at no time was there any question that the Russians would be dominant there.

The really interesting countries in the Churchill-Stalin deal of 1944 are Hungary and Yugoslavia, where the two statemen agreed on a 50:50 division of influence. And oddly enough Hungary is the only country where there were free elections under a Soviet occupation—at least until the Cold War began in earnest. Also, evidence has come to light that Stalin encouraged Tito in 1944 to make a compromise with the British-based Yugoslav government in exile. Most people today, even if they know of this spheres-of-influence deal, do not remember that the subject of Czechoslovakia didn't even arise in the talks between Churchill and Stalin because at that time Czechoslovakia was regarded as a country to be liberated and was expected, because of its history, to have good relations with both East and West.

So while I can imagine the rage and frustration of the American Minister in Bulgaria just after World War II, who was supposed to sit on a Control Commission which never met, and who felt that he had to respond to the pleadings of the Bulgarian democrats who were being slowly strangled, it never surprised me that Bulgaria came under Communist domination. What irks and chafes and keeps disturbing me is the incredible hypocrisy, the downright lies in the way the Communists rewrite history—and the short memory of the people in the West, and even of some of my diplomatic colleagues here in Sofia.

I don't have the heart, for instance, to ask Olga Lucila Carmona, the Venezuelan poetess who is her country's ambassador here, why Professor Orlando Susa, leading a delegation of the Party of Democratic Action of Venezuela, came here recently to pay a visit to Mr. Petur Tanchev. She might tell me that the Party of Democratic Action is unimportant in Venezuela, or she might tell me that it is important. In either case, if I had gotten that far, I would have to ask why, then, she herself had to attend the meeting. She would probably tell me that it helps relations, that it serves to lubricate them because it pleases the Bulgarians.

And then I would have to say Dear Olga, why does Venezuela have to lubricate Bulgaria? They should be lubricating you. They will have more respect for your country if you don't play the charades that they set up for you. But then I would have to say the same to half a dozen ambassadors here. One of them, probably the most honest among them, gave me a frank reply when I asked him why a respectable party of his country was prostituting itself with Mr. Tanchev. He said: "It looks good at home. They know what they are doing, but it makes them look like statesmen in the eyes of the populace, and they can always say they didn't kowtow to the Communists, they were just talking with their own opposite numbers in Bulgaria."

On vacation in Greece, the author is stung by a news item from Vietnam; compares notes with a colleague about the Buddhists there; and suggests some speculative parallels with the potential of the Orthodox Church in Bulgaria.

September 21. Elisabeth and I went for a week to Tsangarada, Greece. It had become very necessary for us to get away. It is not always recognized that the role of the wife of an ambassador, especially at a hardship post, is far more difficult than that of the husband. We have no children. My wife is a professional woman, a highly skilled gynecologist, and in this Communist country there is no chance whatever for her to pursue her professional interests. The horizon quickly closes in, and psychological troubles can develop to alarming proportions. The husband, who has many of the same hardships as well as some others, does at least have his professional work to keep him occupied. Both of us had an increasingly difficult time during recent weeks, and our rest in the sun on the Pelion peninsula in Greece did us a lot of good.

While we were there, we received—through the ingenuity and initiative of our colleague, the Consul General in Thessaloniki— the *International Herald Tribune* that is published in Paris; so we weren't cut off entirely from news of the world. (Of course we also saw the Greek television news, but not speaking Greek we could only gather the general subjects that were treated.)

Nothing important happened here in Sofia during the period we were away, but there is again an accumulation of annoying and sometimes perplexing problems. For instance, we have two new security problems in our little Embassy. One is due to one of our unmarried staff members sleeping with a Bulgarian who may or may not have been put up to it by their intelligence services. Our handling of this matter requires great delicacy, for the last thing we would want is for that staff member to feel that it would be better next time to say nothing about it to our security officer. There are also other problems, but first I want to set down something that really electrified me when reading the *Herald Tribune* of September 10, 1976. The news item, datelined Paris, was under the headline: "Buddhists Report 12 Immolated in Vietnam," and it reported that according to the "delegation" of the Vietnamese Buddhist "church" in Paris, nine Buddhist nuns and three monks had simultaneously burned themselves to death in a village in the Mekong Delta in November to protest persecution by Vietnam's Communist regime.

What electrified me in that item were the words "in November." Was it possible that such important news could have failed to reach the West for something like ten months? My mind went back, as that of many other readers must have done, to the reports about the monks and nuns who had burned themselves to death in Saigon in 1963. Those reports had a great deal to do with America's disenchantment with the Diem regime and thus with the downfall and eventual death of Ngo Dinh Diem. I was not in Vietnam at that time. Actually we were in Iran from 1963 to 1967, but we were aware of the wave of horror and revulsion against the Diem regime which swept the United States at that time, building up to the point where President Kennedy publicly washed his hands of the Vietnamese leader—which was taken as a signal that the U.S. would not mind to see him overthrown.

Since our Consul General in Thessaloniki is someone who had served in Vietnam during later troubles between the Buddhists and the Vietnamese military government (in 1966), and since we were staying with him on our way back to Sofia, I brought the clipping along and asked him at dinner what his own impression had been when he had read the story. I should perhaps add here that our host was someone who had worked for quite a time on Vietnam, that he is a much younger man than I, and that I myself served in Vietnam from 1968 to 1970, at a time when the Buddhists were not really much of an issue.

The thing that he remembered most was how the Buddhist demonstrators in Hué in 1966 had kept a sharp eye on the American press, making sure that every one of their moves was covered by eye-witnesses. He referred me to the book, *Our*

Vietnam Nightmare by the late Marguerite Higgins, which shows in great detail how the Buddhists of the Xa Loi pagoda systematically played the American media, not only by managing that any immolations and their own interpretations of them would be amply covered, but also by analyzing the "play-back" of American press reports. They held press conferences twice daily, interrogated Miss Higgins about the "play" in New York (by which they meant the extent of press play), and mimeographed for their own organizers and supporters daily sheets about the publicity received abroad, both as an encouragement and to refine their tactics.

Our young host, who is now of course ten years older than he was when he went to Hué in 1966, reported how he arrived in the old imperial capital with every urge of a young liberal intellectual Foreign Service officer to believe that "the Buddhists" were the victims of religious persecution; and how in time he came to realize that there was no religious persecution, that the Buddhists in the Xa Loi pagoda represented only a fraction of the Buddhists in Vietnam, that they were in fact a political opposition organization, and that in their claims for political reforms they were in fact unappeasable since every concession gave rise to further demands.

What struck our friend especially, and what I also found even during my later time in Saigon when I had come up against this problem, was the extreme indulgence with which the American press treated that Buddhist opposition. Their claims were almost always reported as facts; the immolations—often by young priests who had been totally misled by their superiors about what was going on—were reported as if they were proof that religious persecution existed; and the fact that it was a political power struggle between Diem and an extremely unscrupulous and ambitious opponent, who happened to be a political monk (Thich Tri Quang), was either ignored or systematically played down. Entire careers were made by blowing up the Buddhist issue and otherwise working to bring down Diem in 1963. David Halberstam, who later wrote the book *The Best and the Brightest* without referring to his own role in bringing down Diem, received the Pulitzer prize for international reporting in 1964; and Malcolm Browne of the *New York Times*, who played the same role, received the same prize in the same year.

Why am I writing about this now, in 1976, when our Vietnam nightmare is but a memory? Because of the enormous contrast between this one-day story in the newspapers, about twelve Buddhist immolations "reportedly" in Vietnam ten months ago, and the continuous headlines that less numerous immolations received in 1963 and later, with TV coverage that brought them into every American home—when the international press was on hand to report and interpret. It is far from certain that "the Buddhists" were persecuted in 1963 or 1966, but it was certainly made to appear so by our press.

There is also an interesting psychological phenomenon involved, which has perhaps more general validity in our society—that people who act aggrieved and deeply offended, who are willing to be clubbed and beaten (and sometimes provoke such treatment), benefit from a favorable prejudice on the part of our people. As if history didn't prove that a bad cause can also produce willing martyrs.

Marguerite Higgins in her book wrote (in 1965): "In the summer of 1963 American newspapers certainly tended, at first anyway, to give credence to the charges of religious persecution." And she went on to report that one of the most ardent anti-Diem writers of that time, namely Halberstam, later was quoted as saying that he had always emphasized "that this was a political dispute under a religious banner—the only place an opposition had found to gather in an authoritarian regime." But she adds that whatever Mr. Halberstam's intentions, "his and other press dispatches of the time did create the impression in the outside world that some kind of religious crisis was going on in Vietnam."

So where does that leave us today, in 1976, when we read a newspaper report about Buddhist self-immolations in Vietnam in 1975? We simply don't know. According to the Associated Press news report, the 12 nuns and monks "decided to burn themselves to death after receiving orders from local officials to stop displaying Buddhist flags, praying for war victims or observing 'religious silence.'" The Buddhist flag issue was among those of the crisis in 1963 which eventually led to the downfall of Diem as a more or less direct result of the picture of religious persecution built up systematically in America. Today the issue seems of little importance. No Halberstam or Browne was on hand to cover the burnings in Vietnam last year, if they occurred at all, and to interpret them to American readers and others around the world.

We do not know what happened. And the fact that we do not know, and have few means of finding out, illustrates what is meant by the term iron curtain, which still has some validity even today. We do not know if it is true that the present Vietnamese regime really refused to meet with Buddhist representatives and to discuss their grievances—as contrasted with Diem and his people, who again and again met with Buddhist representatives and made concessions to them. But it would not surprise me if the Vietnamese Communist regime had given the Buddhists the back of their hand, for I sit here in Sofia where it would be unthinkable for the government to meet with the representatives of the Orthodox Church to discuss their grievances, and precisely because the government would suspect that the Church might become a rallying-point for political opposition. The Bulgarian patriarch is often trotted out by the regime to show that it is not unmindful of the role of the church, but one only has to attend the Easter service at the Alexander Nevsky Cathedral to get a feeling for the true attitude of the regime.

The Bulgarian Orthodox Church has its most important Easter service from 11 o'clock on Saturday evening until 1 o'clock on Sunday morning. We have attended that enormously moving service twice so far. The first time the whole square on which the cathedral is located was roped off, and men with red armbands checked the credentials of anyone who wished to go to the service, turning people away who had not obtained special permission beforehand. Inside the church, which was only half full, there were more men with red armbands. But last spring the controls were even more stringent: Not only was the square a no-man's land with not a person in sight anywhere, but the controls had been moved further out so that for two blocks in every direction there were barriers; and as we made our way into the church our diplomatic cards had to be produced altogether four times to representatives of the police, most of them in civilian attire.

Later I asked the patriarch why there had been so many controls and why nobody at all had been permitted to stand or circulate in the square. He looked me in the eye and said that he himself had asked that the square be cleared of people; for if admission to it had been free the crush of humanity would have been so great that he could not have carried the cross around the church at midnight. He denied, of course, that anyone had been prevented from attending the service—how could he have, considering that our interview was attended by his political commissar? But there was an obvious contrast between the sparse attendance of the service and the implication of what he had said, that multitudes of the religious— and perhaps of others as well?—would have easily filled the entire square if they had been permitted to do so.

Does this mean that I believe that the opposition in Communist Bulgaria represents a majority? No, it does not. What interests me, in the light of the news item about Vietnam and of my experiences there and here, is the contrast between our open society with its free reporting and the opportunity to find things out, and the closed societies where this is not possible. Our press may abuse its privileges, and sometimes things are misinterpreted to the American audience. But at least there is room for people to express contrary assessments, however unpopular they may be at the time. Marguerite Higgins, who thought the "holy man" of the Buddhist opposition in Vietnam a fraud and a demagogue and quite possibly a Communist agent, is dead. Her book did not sell very well. David Halberstam, who made the same man into a hero, received honors and prizes and wrote a best-selling book about Vietnam in which he perpetuates some of the myths he and his colleagues had originally propagated. But today not even an argument can take place about what happens to any opposition in Vietnam, or in Bulgaria, because we simply don't know enough.

It is ironical that an American novelist recently published a book about contemporary Bulgaria ("The October Circle") in which an oppositionist immolates himself in front of Georgi Dimitrov's tomb in Sofia—and the news is systematically blocked out by the regime so that the outside world doesn't even hear of it. That couldn't happen here because eventually the report would reach the diplomatic corps and thus the press of the West. But the point is certainly correct that the regime would quickly clamp down on anyone who tried to publicize opposition of any kind.

The greatest irony about the report from Paris about immolations in Vietnam is that, according to the Associated Press report, "the spokesman (of the Buddhist church) said the mission purposely refrained from publicizing the mass suicide in the hope of a change in the Communist attitude." What a 180 degree contrast to what happened when the American press was in Vietnam and when Miss Higgins could be asked for instant replay from New York! In her book she reports, aside from the systematic tipping-off of the press when there were burnings, a "most macabre incident" that occurred on a rainy Monday night when a lovely young eighteen-year-old girl was found on the steps of the Xa Loi Pagoda, her right arm bleeding profusely from what was, fortunately, an amateurish attempt to chop it off at the wrist.

Within ten or twenty minutes of this discovery, she writes, Amercian photographers and reporters had converged on the scene. They had been summoned there by spokesman Thich Duc Nhiep in rush calls from the pagoda phones that always kept in close touch with American and other foreign correspondents. "But what gave some observers pause," she writes, "was the fact that the Xa Loi monks kept the blood-drenched girl at the pagoda for at least forty minutes to make her available to photographers and the press. Only after this was the 'emergency case' taken to the hospital." Enough of this. I just wanted to record it in my diary before I have to return Miss Higgins' book to Thessaloniki.

—0—

October 2. It is now two weeks after we returned from Greece, and a number of interesting things have happened; but I must record a post script to what I have written about the Buddhist immolations because we have just had the visit of an old friend of mine, Professor Daniel Lerner of the Center for International Studies of M.I.T. The other evening we were talking about the press and its role during the current presidential campaign and during the Vietnam war, and the Professor—who told me that he doesn't mind being quoted on this—recalled an interesting episode from a visit to Saigon in 1963. At that time he had met David Halberstam, then of the *New York Times*, and that journalist had exclaimed not only to Lerner but to others that he would "get Diem."

It had seemed such a strange thing for a journalist to say, Lerner recalled. Was it the purpose of a journalist accredited to a foreign country to dedicate himself to "getting" its head of state? Yet at that time only the magnitude of the task Halberstam had set himself seemed incongruous. In the event, "getting Diem" was exactly what he accomplished through a drumfire of reports about all the weaknesses and deficiencies and scandals and cruelties of his regime; and in the end Diem was overthrown. And of course, as the Pentagon Papers show, not long after his overthrow came the bill from his successors, asking for still greater involvement of the United States; for by presuming to tell them how to run their country we had also acquired a responsibility to help them when they accepted our advice.

9

Sex and security. Conviviality and ostentation. A visit to the Soviet Ambassador. A glimpse at the Bulgarian Government's "guest house." An attempt to extract information that elsewhere is available from the daily press.

The wheels of State Department security have ground further in the case of the staff member who had been sleeping with a Bulgarian, and I had the welcome occasion to comment on the case in a highly confidential communication to the Director General of the Foreign Service. Even though I helped the employe with my recommendation, I had to be very careful in the phraseology since the employe could sue the State Department (and perhaps me) for invasion of his or her constitutional rights. The whole area of security rules and their infraction has become shifting and unstable in recent years. There is always a tendency to mix up considerations of morality with considerations of security. To those who live in the free society of America it may seem that there really is no problem and that everyone should be free to conduct his private life as he wishes, whether in America or as an American in Bulgaria, but matters aren't that simple. It is entirely possible that our employe was the target of a James Bond type of operation. The fact is that I think we have neutralized any such operation—by making sure that the Bulgarians know that we know. I made it a point to assure the employe that every effort would be made to preserve his or her privacy in this matter, and am glad that so far this has been successful.

Among other matters engaging my attention during recent days were narcotics trafficking through Bulgaria; the possible elimination of travel restrictions on American diplomats in Bulgaria and Bulgarian diplomats in America; a missing diplomatic pouch; an American citizen in a Bulgarian jail for having tried to smuggle someone out of the country in the trunk of her car; two American citizens stranded here because their passports and money were stolen while they were sleeping in the once-fabled Orient Express; an argument about the size of the audience of Radio Free Europe (I think RFE is inflating its estimate of listeners in Bulgaria, and repeated that opinion bluntly and in greater detail when criticized for saying so); the seizure of a Bulgarian fishing vessel that was fishing in forbidden waters off the coast of Oregon; innumerable farewell parties for departing ambassadors; and a number of business visitors including a banker whom my wife and I invited for dinner, and the representative of a firm that has recently signed a major contract here.

But perhaps the most interesting event was a two-hour conversation that I had with the Soviet Ambassador to Bulgaria, Vladimir Nikolaevich Bazovskii. I called on him at the splendid new Soviet Embassy here, which has two auditoriums, a reception hall accommodating 2,000 people, and beautiful smaller reception rooms—as well as sauna, swimming pool, tennis courts, etc. Elisabeth likes to say that by comparison with that and certain other foreign embassies in Sofia, ours looks like a "flea circus," but I much prefer our small Embassy residence to the pleasure domes of others which make one feel one is living on a movie set rather than in a home; and Elisabeth agrees with that point of view, having spent a good amount of time making our residence into a home. Certainly with all its splendor, the Russian Embassy residence has an atmosphere of coldness and formality, whereas ours while more modest has an atmosphere of warmth and hospitality.

Well, the hospitality of my Soviet colleague was of no mean proportions, including two kinds of caviar, lots of vodka, tea, pastries, chocolates, and a good deal of urbane talk. The cordiality between us is genuine, for in Bulgaria he certainly need not fear that the United States will in any way undermine the almost absolute control that his country exercises here. So he is very friendly, and I reciprocate the friendliness. At the government reception on September 9, the National Day, he rather suddenly and ostentatiously kissed my wife on both cheeks, and when I expressed exaggerated surprise at that "intimacy", he kissed me as well. Later it was said that he had been doubly happy on September 9, and not because it was the Bulgarian national holiday: First, the news had just come in about the death of Mao Tse-tung (later to be spelled, at Chinese behest, Mao Zedong); and second, he was celebrating the demise of his dear but unlamented mother-in-law.

Incidentally, the place where the government held its National Day reception, called the Boyana "Guest House," is an eye-popping pleasure dome of the kind that the United States of America could certainly not afford to build for its visitors. It has a huge—about a quarter mile—driveway, an imposing entrance hall, a grand marble staircase (at that time flanked by Bulgarian honor guards in their colorful old uniforms, with an eagle's feather sticking from the front of their caps), a huge upstairs reception hall, and many large rooms for entertainments or conferences. Overhead are magnificent Austrian chandeliers, and the central ceremonial hall has huge floor-to-ceiling windows giving out onto a garden in which there are fountains and marble-bordered walks on ascending terraces. Upon command, the floor-to-ceiling windows glide silently down and disappear into the ground, permitting direct access from the ceremonial hall to the terraces, fountains and gardens in which are located smaller "guest houses" for distinguished visitors. When I wrote that we couldn't afford the like, I meant that our Congress would never appropriate money for such a lavish building for largely ceremonial purposes (except perhaps for itself).

But I have just been describing Boyana, the government "guest house," and thereby risked some confusion with the Soviet Embassy which I had earlier discussed—and which is no less lavish. Anyway, it was in the latter that I was received by my colleague Bazovskii and without much delay launched into the substance of what I hoped to discuss with him, namely the Bulgarian balance of payments situation with its Eastern trading partners, notably the Soviet Union. I explained that we are quite well informed about Bulgaria's problem with its rising deficit and commercial debts to the West, but that I did not regard this as one of major proportions since the economy is growing very fast, industrial equipment is becoming more modern and production thus more efficient, and Bulgaria's Western creditors still regard its credit as good. My question concerned the deficit with the East, which is a much more delicate subject and on which statistics are not published.

It was clear, I said, that after Russian raw materials prices had gone up so steeply in 1975, Bulgaria was bound to have encountered difficulties in stepping up exports to compensate for the higher prices of its imports. Bazovskii had told me earlier, I recalled, that at the end of each year Soviet-Bulgarian trade was in "complete balance," with neither a surplus nor a deficit on either side. Now, however, we had come into possession of figures (actually derived from *East-West Markets*, a publication of the Chase Manhattan Bank) which indicated that in 1975 Bulgaria had had a 129 million ruble (about $179 million) deficit in its trade with the USSR, and something like a 380 million ruble deficit with its Eastern European (CEMA) patners generally. How was Bulgaria going to pay these growing "debts," considering that it is also increasingly in debt to its Western creditors?

Bazovskii said in his most jovial manner that my own credit in Washington should be high because my reporting about a zero deficit between the USSR and Bulgaria had been absolutely accurate and anyone reporting otherwise was just plain wrong. Then he talked about the various Bulgarian enterprises in the USSR which produce raw materials at low cost to Bulgaria: iron ore at Kursk, cellulose at Ust-Ilin near Lake Baikal, lumber near Archangelsk, and of course Bulgarian participation in construction of the oil pipeline from Orenburg. Ah, I said, does this mean that such projects generated rubles for the Bulgarians which they could set off against the cost of imports from the USSR? Bazovskii side-stepped this question and offered figures to show that Bulgarian trade to the Soviet Union (which already is more than 50% of all Bulgarian trade) is increasing, and he said that the prices paid by the USSR for Bulgarian products had also gone up; and besides, the proportion of Bulgarian industrial products, which are more profitable, is also going up.

This is all terribly interesting, I said, and I was grateful that he was taking me into his confidence. But I still failed to understand how Bulgarian industrial exports to the Soviet Union could go up when it was also the policy of the Bulgarian Government to increase industrial exports to the West in order to pay for its imports from that quarter. How would they manage to do both? Was it not logical to suppose, since Western banks were giving credits to Bulgaria, that the Soviet Union was doing something similar?

Absolutely not, said Bazovskii, all that exists is an agreement providing for a temporary "swing" credit of 100 million rubles. Per year? No. at any time during the entire length of the current five-year plan. Well, then, I said, how were the Bulgarians going to make ends meet? By tightening their belts a little, Bazovskii replied, by scaling down some of their more ambitious programs, and by reducing imports from the West. He then went into some details, which are not of interest here.

In such conversations there is perhaps 95 per cent chit-chat, evasion, prevarication and sometimes downright deception. But there is also sometimes a residue of useful information. It may seem odd that I was asking the Soviet ambassador about matters that, in other circumstances, one should have been able to obtain from the central bank, or the trade ministry, the planning ministry, or from higher Bulgarian policy officials. But the situation here is different. Although according to visiting American bankers the personal capabilities of Bulgarian bankers are quite high, they give out unusually little information. The trade ministry and other officials had already been queried either by myself or by members of our staff. Incidentally, to reveal the size of Bulgaria's gold and foreign currency reserves is a crime under the Bulgarian espionage law.

Nor is that all. Two years ago we made an analysis of the entire Bulgarian penal code as it pertains to espionage (we entitled the report "Catch-22: 'Economic Espionage' in Bulgaria") and summarized our conclusion that in addition to the article about gold and foreign currency reserves there were these provisions: "Article 32 does the same [i.e., makes revelation a crime] with respect to information on the balance of payments. Article 33 is so broad that it covers also information 'on the financial results of exports.' Article 34 relates to clearing balances in foreign trade. Article 35 makes it an act of espionage to reveal information on 'licenses which must be imported from foreign countries.' Article 36 also covers 'summarized information on the demands for all or different kinds of goods for import, which harm or may harm the interests of the national economy.'"

Later, when we discussed some of Bazovskii's responses and other fragmentary information available to us among a group of Western ambassadors here in Sofia, someone came up with an interpretation of the Soviet ambassador's reference to Bulgarian enterprises in the Soviet Union which I find quite ingenious and possibly close to the mark: It may be that the figures on the trade deficit were derived from Soviet export and import statistics, but that those statistics include the raw materials that were produced by Bulgarians in the USSR and then shipped from there to Bulgaria. The way in which the Bulgarians pay for the privilege of exploiting, for instance, Soviet timber resources, is that they turn over half their production to the Soviets and can export the other half free to Bulgaria. So a portion of the Soviet exports to Bulgaria may be "already paid" by having been produced under such ground rules by Bulgarians in the Soviet Union. Obviously we shall have to explore this angle.

I cite this conversation as an example of the work that is done here by the Embassy. All information we get is fragmentary. The press, as a source of information, is often worse than useless. Statistics are often contradictory, and in any event very scarce. In our small embassy we have only one officer who handles both economic and political analysis, and he nearly goes crazy trying to compare the data of one year with those of another, because sometimes increases are given only in terms of percentages, and later published figures do not check out; the categories are quixotic (for instance, all machine tools are listed under "lathes"); and much information is so fragmentary that it is almost impossible to analyze. Yet Washington quite rightly insists that we digest the available information and transmit it, because it is of use not only to our economic departments there but also in assessing Bulgaria's performance with respect to its undertakings in the Final Act of Helsinki.

With respect to the adequacy of published information of an economic nature—something which Bulgaria supported at Helsinki—our analysis concluded that "if we had a large staff fluent in Bulgarian with adequate time and full access to all published data on the Bulgarian economy, as well as the capacity to stitch available data together in a comprehensive fashion over a long period of time, it would be feasible to know a lot about Bulgaria's economy and the commercial possibilities here. But failing that, it is necessary to characterize the Bulgarian economic and commercial information that is readily available as tardy, irregular, sparse, acquired only with considerable difficulty, and not easily subject to analysis." The same situation, incidentally, does not prevail in Budapest where much economic data is published and where Hungarian officials will gladly answer detailed questions because they realize that it is in their country's interest to do so.

I don't like to brag, particularly since I really didn't have all that much to do with it, but American trade with Bulgaria has risen considerably since I arrived here in April 1974. In that year our trade rose from $10 million to $30 million, both ways. In 1975 it topped $50 million. And I estimate that by the end of this year 1976 we will have reached over $75 million. This isn't much in absolute terms, and it is still minuscule compared for instance with Bulgaria's largest traditional Western supplier, West Germany (half a billion dollars both ways), but the trend is heartening. And I make it a point to support American businessmen whenever I can. At the Plovdiv Fair, which gave us a lot of work at the embassy, I think we had a better-organized pavilion and in comparison to its size did more business than most of the other nations represented. My wife and I were there twice, we talked with all the American exhibitors, we escorted Zhivkov through the pavilion, and then tried to be helpful in the follow-up.

10

How private remarks can become the undoing of public officials. President Ford puts foot in mouth on Eastern Europe. The non-existent Sonnenfeldt Doctrine. "Considerable vertical disagreement" about a message sent to Washington.

We had two people from the Agriculture Department here last week, one of them is our newly assigned Agricultural Attache who is resident in Athens and will just come to Bulgaria from time to time, another a fine gentleman who worked out of Secretary Butz's office in Washington. I always make it a practice to invite such visitors to the residence for an informal chat and if possible for a meal.

Naturally the conversation turned to the recent resignation of Earl Butz over the "gross indiscretion" (his own words) in making certain remarks about black Americans. According to the *Washington Post,* Pat Boone, an entertainer, asked Butz during a flight from Kansas City just after the Republican convention, why his party did not attract more black voters; and Butz responded "because coloreds only want three things . . . first, a tight [woman's sexual organ], second, loose shoes, and third, a warm place to [defecate]."

What struck me about that remark, which certainly was grossly offensive, was that it was made in a private conversation. However, it was made in the presence of a newspaper reporter, in that case John Dean, the former White House legal counsel who was working for *Rolling Stone,* the counter-culture magazine, when he overheard the conversation.

How well I can remember John Dean, how his name inspired terror in high places in the State Department, how he was regarded as the ultimate arbiter of White House thinking on matters constitutional, and how some of my superiors (when I was Deputy

Assistant Secretary of State) were reluctant to take him on in any controversy. At that time the question was whether the United States Government was responsible for the security of foreign diplomats accredited to the United Nations, who were being subjected to harrassment and in some cases physical injury by various demonstrators. John Dean had taken the "high ground" that under the American constitution the states and local authorities are responsible for local security—a position that had seemed to me to beg the question since the City of New York had stated that it was simply unable to devote the necessary resources to protecting UN diplomats. By a miracle, no Russian had yet been killed by the activities of the Jewish Defense League, but there had been firing into a Russian apartment.

As for Butz, my perspective on him is also colored by the particular angle from which I saw him. He received me twice during my present tenure as ambassador to Bulgaria and was genuinely concerned about expanding cooperation with that country in the agricultural field. At my urging, he came to Sofia last year and did a great deal for the United States—not only in the field of agricultural cooperation but also in extracting a commitment from the chief of state that the problem of "divided families" (Bulgarians who were being prevented from joining family members in the U.S., the latter usually people who had originally left the country illegally) would be settled.

My visitors recalled that Butz had already once gotten himself into trouble politically because of an alleged "ethnic slur" which consisted of telling a story about Italy in a mock Italian accent. I had actually thought it pretty funny and not so offensive. (Referring to the Pope's opposition to birth control, he had quoted an Italian lady's reaction as: "He no playa da game, he no maka da rules.") It isn't clear to me why the Secretary of Agriculture had to apologize for that mild joke about Italians, but he did. Yet it must be recognized that his remark about blacks was much worse—and of course it got into print just during the presidential election campaign.

As an example of Butz's joyous playing with words and foreign accents, one of our visitors quoted him as having invented a sentence using the word Euripides. The sentence is spoken by an

Italian father who has just given his young son a new pair of pants after the boy had ripped another one. "Thesa new pants; Euripides pants and I giva you a spanking."

Funny or not, the mind returns to the fact that Butz, a highly competent Secretary of Agriculture, has been forced out of his cabinet position due to a private remark made on an airplane having been overheard by a journalist. And then, of course, the usual cross-ruffing took place. Dean had reported the remark as having been made by an unnamed cabinet officer, in a conversation between four persons—the singers Pat Boone and Sonny Bono, Dean, and the cabinet officer. It was easy, once that report appeared in *Rolling Stone*, to seek out Boone and Bono and to extract from them the identification of the cabinet officer.

It reminds me of a press conference in Saigon at which all participants undertook not to publish a certain item of military information—and they kept to their bargain. But then they talked in a bar with other journalists who had not been invited to that press conference and told them what had happened. Whereupon one of the uninvited journalists, Beverly Deepe, published the information, which was highly sensitive, with a paragraph inserted that said something like this: "The revelation was made in strict secrecy at a press conference to which this reporter was not invited."

Well, in this case Butz does have himself to blame for not recognizing that his erstwhile friend and colleague John Dean had changed considerably since the days when he had known him; and political figures are responsible, I suppose, for what they say not only publicly but also privately—and, being politicians, should know when they are dealing with harmless fellow passengers on a plane and when they are dealing with representatives of the press who will not protect the privacy of remarks made in private.

There was another incident involving private remarks not so long ago which caught my attention. That was the conversation between Vice President Rockefeller and Speaker Albert, at the time when the President of Liberia was visiting the Congress. The two apparently thought that they were talking in private, but their microphones were "live" and journalists in the press gallery were able to hear and even record what they said. Rockefeller and Albert were presiding over a joint session of the Senate and the House to honor the visiting President of Liberia, and in their unguarded conversation the two presiding officers made some mild jokes about the distinguished visitor and his country and about his host, who was a black member of the Congress.

Congressional officials, the story said, tried to prevail upon the journalists in the press gallery to treat the remarks that they had overheard (and recorded) as private and off the record, but to no avail. The remarks, inane but uncomplimentary, were published to the embarrassment not only of Rockefeller and Albert, but of the United States and its relations with one of the few African countries that has a favorable prejudice toward us. It appears that when you are in public life, there is no such thing as a private conversation if it can either be overheard by or reported to the press. But to those of us who belong to the diplomatic profession there is a lingering question whether the "cost/benefit ratio" of publishing this item was a reasonable one: Much damage was done to our country's relations with an African country that is important to us, for the sake of reporting some inconsequential but mildly titillating chitchat that provided a passing snicker to some newspaper readers.

Of course, if Rockefeller and Albert had exchanged remarks that reflected important policies or positions, if they had let slip something truly significant, I could understand that a conscientious journalist would feel he owed it to the public to record what he had heard; although even then much would depend on the context, on how the remarks were presented—whether as something odd and unrelated to the larger picture of our relations, or as a reflection of a reasoned position taken by senior government officials. In this particular case, "investigative reporting" might have consisted in trying to find out whether what the two men had said represented government policy; but no such investigative reporting took place because it would have resulted in killing the story.

—0—

Having written the foregoing, I dug out the newspaper account of September 24 and find that things were not as simple as I recorded them—and even more damaging. "Staff aides," the *New York Times* reported, "asked reporters not to use the recordings, pleading that under the rules of the House any remarks made on the speaker's dais were privileged. However, the National Black Network in New York and National Public Radio decided to treat the remarks as news and commented on them during a news program yesterday afternoon." Thereupon the rest of the press featured the whole story—the whole chain broke because its weakest link had broken, because someone had violated the voluntary embargo.

And so the once-venerable *New York Times*, which prints "All The News That's Fit To Print," found it fit to print this kind of exchange: Rep. Albert: "Are there many Liberians that are mulattoes?—There are?" Mr. Rockefeller: "Most are strictly blacks." Rep. Albert: "Really black, huh." Mr. Rockefeller: "But they've got a class system—the blacks that went back to Liberia and took on all the characteristics of the Southern whites. And they treated the local blacks. . ." Rep. Albert: "They never let the local blacks get in on anything?" Mr. Rockefeller: "Oh, no. (Pause). They've slightly changed their speech, but only slightly." Rep. Albert: "But only slightly." These pearls of wisdom were dispensed while the highest officials of our House and Senate were waiting for the entrance into the chamber of President Tolbert of Liberia, who was being honored by our Congress. One can imagine how honored he felt when he read the *Times* the next morning.

—0—

I promised earlier to explain what was the difference of opinion that I had with the State Department about a policy meeting that I had attended in Washington in April. There can be no better way to do this than to discuss, first, the Ford-Carter television debate on foreign policy in which the President said something rather hair-raising about Eastern Europe. It went like this:

Frankel (of the *New York Times*): "I'm sorry. Could I just follow? Did I understand you to say, sir, that the Russians are not using Eastern Europe as their own sphere of influence and occupying most of the countries there and making sure, with their troops, that it's a Communist zone? Whereas on our side of the line, the Italians and the French are still flirting with. . ."

President Ford: "I don't believe, Mr. Frankel, that the Yugoslavians consider themselves dominated by the Soviet Union. I don't believe that the Romanians consider themselves dominated by the Soviet Union. I don't believe that the Poles consider themselves dominated by the Soviet Union. Each of those countries is independent, autonomous. It has its own territorial integrity. And the United States does not concede that those countries are under the domination of the Soviet Union. . ."

It was not surprising that Governor Carter moved into this opening, which was as large as a barn door: ". . . We have also seen a very serious problem with the so-called Sonnenfeldt document, which apparently Mr. Ford has just endorsed, which said that there's an organic linkage between the Eastern European countries and the Soviet Union. And I would like to see Mr. Ford convince the Polish-Americans and the Czech-Americans and the Hungarian-Americans in this country that those countries don't live under the domination and supervision of the Soviet Union behind the iron curtain."

Now, let us disentangle this confused skein of arguments and countries. First of all, it is true that Yugoslavia is really independent of Soviet control, ever since Tito broke with Stalin in 1947—although that doesn't mean that Yugoslavia doesn't line up with the other Communist countries on many world issues to the detriment of the United States. Second, it is also true that Romania is not completely dominated by the Soviet Union. It has no Soviet troops on its territory, and it was the only Warsaw Pact country that didn't participate in the 1968 invasion of Czechoslovakia. It is fairly independent in its foreign relations, but controls its people just as tightly as the other Communist countries.

But when it comes to Poland, a country that does have Soviet occupation troops and is controlled to a considerable degree by the Soviet Union, the matter is much more complicated. If President Ford had said that Poland will have every encouragement from the United States to maintain the modicum of individual personality that it has been able to preserve or regain in the framework of the Communist-dominated Warsaw Pact; if he had said that our policy is to deal with Poland on many matters as if it were independent or at least autonomous; if he had said that we accord Poland special treatment because of the long tradition of friendship between our countries and the large number of Polish-Americans in our country—if he had said those things he would have been unassailable.

The trouble is that each Eastern European country is different and that it is an awful vulgarization of the debate to make it appear that they are all equally dominated by the Soviet Union. If Carter clearly got the better of the argument with respect to Poland, he had an even stronger case with Hungary and Czechoslovakia (which Ford hadn't mentioned), two countries which have even less room for maneuver than Poland. The United States has granted most-favored-nation treatment in the matter of trade to Yugoslavia because of its independence; to Romania because we hope to nurture and encourage the modicum of independence that it displays in foreign affairs; and to Poland largely because of the traditional ties between the two countries and because we hope eventually to move the situation there—and elsewhere in Eastern Europe—in a direction where those countries will be able to exercise their sovereignty even while retaining the ties to the Soviet Union that the latter regards essential to its own security.

And that is where the "Sonnenfeldt document" comes in. Poor Hal Sonnenfeldt! As so often happens, a man who can be criticized on many counts is attacked, and perhaps brought down, for entirely the wrong reason. I have many things to criticize about Hal Sonnenfeldt, who handles Eastern Europe for Secretary Kissinger, but there is absolutely no doubt in my mind that he was unfairly accused by a number of newspaper writers over the lecture that he delivered to the London conference of ambassadors in December 1975. At that time he said that we are looking for an "organic relationship" between the Soviet Union and the Eastern European countries—and this was misinterpreted as meaning that we are complacently looking for their absorption into the Soviet Union. Clearly, Sonnenfeldt had exactly the opposite in mind, but he had phrased his thought so unfortunately that he was subject to misinterpretation.

I was at the conference, and I took shorthand notes of what he said, and it was that our policy should be to influence events in Eastern Europe in such a way that the present "unnatural" relationship doesn't explode and become the source of a major conflict. Consequently, Sonnenfeldt said, we should encourage the Soviets to loosen their grip, to develop a more organic and viable relationship, one that will not be solely based on raw Soviet power. The problem, Sonnenfeldt said, is to make the Russians aware that this is in their own interest. If we display excessive zeal in trying to exploit the increased maneuvering ground sought by some Eastern European countries, the Russians may just tighten their grip. We and our allies should so conduct ourselves that the Soviets themselves will participate in the process of loosening up.

There was nothing in this that could give offense to any reasonable person except the phrase about the more organic relationship, which malicious persons could misinterpret as meaning that Sonnenfeldt, who is rather a hard-liner, wanted the Soviets to digest the Eastern European satellites in quiet and without outside interference. In fact, he went on to say at the London conference that we must pursue a policy, in this administration or in any one that is likely to follow, of "responding to the clearly visible aspirations for a more autonomous existence" by those countries, but "within the geopolitical realities"—by which he meant that it would be both unrealistic and unethical, indeed self-defeating, to give them the hope that we could come and free them from the Soviet yoke, for an attempt to do so would precipitate World War III.

The trouble with Sonnenfeldt is that he is arrogant and impatient with anyone who tries to modify some of his constructs even in detail. The manner in which he lectured the London conference of ambassadors—bored, supercilious, as if he were talking to people who ought to know all this but probably didn't have his grasp of the subtleties—was typical. People generally agree that he makes good sense most of the time, but he manages to get their backs up by his manner. He is a bad listener, especially for subordinates. So I would not be surprised if the malicious leak had occurred from among his own entourage rather than from the Pentagon or some other place in the government. But the leak (of the so-called Sonnenfeldt telegram) could not have occurred if the vanity of the man hadn't caused him to send a summary of his London remarks by cable to all the ambassadors who had already heard them; and of course such telegrams, despite their restricted distribution, can easily find their way into the wrong hands, particularly since the invention of the Xerox machine.

Actually his policy is quite subtle—perhaps too subtle for President Ford to have understood it clearly enough before the TV debate. We conceive of Eastern Europe (minus Albania, which is a special case) as consisting of two tiers, an upper tier consisting of Yugoslavia, Romania and Poland; and a lower tier consisting of the others. This is a schematic way of looking at the area, which is helpful as a shorthand formula for a rather sophisticated policy; for just as there are major differences between Yugoslavia, Romania and Poland—the three Eastern European countries that receive "most favored" i.e., non-discriminatory treatment from us in trade—so there are major differences (not quite so major, but still respectable) between Hungary, East Germany, Czechoslovakia and Bulgaria; and each country has to be dealt with on its own merits and in its own way. [Note: Since this was written Hungary, for good reasons, was moved to the "upper tier."]

If one considers, for instance, that at least the people, if not the governments, of Czechoslovakia and Hungary would like to see a loosening of Soviet constraints and controls, it must be recognized that the same is not true of Bulgaria, which has no Soviet occupation troops because none are needed, and whose government, far from wishing increased maneuvering room, calls for "ever closer integration" with the Soviet Union. My own impression of the Bulgarian leaders and a substantial number of their followers is that they probably congratulate themselves on having bet early on a winning horse, that they genuinely cheer when they see Soviet power expanding, because they consider themselves part of it and not among its victims.

By applying strict logic, which is always a very dangerous thing to do in foreign policy, Bulgaria would qualify for first prize in the "organic" nature of its relationship with the Soviet Union since that relationship is not based on force as it is currently in Hungary and Czechoslovakia. But it would be sheer idiocy for us to favor Bulgaria over the other Eastern European countries on such grounds, which nobody is proposing to do. What I am proposing, and have been proposing since shortly after I got here, is that we do exactly what Sonnenfeldt seemed to be saying in a larger context in London, that is, respond to the desires for closer relations on the part of the Bulgarians in strict accordance with our own national interests and without illusions about loosening their ties with the the USSR. Only, I also propose that this not be done in accordance with some rigid scheme of priorities, mainly because such a rigid scheme wouldn't work.

This seems like a very minor point, and it probably is, for I fully accept that the upper-tier countries are a lot more important to us than the others, and that Bulgaria should receive no specially advantageous treatment. But when it is a matter of mutual advantage, I do not believe it is in our interest to wait until something has been done with Hungary or Czechoslovakia because of some over-subtle schematization of our policy toward the minor Eastern European countries. And that is what I said at the meeting in Washington, and that is what seemed to be generally accepted at that meeting—until four months later a telegram arrived from there which purported to summarize the meeting and which obviously had been re-written in Sonnenfeldt's office to conform with his own ideas, even though he had never found it worth his time to listen to contrary argument.

So it can be seen that while I defend Hal Sonnenfeldt, I see his trouble in his operating style, not in his political beliefs. While I agree that we should not write off any of the Eastern European countries, I do not think it fair to have cited a Sonnenfeldt "document" or doctrine because no such doctrine exists, at least not in the terms attributed to it. When it comes to the problems of our policy toward Eastern Europe, there probably isn't much difference between what has been done under Ford and what might be done under Carter—any more than, despite the fulminating rhetoric, there was much difference between the policies of Truman and Acheson on the one hand, and those of Eisenhower and Dulles on the other. The overriding reality in Eastern Europe is Soviet power. The question is how best to come to terms with it.

The most convincing argument against the existence of a "Sonnenfeldt doctrine," incidentally, came from Henry Kissinger himself, who is supposed to have asked a journalist who tried to confront him with the telegram as a new departure in American foreign policy: "Do you really think," he is supposed to have asked, "that when we announce a new doctrine, I will let Sonnenfeldt be the one to announce it?"

In the infinitely careful and almost Aesopian language used by our director for Eastern Europe in the State Department, whom I had queried about the reaction there to my protest over the account of the policy meeting, I was informed in a letter that there had been "considerable vertical disagreement" with my message; which I interpret to mean that Sonnenfeldt blew his stack. But I was told by another source that a snappy reply to my telegram had "not been cleared" in the Department—which may mean that there was at least one major participant in the April meeting who refused to put his name on a telegram that took issue with my differing account of it. Hooray for that one courageous bureaucrat, whoever he may be!

On the other hand, those people who were willing to go along with a message censuring me (or, shall we say, putting me in my place) may get promoted to more important positions in the government; and as for me, I may have acquired the reputation of being querulous way out there in Sofia from where everything is seen in a distorted perspective. On the other hand, I cannot really have acquired through this little incident the reputation of making a nuisance of myself when I find that people are playing fast and loose with the facts. I've had that reputation all along—and if I suffer for it, so be it. All through my professional life my motto has been "Capitalize on your liabilities!"

11

Fringe benefit of being an ambassador: A luncheon with Barbara Tuchman. And how the writer, instead of acting the genial host, tries to probe her views on what might have been in China—an exercise in futility for any historian.

October 8. The other day Al Schrock, our General Services officer, asked to see me in the morning, and he told me that the previous night he had come back to the office to pick up some personal papers and had found "two damsels in distress" who had rung the bell of the embassy and were talking with the Marine on duty. It turned out that they had thought they had hotel accommodations in Sofia arranged through the government tourist agency, but when they came to Sofia they found that the hotels were full and there was no record of a reservation. In their distress, they asked for any help the Marine could give them; and the top sergeant came downstairs and offered to put them up in his own apartment, while he would presumably sleep elsewhere in the Embassy.

Nothing particularly remarkable about that story, except that our Marines had once more done themselves proud by their intelligent and helpful approach to an unusual problem. But it turned out, Al Schrock said, that one of the two ladies was a rather well-known American: Barbara Tuchman, the author and historian. The ladies had then inquired about a restaurant in the nieghborhood, had been sent to the Balkan Hotel, and had later called to say that they had found a room there. Al just wanted me to know that a rather celebrated American was in town.

So I profited from one of the few really valuable privileges of being an American ambassador in such a small and out of the way country, and put in a telephone call to Mrs. Tuchman and said to her that my wife and I would be pleased if she and her traveling companion would do us the honor of coming to lunch before they

77

continued their voyage; and so we had a fascinating lunch in which my deputy, Harvey Feldman, and his wife, both of whom are China specialists, joined. Barbara Tuchman is of course the author of *Stilwell and the American Experience in China*, in addition to her superb books *The Zimmermann Telegram, The Proud Tower* and *August 1914*. She said she is currently working on a book about Europe in the fourteenth century; and she talked for a while about the fascinating considerations that led her to write about that period.

In the course of our conversation I brought up a question that nettled her a little—whether she really thought that if Washington had followed the advice of the dissidents in the American Embassy in Chungking and had invited Mao Tse-tung [Mao Zedong] to visit America just after the war, things would have come out differently in Sino-American relations. She denied ever having said this, and of course she must be right. I had probably read some extrapolation of the remarks she made to the luncheon given by the American Foreign Service Association in honor of John Stewart Service. But I had been present at that occasion. At that time she had cited the recommendation of such a visit as one of many by our experts in Chungking who later were savagely disciplined by their own ambassador, an ignoramus named Patrick Hurley who remained convinced to the end that America must stand behind Chiang Kai-shek, even when it was obvious to all experts that the Generalissimo had no chance of prevailing over the Communists.

Mrs. Tuchman, who had taken up the cudgels in behalf of the China experts of the Foreign Service who suffered such persecution first by Hurley, later by McCarthy and finally by Dulles, had an interesting remark about how things turned out in China after World War II, a remark which is not contained in her book about Stilwell because she had come upon the evidence only after it was published. She said that when looking through the records of the election debate in America in 1944, she had come to realize that the margin on which President Roosevelt was operating was actually much smaller than she had believed—because even in 1944 Thomas Dewey, the Republican candidate, was belaboring the China issue and warning against any abandonment of Chiang Kai-shek, as if abandoning him were the same as abandoning China.

I find it entirely plausible that the political margin on which Roosevelt, who alone could have shifted support from Chiang Kai-shek to Mao Tse-tung, was smaller than she had thought, for I well remember how the Generalissimo was lionized during the war by the American press. But my question, of course, was whether even a sudden shift to Mao would have resulted in anything like a viable and friendly relationship between the new revolutionary regime in China—whether Russian-controlled or not—and the United States; and I recalled that the Soviet Union, which we had supported with enormous masses of economic and military supplies during the war, still had found it to its own interest to roll down an iron curtain between Eastern and Western Europe after World War II. Even Castro, I said, had been approached not long after he came to power to see whether the United States might come to some civil relationship with him, and there had even been a timid offer of aid which he instantly turned aside, since—in my opinion—Castro *needed* bad relations with the United States in order to consolidate his own regime.

To which Mrs. Tuchman answered by referring to the last sentence of her book about China, which she said reflected the essence of any wisdom she had been able to distil from this traumatic chapter in American diplomatic history. I went to my library and dug it out. That passage reads: "(Stilwell's) mission failed in its ultimate purpose because the goal was unachievable. The impulse was not Chinese. Combat efficiency and the offensive spirit, like the Christianity and democracy offered by missionaries and foreign advisers, were not indigenous demands of the society and the culture to which they were brought. Even the Yellow River Road that Stilwell built in 1921 had disappeared twelve years later. China was a problem for which there was no American solution. The American effort to sustain the status quo could not supply an outworn government with strength and stability or popular support. It could not hold up a husk nor long delay the cyclical passing of the mandate of heaven. In the end China went her own way as if the Americans had never come."

Much wisdom here, but it does not answer the question—which is inherently unanswerable, as are most questions about what might have been in history—whether the attitude of the Chinese

Communists toward the United States would have been friendly after the war if we had in 1944 ceased our support for Chiang and transferred it to Mao. One-half of the answer to that question was provided by Mrs. Tuchman at our lunch when she pointed to the constraints on Roosevelt which in effect made such a transfer politically impossible. But the other half, whether we would have embarked on an era of friendship with the Chinese Communists if we had supported them, will always remain moot. My own opinion is that it is very doubtful that Mao would have wanted friendship with Western barbarians whose credentials, to his fanatical Marxist turn of mind, would always have been highly suspect. To the conspiratorial mind, to the spirit devoted to perpetual revolution, the United States must seem inherently hostile and dangerous.

And we *are* dangerous to them because despite all our shortcomings we represent the ideals of freedom of the individual, freedom of political choice, economic betterment through private initiative, and political diversity. Our ideals are really quite revolutionary, but to Communists we quite naturally appear quintessentially counter-revolutionary.

[A little later, I managed to find the quotation from Barbara Tuchman which she herself had apparently forgotten. It was in the address which she delivered to the Foreign Service Association luncheon in 1973 which honored John Stewart Service, and through him others who had suffered unjustly during the period of Senator Joseph McCarthy. In that address, Mrs. Tuchman referred to the Nixon visit to Peking and the apparent drawing-together of the anti-Communist U.S. government and the hitherto anti-American Chinese government. She said:

"Yet it could have happened 25 years earlier, sparing us and Asia immeasurable, and to some degree irreparable, harm, if American policy had been guided by the information and recommendations of the staff of the Chungking Embassy, then acknowledged to be the best informed foreign service group in China."

That, precisely, is the point that I question. There is no doubt that Service, Clubb, Vincent and others were treated very unfairly and that their assessments of the Chinese Communists as the likely winners in the Chinese civil war have been vindicated. However, whether a meeting between an American President and Mao Tsetung after World War II would have produced good feelings between the two countries rather than the antagonism that existed for almost thirty years, depends on how one assesses the reasons for that antagonism.

It wasn't necessarily only because of our assistance to Chiang Kai-shek that the Chinese Communists launched their anti-American campaign almost immediately after their victory. In fact, we had ceased to support Chiang well before the end of the civil war. Just as Fidel Castro turned toward the Soviet Union despite the fact that he was very well received in Washington and even offered a loan—and we had not supported the Batista regime in Cuba against him—so the Chinese Communists seemed to have very specifically Chinese reasons for humiliating Americans and excluding all American influence from their country after they won their revolution. After all, they turned even against the Russians who did help them, contrary to their undertakings at the Yalta Conference; just as the Russians, whom we helped so much during World War II, turned against us after that war for very specifically Russian reasons.]

—0—

October 12. Among the things we discussed at our staff meeting today were some that may be of general interest: The Bulgarian Government has signified its agreement to removal of travel restrictions which were a remnant of tit-for-tat retaliation during the height of the Cold War. On the other hand they have refused to waive visa fees, pleading that these constitute a major source of revenue for them.—The Bulgarian ship that violated our fishing zone off Oregon was fined $350,000, but it turned out that it carried insurance against just such an outcome. The situation was somewhat complicated by the fact that three Bulgarian seamen refused to get back on their ships and asked for asylum.— Meanwhile, the American who has been in jail here for trying to smuggle someone out of Bulgaria was visited by our Consul (after we sent a stiff note to the Foreign Ministry recalling that our Consular Agreement provides for consular access after no more than four working days), and the Bulgarians apparently will not only let her out on bail but give her back her passport.—We have sent to Washington an analysis of the Bulgarian propaganda which describes Western insistence on "freedom of information" as a weapon used to revive the Cold War.

Had a visit from our Embassy doctor, who resides in Belgrade, and who looked at one of our staff members whom we had considered evacuating by air to Frankfurt, since the treatment he received here seemed to do no good and there were doubts about the diagnosis.—We received amended instructions (which we had had to seek in lengthy exchanges) that will enable us to make a sensible compromise with the Bulgarian government over their insistence that all Bulgarian employes of foreign embassies must be covered by a standard labor contract.—Elisabeth and I attended a reception in honor of a distinguished American librarian, at which we learned for the first time that the head of the Sofia public library will be going to the United States (on a UNESCO grant).— Received by pouch from Embassy Moscow a telegram that we had requested, with one page missing.—Finally buttoned up an invitation to the Director of Customs, whose organization is working well with U.S. Customs in the matter of narcotics, to visit the United States.—Exchanged messages with some ambassadorial colleagues at other Eastern European posts in connection with a trip that I am preparing.—Talked with the representative of Lufthansa about our missing pouch which seems to have disappeared after they received it from Pan Am at Frankfurt; with our cultural officer about a private performance of the visiting American harpsichord artist; and attended two more receptions in honor of departing colleagues, at one of which I had a useful conversation with another guest. The cocktail party circuit is, of course, for us a place of work and a very disagreeable but necessary one.

12

On getting nominated for a "presidentially appointed" position: a glorified (and infamous) shell game. How the prolongation of that game can break a strong man's spirit. Case study of a big man being slowly made smaller.

October 14. About a month ago I had written a letter to a friend in the State Department asking his advice in a personal matter. I said I would be traveling to Warsaw to compare notes with our ambassador there and his staff. I could save the government money by combining such informational ("orientation") visits with other travel, and in this case I was due for a physical checkup at the Air Force hospital in Wiesbaden. Berlin, I pointed out, lay on the route from Warsaw to Wiesbaden. But as my correspondent in the Department knew, a few months ago I had received a telephone call from Washington asking whether I minded if my name were put up as one of four among whom the Secretary of State would choose one to recommend as Ambassador to the German Democratic Republic. Naturally, I had consented. Now, however, I wanted to know whether a visit to East Berlin might give rise to remarks in the Department that I was perhaps taking things for granted and already looking over what I thought would be my next post.

Nothing, I said, would be further from my mind. It just so happened that after visiting Warsaw I would have visited all our Eastern European embassies except Berlin; and it might be taken as an excess of delicacy and concern over being misunderstood if I skipped the last remaining capital, particularly since it would be on the way.

What I did not say in the letter is that I knew that Secretary Kissinger had in mind someone quite different than myself for that position, and that that person had in fact turned it down; and that the higher rank and longer experience and greater stature

83

of that candidate had convinced me that Kissinger was not likely to recommend me, since I have never been close to him and am probably not regarded by him as one of the most deserving career chiefs of mission. Anyway, I finally received a reply to my letter (encouraging me to proceed with the visits), and attached to that reply was a small piece of paper, scotch-taped to show it was very personal, which said something like this: "I'm a bit down at the mouth because have just learned that the White House will make no recess appointments to (the post for which he had been waiting for a long time), and also not for East Berlin."

And thereby hangs a tale. It is not a tale about my angling for another ambassadorial appointment; anything I might write about that would seem self-serving. The tale is that of my colleague, who shall remain anonymous, whose current experience while waiting for an ambassadorial appointment can be taken as fairly typical for many others that I have known, including myself when I was waiting for the presidential appointment. To put it in a nutshell, he has been kept dangling now for almost two years. In his correspondence with me he keeps a stiff upper lip, but he's been on an emotional roller-coaster with ups and downs that would tax the character of a saint. His appointment as ambassador to a certain country was about to be announced some two years ago—people were already congratulating him on it—when it mysteriously fell through. The most intriguing and distressing feature of such situations is that one never really knows where one stands, where matters are, where a holdup might be—and whether the people one is dealing with are telling the truth.

I know, I've been through that situation myself. In the case of my friend, his first disappointment came almost two years ago when it was decided, first, not to fill the ambassadorial position for the time being, then to offer it to someone else; and finally it went to someone still different who has very good connections outside the government with an organization that has a good deal of influence in the White House. And my friend was left out in the cold, i.e. continuing in his present responsible but highly unrewarding job, and placing his faith once more in "the system" which is supposed to reward, ultimately, those career officers who are most deserving of promotion and who manifestly would be well qualified for a particular ambassadorial job.

I am not talking here of political appointees knocking out the candidacies of better-qualified career officers. That, too, is an interesting subject and one on which I love to express my views. I am writing, instead, of the incredible competitiveness among career officers and the heartbreak that comes not only from seeing· younger and perhaps less well qualified people pull ahead of someone who has devoted a lifetime to diplomacy, but the almost completely impenetrable curtain behind which the decisions on such matters are made. Obviously, the White House is involved but the first steps have to be taken in the State Department. That is where peer judgment comes in, and maneuvering and backbiting and stiletto work, and frequently also unbelievable dishonesty on the part of the people who make the final recommendations—who, of course, are subjected to all kinds of pressures. A number of times my friend remarked to me already during his first ordeal that if he knew that he wouldn't get the embassy for which he was being told he was the leading candidate and for which he was ideally qualified, he could arrange his life differently. Instead, however, he continued to be told to be patient, that everything would work out. That is what he is still, or again, told today. Only, a number of other people competing with him are probably being told the same.

Well, after he failed to get the one embassy for which he would in my opinion have been ideally qualified, another one fell open and he was a candidate for it. After many months of waiting and getting mixed signals, he was finally informed one day that the Secretary had "signed off" on a paper to the President recommending his nomination. As it turned out, however, that was not the end of his troubles but more like the beginning of another game of roulette: at the same time the head of another agency of the government put up to the White House another candidate who also had some good qualifications although he did not have the experience of my friend. Paralysis ensued. Months later I learned that what had happened was that the White House sent both proposed nominations back to Kissinger, asking him to choose between them. One might think that having already nominated my friend as the best qualified career officer, this would have been an easy task. However, with Africa and the Middle East and a number of other things to worry about, Kissinger apparently laid the whole business aside. Also, he may have been genuinely unsure who was the better candidate. Meanwhile the other candidate, who is no fool, called on several of the top State Department officers to make his own candidacy better known; while my friend, who works there, is dependent on the support of his own superiors who presumably are well aware of his better qualifications. Now, having already waited over half a year, he will have to wait still more—while being completely uncertain about the outcome.

His wife wrote Elisabeth a letter that brought twinges of recollection to us, since it recalled so many of our own experiences. She recounted how one evening her husband [let's call him Ted] came home with news that the Secretary had sent his name to the White House. "He was so excited and I was completely amazed that he would react like that for we had gone through the whole thing so many times and been let down each time. I asked Ted why he was letting himself in for another letdown and he said—Muriel, this has to be it. The thing had actually gone to the White House this time, K. had personally endorsed him, etc., and then he said that if he didn't get this appointment he knew he was really finished as far as the Foreign Service was concerned—it all had to do with his being rejected for (the other post) which would have been so right, and if the powers that be didn't think enough of him to give him this appointment then he certainly wasn't going to get any other. Well, we talked it over then and said why not, why not make this into something, no holding back, enjoy whatever excitement we could get out of the whole thing. I remember feeling that this was wrong, that we would regret it, but Ted seemed so happy, or maybe he was forcing it to make me happier, I don't know, but we consciously decided to 'go' with this appointment.

"We talked about all the things we'd do, places we'd see, the fun of visiting with you if we could manage it. This was idiotic. We should have known better, so in a way all that happened was our own fault. For the basic thing that happened as each damned day went by and nothing came from the W.H. was that we began to live in a vacuum, a sort of coma; I'd think when I'd get up in the morning, well, today we will hear; by nighttime when somehow the day had just gone by, I'd go to bed thinking we'll hear tomorrow, and so it went. Just about the time we'd be the lowest something would happen—like first the FBI investigation, getting the list of forty friends, then people writing or calling to find out what appointment was coming up, etc. Then the call from the Dept. to have the physicals. A few more signs of encouragement, though not many. Meanwhile I began to have trouble with my blood pressure and started worrying that that might disqualify Ted for the assignment. But I passed anyway. Then, while I tried not to do too many things based on our being posted there, some things I felt I just had to do, like buying up the dregs of winter clothing, feeling it would be my only chance to supplement my wardrobe in time. Then I had all our winter clothes cleaned, blankets, etc., for I felt they would be in storage, or en route for a long time and must be clean in case of moths, etc. Then, at the end of summer, I bought dregs of summer clothes for the same reason. Then we needed a new washing machine, so with the thought that we'd be renting our house it seemed best to buy it when the sales were on, also we thought our house should be painted on the outside if we were to rent it and we should certainly go ahead and do it rather than wait for the last minute when we'd be showing it for rental."

It is a touching letter, especially poignant because every detail recalled by this gifted and perceptive woman touched chords of our own recollection. First my nomination had been held up because Sofia was to be kept in reserve for a candidate who might not get White House approval for a better post. Then, when the man (who was not a Foreign Service officer) got that better post, my name went to the White House recommended by Secretary Rogers, and after the FBI investigations had just been concluded Mr. Rogers resigned and Mr. Kissinger took over, and of course everything went back to square one. But rather than detail the frustration that *we* went through, let me quote more from the letter of the wife of my friend [with her permission, of course]; for she puts it so much better in terms of what all this means in the lives of a middle-aged career couple who have devoted the better part of their lives to serving the government abroad.

"Thank God we put off selling some furniture we thought we'd have to sell," she continued, "but we gave some away to (their son and daughter-in-law) that I'd give anything now if we still had. So now, a good bit poorer financially and tremendously poorer in spirit, here we sit. Ted has now heard that there will be no interim appointments. The Congress has adjourned. That means even if there were any hope at all, which I'm now quite sure there isn't, it won't be until after the first of the year. And you know, my friend," she wrote to my wife, "I tell this only to you, I honestly don't think I can take it any more. Just what I'll do I don't know. I've felt so damned sorry for Ted all this time, the humiliation and all, other people who can't hold a candle to him are getting appointments, I've tried with all I have to be fun and gay and keep his spirits up. But now I'm drained. I can't do it any more. I must do something and I will. As it is, I never go out of the house except to the market. We have no one in, all seems too much effort. The thought of entertaining is abhorrent. I'm bored to death and I'm boring to be with."

And her letter ends, after she describes some more private matters: "Add to all this the dreadful frustration of indecision, and the burning fury that we could be put in a position like this, and fury against who—what—if only—only—only there were one person or maybe there is one person and I just don't know who it is, but somebody I could go to and just ask 'why', 'why', 'why'. For God's sake—either give this assignment to a politico, or give it to (the other candidate), or give it to us, but do something!!!!! Well, this is the first and only time I've tried to put down on paper, to verbalize what I feel and think about it all, and now you will understand why I have not written before. But how could I have written you anything else when all this has been occupying my days and nights ever since you left? Forgive me, it is a horrid thing to do to a dear friend but maybe it is the therapy I need. Let's pray so, for I am indeed desperate."

Elisabeth and I read and re-read this letter and relived the very similar experiences through which we had gone. As one gets higher in a hierarchical and competitive service, there are always fewer and fewer jobs with more and more applicants. The Foreign Service itself would provide a terrific amount of competition, but we also have to face competition from people outside, a subject about which I would rather not explode at this time.

But there is a post-script that I must add to the above glimpse into the perils that attend the transition from career Foreign Service officer to presidentially appointed (and Senate-confirmed) ambassador, and that point has fairly general application to people in large organizations, in responsible positions, who are put under such psychological strain. It is my experience, which I must humbly acknowledge, that under such circumstances not only the ego suffers but inevitably also the performance—and this, in turn, affects the prospects for the expected preferment. There are some officers in the Service who have become ambassadors at a very young age, and not necessarily due to luck—many of the younger ones, I have felt for a long time, are really better than most of the older ones. They probably have little sympathy for this phenomenon, but it is a very significant one: The more responsibility you get, the more you can show what you can do; the more you are sat upon and baffled by doubts and kept in the dark and in effect pushed around, the smaller you are apt to become, no matter how highly placed you may seem to be in the hierarchy.

The policy-making process has once been described by a brilliant sociologist as a mountain stream, with ideas—like salmon— fighting their way up over the rapids. Very few reach the spawning grounds at the top. This certainly is true of ideas and policy proposals in the executive branch; but it is also, in my opinion, true of people. Those who can go up the rapids leap by beautiful leap, emerge at the top in excellent form; but those who for one reason or another are tossed back, who have special obstacles to sur- mount, are naturally apt to tire—and then the process of natural selection sets in. I myself went through one such experience, and it took me some time to surmount it. It wasn't a matter of missing promotions—this, too, has happened in my career—but, rather, involved one superior who decided that I wasn't any good and treated me that way.

The episode, if one can term it that, was many years ago. I was a second secretary in our embassy in Paris, and a new minister came in who gave me a few things to do which interested him but for which I had no aptitude and which, actually, lay outside the area of my normal duties. I did them badly, and then noticed that he started giving me easier and easier things to do. His courtesy toward me, if anything, became greater and greater; but when I spoke at staff meeting he seemed not to listen, being convinced that what I said wasn't worth listening to; and once, sitting with him in a car and chatting while on the way to some appointment, he reminisced about some episodes in his career and then, rather casually, remarked that he wasn't sure that those stories interested me since "he didn't know if I wanted to make the Foreign Service my career." It was clear that he had written me off as sub- standard—and the awful effect of this was that I did turn in less useful work, I saw myself slowly and dreadfully conforming to his image of me.

That particular story has a happy ending, for about six months later he had changed his mind 180 degrees, recognized that I had very useful services to offer, and in fact used to come to my office early in the morning when I had read the cables and scanned the newspapers, to discuss the political situation in order to get some angles on it that he could put forward at the ambassador's staff meeting. But it took me a good long time to get to that point, and I was a lot younger then. It is a truism that people grow with responsibility. The trouble in the State Department is that not all positions have the authority that goes with their responsibilities. The last position I had before being named ambassador was one with much responsibility and very little authority—Deputy Assistant Secretary of State for International Organization Affairs, which means that I was dealing, or trying to deal, with the hydra-headed United Nations and all the issues confronting us there, actually more a coordinating than a policy making position. A glorified broker. But that position sometimes required me, by the nature of the job, to put to my superiors some very unpleasant alternatives or rather dilemmas, with none of the choices apt to cover them—or me—with glory.

The reason I am making these observations is that I have seen my friend at various stages of his career. Once he was in a job in which he was handling a lot of rather grubby and unattractive problems, and I well recall telling Elisabeth that I had doubts whether he could handle a great deal of responsibility. Then another time I saw him in a very difficult and demanding position in which he had maneuvering room, and he performed superbly— he was a fine executive who got the best out of his people, was quick to go to the essence of problems, articulate in developing the policy choices, and persuasive in "selling" the right solution at meetings with some very prickly adversaries. Now he is in a position which has still more responsibility but rather less authority, and I can well imagine that in his present frame of mind he may not project the same image of the happy warrior, thoughtfully sardonic analyst, gregarious companion or artful advocate that others might project because they aren't burdened down with the personal problems that he has to carry in addition to all the responsibilities of his office.

13

The Bogomil heresy, and the Bulgarian origin of the word "bugger." The Museum of Revolutionary Vigilance features a book by Henry Kissinger as an example of subversive literature. Poor Mr. Levchev offers to be helpful.

Our discussion with Barbara Tuchman about Bulgaria in the fourteenth century sent me back to the history books, for in that conversation the subject of the Bogomil heresy had come up; and with it the question, which nobody was able to answer, whether that heresy had anything to do with the demise of the second Bulgarian empire and the 500-year occupation of the country by the Turks. The Bogomils are a little-known chapter of Bulgarian history. The English word "bugger" probably goes back to them because it was believed that in their religious zealotry they advocated sexual abstinence with members of the opposite sex, not to mortify the flesh but to prevent the further propagation of the human race. The Bogomils were a subversive sect of reformers who attacked the laziness and luxury of the Orthodox Church hierarchy, but they went to extraordinary lengths in constructing a new version of the Old and New Testaments, which resulted in the conclusion that the devil was not only responsible for the crucifixion of Christ but also for the creation of the whole Orthodox community, with its churches, vestments, ceremonies, sacraments and fasts, and all its bishops, monks and priests.

There was a certain structured consistency in their beliefs, which started with the notion that Satan had not always been the Prince of Evil. He was, together with Christ, a son of God, in fact the first-born. But his ambition was to be the equal of God, and he won over a part of the heavenly host in an attempted coup which failed, resulting in "Satanael" and his rebel angels being cast out of heaven—whereupon he built his kingdom on earth. When God breathed life into Adam and Eve, they had to sell themselves to

Satanael who ruled them until Christ came to earth. It was through Satanael's machinations that the crucifixion took place; but while seeming to go to heaven Christ actually went to hell, defeated Satanael and took away the divine suffix "el" which made him simply Satan, the Devil. Satan thereupon became the inventor of the entire Orthodox Church. Those Bulgarians who wished to worship God and Christ therefore had no choice but to do it in the privacy of their homes.

The Bogomils, writes David Marshal Laing in his book *The Bulgarians*, based their morality, as the Manichaeans had always done, on the view that the visible world was inherently evil, and that salvation could only be found in deliberate withdrawal from it. Some scholars, notably those with a Marxist background, however, regard them essentially as "rationalists" because they denounced many of the features of the Orthodox Church which dealt with supernatural phenomena. Thus Professor O. Angelov points out that the Bogomils saw no special virtue in baptism, since ordinary water or oil possess no miraculous power, and that they especially rejected infant baptism "because babies are incapable of understanding what is going on." About Holy Communion they were equally categorical: its elements were nothing but ordinary bread and wine. They also rejected the cult of relics, declaring that the bones of dead men differed in no way from the bones of dead animals. And they detested the cross, as the instrument that had been used by the devil to torture Christ.

Persecuted throughout their existence, during the first Bulgarian empire (9th to 11th century), then under the Byzantines, and again under the second Bulgarian empire (13th to 15th century), the Bogomils provided a rallying-point not only for religious opposition to the church but also for opposition to the state. As Laing puts it, "As a result of their intransigent hostility to all feudal or 'capitalist' institutions, the menace of the Bogomils provoked a reaction comparable to that inspired by modern Communist parties among regimes in many parts of the world." And this seems to have been not entirely unjustified since they did not seek only religious reform but wanted to bring down the state itself. While they possessed no armed forces, as did the Paulicans of Asia Minor, they went in for assassinations and, according to some historical authorities, made an alliance with the fierce Pecheneg tribe in the year 1086 and apparently encouraged those barbarian invaders to ravage the Balkans. "They constituted a 'fifth column' in Bulgaria," writes Laing, "both under the Bulgarian tsars and during Byzantine domination. There is no doubt that they helped to destroy Bulgarian national unity, and pave the way for ultimate Turkish conquest."

They were, in other words, a counter-culture, so fiercely opposed to the basic beliefs and social and political structures of the society in which they lived, that they did not care if it was destroyed even by their country's enemies. There was no chance, of course, for the Bogomils—or for any Bulgarian community whatsoever—to prosper under the Moslem yoke of the Ottoman conqueror. But apparently the Bogomils did not see that the Moslems represented a greater danger than their internal Bulgarian enemies. This of course is a phenomenon that we see again and again in history. As the Indian sage Kautilya put it two thousand years ago, to many a statesman "the enemy of my enemy is my friend." Often this makes sense, but in practice it doesn't always work out that way. In practice one sometimes has to choose a lesser evil, and even support it, in order to ward off a greater evil.—As I am writing this two weeks before our national elections, I am wondering if many a voter won't approach them in that spirit.

—0—

I mentioned before that we had met some interesting people, including the head of the National Library here, at a cocktail reception in honor of a distinguished American librarian. Thereby hang a number of tales. First, Elisabeth and I had already met the head of the National Library when, about six months after our arrival here, we asked to be shown around the Library and especially its map collection, since I am a collector of old maps. The librarian, a lady, had been charming and had entrusted us to some English-speaking subordinates who took us through the building. We found the visit very interesting. We saw how foreign periodicals are accessible only to persons with special permits, we saw how with relatively small resources a truly excellent public institution was being run for the benefit largely of students and scholars. We also met there a "paleonto-geographer," a delightful man not connected with the Library who specializes in the early cartography of the Balkans. He apparently had "clearance" to accept invitations from us, as he did later; but the librarian—who, it turned out the other day, actually speaks very good English— never accepted our invitations, about which we were genuinely sorry. She is an interesting intellectual, and obviously it would have been pleasant to chat with her about matters of mutual interest.

At the same cocktail party I had a conversation with the Deputy Chief of the "Committee for Art and Culture," which is really something much more important than its name would indicate. Run by Lyudmilla Zhivkova, the daughter of the chief of state and party secretary, the Committee is for all intents and purposes the Ministry of Thought Control, for it controls not only art and culture but also radio and television in Bulgaria; and it is supposed to see to it that artists and media people—all who communicate to the public—are properly inspired with the "socialist" ideals and inculcate the doctrine of "socialist" discipline and proletarian internationalism (i.e., dictatorship of the Communist Party and leadership of the Soviet Union) in those who see or read or hear their output. The Deputy Chief, Mr. Lyubomir Levchev, whom I had not met before, is a poet and a man of great charm. We talked, in the presence of the visiting librarian from Washington, about the forthcoming visit here of Daniel Boorstin, the Librarian of Congress, and in that connection also about the possibility of an exchange of book exhibits. Each side seemed to think that an excellent idea.

At that moment I was seized by an uncontrollable desire, which as a "seasoned diplomat" I surely should have controlled, to speak to Mr. Levchev about another book exhibit that I had seen here in Sofia. I told him that about a year ago I had gone to see something called the Museum of Revolutionary Vigilance. It is a dingy place which no one is likely to visit unless required to do so , but one could see school children being taken through that little museum as part of their curriculum of indoctrination. The museum showed the various instruments foreign powers use in their attempts—doomed to failure by the revolutionary vigilance of the people—to sow confusion and disaffection, to spy and sabotage, and otherwise to harm the interests of Bulgaria and international

Communism. One could see radio transmitting sets that had been parachuted into Bulgaria (apparently during World War II), weapons, codes used by spies, instruments of concealment and deception—and, in the last room, books that could be used to subvert right-thinking Bulgarians.

Since I am interested in books, I took a rather leisurely look at that display case. It contained, by and large, sociological books published in England, France, Germany and the United States about Communism, or the cold war, or the Soviet Union. Some of the authors were well-known scholars, others I had not seen before. And right in the middle of those books was the one called *American Foreign Policy* by a certain Henry A. Kissinger, the edition that was published just before he became national security adviser to President Nixon. I was noting down the titles of the books when a lady custodian of the museum came up to me and said, in a slow Bulgarian that even I could understand: "Please, mister, this is a private exhibition just for ourselves. It is not for foreigners. We must ask you not to take notes. That is forbidden."

So I expressed to Mr. Levchev my surprise that a book by Mr. Kissinger should have been so prominently displayed in the Museum of Revolutionary Vigilance; but I added that I had seen it quite a long time ago and perhaps it had been removed in the meantime. Mr. Levchev, quite properly, asked whether I had mentioned this before to a member of the government. I said no, it had seemed to me pointless since Mr. Kissinger is so frequently reviled in the press here that displaying a book of his in English as an example of "anti-revolutionary" activities had seemed to me too trivial to mention. Well, said Mr. Levchev, he would certainly look into the matter. Don't bother, I said. Well, he added irrelevantly— and this is the point of the story, for he obviously needed to find some justification—"there is no censorship in Bulgaria, but we do have a strict policy of prohibiting all books that are pornographic or that advocate war or fascism." Since the occasion was a cocktail party and not an official meeting, I let this pass with the remark that "I had not been aware that Mr. Kissinger had written anything pornographic." By which I meant to imply that if Mr. Levchev were to characterize Mr. Kissinger's book as advocating fascism or war, he would have a real incident on his hands; and he understood and said nothing more.

After my visit to the Museum of Revolutionary Vigilance a year ago, I went to my bookshelf and took down *American Foreign Policy* by Kissinger, to see if it contained any particularly inflammatory anti-Communist passages. It is a clinical book and not a polemical tract, being concerned mostly with analysis of our own failures and offering prescriptions for how to deal with the other great powers of the world. But I find this passage which certainly would not make agreeable reading to a Bulgarian Communist: "The ironic feature of the current situation is that Marxism, professing a materialistic philosophy, is accepted only where it does not exist: in some new countries and among protest movements of the advanced democratic countries. Its appeal is its idealistic component and not its economic theory. It offers a doctrine of substantive change and an explanation of final purposes. Its philosophy has totally failed to inspire the younger generation in communist countries, where its bureaucratic reality is obvious."

I am writing this just prior to my departure for Warsaw. But at the airport I intend to ask Harvey Feldman, who will be in charge during my absence, to send someone to the Museum of Revolutionary Vigilance to see if Henry Kissinger's book is still displayed there among the weapons used by the enemy to undermine and subvert Communism in Bulgaria.

14

Bringing back impressions from Poland and East Germany. The accumulated agenda of a small embassy. Dealing with a foreign government over the head of one's own ambassador: Disadvantages of "personal" diplomacy.

October 28, I have just returned from a trip that took me to Warsaw, East Berlin, West Berlin and Frankfurt. Harvey met me at the airport, and one of my first questions was whether the missing pouch had been found. Unfortunately the State Department, Pan American and Lufthansa all agree that nothing more can be done to trace it. The pouch, containing 11 pounds of personal mail, left Washington on September 8, and since it hasn't turned up anywhere it may be resting underneath some piece of freight in a warehouse in Singapore or Reykjavik, and may not be discovered until that piece of freight (or perhaps furniture) is moved.

Meanwhile—and sometimes pouches don't turn up until more than a year after they have been missent—what love letters, pleas for help, financial opportunities or disasters, and irreplaceable mementos may have been lost? I myself have been expecting to hear from a friend in trouble, a bank, and a publisher (about the draft of a novel), and am increasingly worried by their silence. Others have different problems. Such an uncertain dead space in the flow of communication with our country is one of the many hardships one has to accept as part of serving at an isolated post abroad.

I am full of impressions of Poland and East Germany, having managed to compress a great deal of information and observation into very little time. And I must confess to a certain amount of envy of my colleague in Warsaw because he has "real problems" to deal with. The political and economic situation there is infinitely more complex and unstable than in Bulgaria, and a foreign

97

embassy in Warsaw comes into possession of infinitely more information to analyze and report—and of course (why do I say of course?) Poles talk freely to foreigners, and this includes the government, the party and the press—to say nothing of the church and the opposition, for there is a much greater play of political forces in Poland than I had supposed, especially in contrast to Bulgaria.

Even though I had been aware of the importance of the Catholic Church in Poland, I had not realized that sixty per cent of Poles above the age of 18 go to church at least once a week there. It would be a mistake to equate the Church with the opposition, but a story illustrated the degree to which church and opposition are intertwined, at least in the opinion of some Poles. The story, as told to me by a foreign diplomat, went somewhat like this:

At a service in a crowded church, the priest from his pulpit notices a man standing in the back of the congregation, a man who is wearing a hat and who doesn't participate in the service—he doesn't kneel, doesn't genuflect, doesn't pray, nor does he join the others in Holy Communion. So after the service the priest goes up to the man and asks him if he belongs to the police. Oh, no, not at all, says the man. Well, then, why didn't you kneel with the others or pray or come up to partake of communion? Oh, I can explain that, father, says the man, you see, I'm a Jew. A Jew? Why are you coming to a Catholic service, then? But don't you see, replies the man, I, too, want to show that I'm opposed to the Communist regime.

One mustn't exaggerate the significance of this story, but one cannot help comparing it with the carefully screened attendance, mostly by old women, of religious services here in Bulgaria where the church has long been kept under tight rein. And having remarked upon how the Vietnamese Buddhist opposition had served as a rallying-point for all kinds of elements opposed to the Diem regime and its successors, to the point where (after the war) Communists admitted that they had infiltrated the ranks of that seemingly religious opposition; and having noted earlier how important the Bogomils had been at one time in the history of Bulgaria, one can imagine that the rulers of Poland look with some envy on the rulers of Bulgaria and how they have been able to bring their church to heel.

As far as talking informally with Poles is concerned, our ambassador in Warsaw said to me, "The extent to which we do that (in our homes) is only limited by the availability of time and representation funds." But then, of course, there are between 6 and 8 million Americans of Polish origin; for that reason alone there are thousands of strands of connections between the two countries. "You have to think of this country as a western country," someone explained to me, and he noted that Warsaw is actually on Western European time—which makes the evenings come on unusually early. How many more contrasts there are with Bulgaria! In Poland private enterprise in service industries is encouraged, whereas in Bulgaria the small independent craftsman has all but disappeared. Economic information is published to a much larger extent than in Sofia. My colleague in Warsaw received two months' advance notice for his invitation to speak on Polish TV on the 4th of July (and he was immediately followed by the party chairman (the equivalent of Brezhnev in the USSR) who also hailed our Bicentennial. 30 American universities have private (non-government-sponsored) relationships with Polish universities. The target for trade between Poland and the U.S. for this year is $1 billion, compared to one-tenth that amount in Bulgaria. And an interesting sidelight—at public functions the Soviet ambassador doesn't stand separately from the other diplomats, as he does here where he stands together with the government and party leaders.

Perhaps President Ford was right? Perhaps Poland is an independent country? Of course not. They are an occupied country which is run by dedicated Communists whose ideological and economic ties to the Soviet Union are only slightly less tight than those which link Bulgaria to the USSR. The difference, once again, lies in history. Through all its existence, Poland has had to struggle against the Germans, the Russians, or both. It has always regarded the Russians as barbarians of the East, whereas in Bulgaria for a century they have been regarded as liberators and benefactors. And in World War II Poland was attacked by both the Germans and the Russians, and then conquered and occupied by the Red Army— after that army sat idly by while Warsaw was pounded to bits as the Nazis beat down the insurrection of the (anti-Communist) Polish underground in 1944. Much more than the country to which I am accredited, Poland has a tradition of valor, individualism, and religiosity. It also has a strong tradition of democratic socialism and land reform. Enough said. I've not become an expert on Poland, but I have learned once more how different are the various countries "behind the iron curtain."

—0—

Here we have problems with the proposed visit of a Congressional "commission" to investigate compliance with the Helsinki agreement—what we call CSCE (the acronym that stands for "Conference for Security and Cooperation in Europe"). It is unlikely, but not impossible, that the Bulgarians will allow members of our Congress to come to Bulgaria to investigate what the Bulgarians are doing in their own country, but there may be ways of smoothing the entry of the group, and we are working on it. Harvey has completed the negotiation of the labor contract. We have made some further progress in connection with the possible acquisition of land for a new embassy chancery. Things are moving ahead for the harpsichord concert by a visiting American artist. The film to be introduced by myself on Bulgarian TV has arrived, and as Harvey put it, "just misses being excellent because of rather too much focus on portraits of the Founding Fathers and a bit too much bombast in the narrative." The American who was arrested for trying to smuggle her fiancé out of Bulgaria has been released on bail, but refuses to leave the country and to forfeit her bail, which may have the result that she will be re-arrested and tried here after all, something the Bulgarians are apparently trying to avoid.

The young American couple who lost their passports and money and to whom I lent $200 (there being no official fund for such purposes) have lost their new passports in Istanbul, raising the question how such a thing could have happened twice in a row—and also some misgivings about getting my money back. We have made a new and much more thorough, analytical study of all pending "divided family" cases. The sale of a sizeable American computer is again stymied because of a chicken-and-egg situation with export control. The Bulgarians have worked out arrangements for the showing of their exhibit of Thracian Art (which I saw in Leningrad last year, and just now in Warsaw) at the Metropolitan Museum of Art in New York next year. The visit of

Librarian of Congress Boorstin in mid-November is on the tracks. So are arrangements for the machine tool seminar, which I am going to open next week. We have an impasse, which I will have to break soon, in the negotiation of the program document for the cultural/scientific/technical agreement. There are two serious cases of sickness in our small embassy, and one of them has been evacuated to Wiesbaden. In other words, while everyone has been busy, and while I have my work cut out for me, nothing has happened that I would write down if it weren't for my purpose of giving a picture of what things are like in a small embassy such as ours.

—0—

Incidentally, I now have the answer to my question about the Museum of Revolutionary Vigilance. Our junior officer, Bill Black, dropped in there and found that Kissinger's book was still displayed along with other books identified as having been seized from the Bulgarian mails as they entered the country, obviously as material subversive to the system of government in Bulgaria. Among other books in the same category he noted such dangerous works as *Parties and Politics in America* by Clinton Rossiter, *The Truman Memoirs, Essays in Honor of Henry Steel Commager,* and *Modern Capitalism* by A. Schonfield. The captions on the display cases made clear that these books were regarded as examples of "anti-Communist literature."

I wonder whether Mr. Lyubomir Levchev, the First Deputy Chairman of the Committee of Art and Culture, really meant it when he said that he would look into the matter of Kissinger's book being displayed as an example of subversive literature. Mr. Levchev is a poet, and although he is an establishment poet he is not likely to be the type of person who will throw his weight around. The people who have jurisdiction for the Museum of Revolutionary Vigilance, on the other hand, are likely to be pretty tough customers, the kind who deal with counter-intelligence and the identification of people—even people in the government, and perhaps *especially* people in the government—who are lacking in the proper spirit of anti-imperialist vigilance. My guess thus is that Mr. Levchev decided not to report our conversation and not to mess into matters involving state security.

But I hope I'm doing him an injustice.

By the way, while on the plane from Sofia to Warsaw I read a Bulgarian newspaper and ran across something that Mr. Levchev had said at the "Festival of Political Songs" held a week before in Blagoevgrad. "Art is always politics," he had declared on that occasion. "It is always a policy. And this is by no means new, it has been that way since time immemorial—from Homer to today. . . When it comes to songs of commitment, the songs which gathered us in Blagoevgrad, I must say that they are among the best proofs that art—since it serves people, since man's life has always been the defender of some policy—is always one of the best examples of the eternal friendship between politics and art." By friendship, of course, he meant political control. Few accusations against an artist can be more damning in Bulgaria than that he had placed art ahead of the cause of Communism.

—0—

Just a few words about my visit to East Berlin, where the political situation is much closer to that in Bulgaria. East Berlin is very impressive. There are many new and tall and shiny buildings, a huge television tower, and there is evidence of a modicum of prosperity—East Germany being the most prosperous, or economically the least miserable, of the Eastern European countries. But all these impressions pale into insignificance when one has crossed the boundary into West Berlin, which is a place of real affluence, of crowded stores displaying a hundred times the goods that one can see in the eastern part of that divided city, and where—on top of a volcano that now seems extinct—people live even gay and carefree lives. If this is "decadent capitalism," it certainly displays great signs of vitality, but all this is at the cost of enormous subsidies from the German Federal Republic.

In West Berlin I read the valedictory telegram of Martin Hillenbrand, our ambassador to West Germany who had just been fired by Kissinger. (The fact that he had been forced out was leaked to the press, and it appears that Hillenbrand himself gave some interviews which made it clear that he felt Kissinger had always been uncomfortable with people who, like himself, knew more

about a particular subject than the Secretary of State.) Hillenbrand, who in the manner of the traditional Foreign Service doesn't
put things in flamboyant terms, merely mentioned at the end of his
message that it was deplorable that the Department of State didn't
always make full use of the knowledge and expertise that it had
available on the spot, preferring sometimes to deal with the leaders
of West Germany over the head of the American Ambassador who
sometimes had to learn of positions of his own government from
conversations with officials of the host country.

This, of course, is nothing new. For years Kissinger has preferred
to deal with the Soviet Union either through personal meetings
with leaders of that country or through the Soviet ambassador in
Washington, Anatoly Dobrynin, which tended to leave our ambassador in Moscow in the cold. Not that there aren't good reasons
for Kissinger to talk with Dobrynin—this enables him to express
exactly what he wants to say, in his own nuances, in his own
personal way and perhaps sometimes with well-calculated indis-
cretions, speaking to a man who is held in high esteem in Moscow
and certainly reports what Kissinger said promptly to his superiors.
But for the advantages that he gained by this procedure, Kissinger
and the United States have had a major price to pay, namely that
the views of Kissinger were presented to the Soviet leadership by a
Soviet diplomat rather than by an American diplomat. And who is
more likely to present those views objectively and in a manner best
calculated to serve American interests?

This problem exists for the bilateral relations between all states,
for if country A has an ambassador in the capital of country B, it
also has an ambassador of country B in its own capital. How to
conduct business with the other government thus depends on the
judgment of each government as to how it will best be able to
explain its position and advance its interests in the capital of the
other. In my own case, I benefit from the utter unwillingness of
Kissinger to see someone as lowly as the ambassador of Bulgaria.
So, although the Foreign Minister here will mildly complain from
time to time that his ambassador doesn't seem to have ready access
to the top levels of our government, he does receive me whenever I
ask to be received—and my superiors quite rightly find that it is
more likely to be effective if I convey our views to the government

here than if they called in the Bulgarian Ambassador and tried to explain everything to him. But the fact remains that the position of our ambassadors in a number of world capitals has been downgraded by Kissinger's penchant for personal diplomacy.

15

Non-substantive diplomacy: Agostinho Neto, the leader of fraternal Angola, comes to Bulgaria. Ruffles and flourishes, pomp and circumstance, are an integral part of diplomacy. Brezhnev and wife travel through Eastern Europe.

November 2. Among the things that happened during my absence was the state visit to Bulgaria by Agostinho Neto, the President of the People's Republic of Angola and Chairman of the MPLA, the "Popular Movement for the Liberation of Angola" which won the civil war in that country thanks to the active support of the Communist countries including the intervention of Cuban troops. Substantively there was very little of interest in that visit, but it was an excellent example of what I call "non-substantive diplomacy" which is conducted with consummate skill by Bulgaria and the other Communist countries.

I have been unable to get the Department of State very interested in the subject of non-substantive diplomacy, and this is understandable because we have our hands full with substantive diplomacy and thus have little time for the panoply, the image-building, the flattery, and the appearance of seriousness and dignity with which the Communist countries are able to treat visitors of all kinds. Just to get some foreign leader five minutes of our President's time, or ten minutes of the time of the Secretary of State, is often a labor of major proportions. For the reception of visitors, for the purpose of impressing them with what the Communists have to offer them in friendship and support, the Communist countries put out a great deal of effort and ingenuity—and time.

Let us just see who was out at the airport when Neto arrived: There were chief of state and chief of the party Todor Zhivkov, Prime Minister Stanko Todorov, four leading members of the Politburo, three vice premiers, several members of the Council of

State, the president and vice presidents of the National Assembly, and of course a gaggle of ministers and the inevitable representatives of the Bulgarian Agricultural Union and the Fatherland Front. And the Soviet ambassador.

Neto was awarded the Georgi Dimitrov Prize at a special ceremony which featured an effusive speech by Zhivkov, to which Neto replied by paying tribute to the help that Bulgaria had rendered his country during its struggle for independence, "in the form of arms, industrial products, food and other materials." The people of Angola, he said, know that their victory was facilitated by the fraternal aid of the Soviet Union, Cuba, Bulgaria and the other socialist countries. That, he said, is why "Angola understands the value of proletarian internationalism. That is why it associates itself with the idea of socialism which alone, in tune with the march of history, can bring the liberation of peoples, and open perspectives for peace and for human progress."

Remembering how difficult it was for the Federal Government in Washington to persuade its employes to go out on the street to welcome some visiting dignitaries, I find especially poignant the cheering multitudes who received Neto in the square in front of the Dimitrov mausoleum, the flags, the march-past, the martial music, and the full-throated cheers that were amplified a hundred times by loudspeakers around the square. (I heard those cheers, for the rehearsal for the event took place before I departed on my trip, and roars of carefully prepared "spontaneous" manifestations of brotherly enthusiasm were carried right into my office.)

After the arrival ceremonies, there was a working meeting at Communist Party headquarters between a phalanx of BCP officers and their African guests. The papers only announced that "in an atmosphere of friendship, cordiality and complete understanding matters were considered which relate to the relations between the BKP and the MPLA, between the People's Republic of Bulgaria and the People's Republic of Angola. It was pointed out that conditions are at hand for the promotion and expansion of all-round Bulgarian-Angolan cooperation in the political, economic, scientific, technical, cultural and other sectors. A complete concordance was noted in the views on major international problems, etc. etc."

Then, of course, came a huge state banquet at Boyana. No

African leader, whether Communist, anti-Communist or neutralist, has ever been treated to such pomp and circumstance in Washington. Next came a helicopter trip to Plovdiv, and another ceremony in that second city of Bulgaria. Then a visit to Varna, on the Black Sea, and visits to factories and an "agro-industrial" complex. And back again to Sofia, for more celebrations of brotherly love and socialist cooperation. A five-page communiqué—how I can see the fright on the faces of officials in Washington when a visitor asks that a communiqué be issued to mark his visit—with rolling cadences of generalities that come from the skillful pens of Bulgarian specialists in such documents. But a communiqué was not enough: There was also a high-sounding Declaration of Principles which are to govern not only relations between the People's Republic of Bulgaria and the People's Republic of Angola but also the "development of contacts and cooperation between the Bulgarian Communist Party and the Popular Movement for the Liberation of Angola, and between the public, scientific, and cultural organizations of the two countries." And for good measure there was also a pact between the MPLA and the BKP.

Who really cares about such things? Isn't Angola already gone, and irretrievably part of the Communist camp? Well, there are two observations: First, I do not know if Angola is irretrievably part of the Communist camp, but in addition to being government and party officials the Angolan visitors are also human beings and as such are subject to being impressed and even deeply moved by displays of affection and esteem and a desire to cooperate. Second, this treatment is not only accorded by Bulgaria to Angola, but by all the Eastern European totalitarian governments to all kinds of state visitors, some of whom are certainly not, or not yet, in their camp.

But it would be absurd to expect the President of the United States, the leaders of Congress and the Supreme Court, and half the cabinet to be out at Dulles Airport to meet any foreign leader whatsoever. Our political leaders have work to do—they are part of a system which requires constant struggle and competition, the adjustment of differences, checks and balances, cultivation of the press and the constituents, a constant look to the other branches of the government, and so our representational functions are focussed especially on the people at the very top. In Bulgaria the "President" of the country can afford to take as much time as he likes with a guest, if necessary one whole day or even several days. The Prime Minister doesn't have to worry about his parliament, and the parliament doesn't have to worry about any debates or investigations because it isn't authorized to debate or investigate, only to approve. And the Foreign Minister cannot be very busy formulating or conducting foreign policy, because essentially Bulgaria follows the foreign policies of its big brother.

So what am I proposing? Why don't I recognize that in our system of government "non-substantive diplomacy" is simply a luxury that we cannot afford? Because we have to take the world as we find it, we can no longer simply say we are the Joneses, let others keep up with us. I think we will have to develop people and positions, we will have to appropriate money, we will have to find time to do more to make foreign dignitaries—and not only those who are most important in the world—feel more wanted, more welcome when they come to the United States. Bulgaria has a number of excellent front men and women, persons who project an image of unhurried empathy and broad and tolerant understanding, who are well-schooled in Western politeness as well as Communist dialectics, and who have high-sounding titles without much substantive responsibility. Odious as it may seem to some, I think we need quite a few such people in the White House and the State Department to take care of visitors; and the Congress, too, which is so free in sending delegations to countries all over the world, will have to learn that this also entails an obligation to give reciprocal treatment, simply because a large part of the world has come to expect that the red carpet will be rolled out for its leaders, even if they represent unimportant countries. The leader of the Cape Verde Islands, which is now a member of the United Nations, was feted up and down in Bulgaria for three days. Perhaps we should contrive to accord him, or similar personages representing small states that could some day become important to us, at least a modicum of "class" in the way we receive them in our country— with bugles and ruffles and flourishes, and with time and attention paid to them, even if we cannot provide cheering crowds.

—0—

And another political joke. Brezhnev and his wife are traveling by train from Geneva back to the Soviet Union. It is night. The train stops. Mrs. Brezhnev asks her husband, "Leonid, have we arrived in the Soviet Union yet?" He opens the window, puts out his hand, withdraws his hand, closes the window, and says no, my dear, we have not yet arrived in the Soviet Union.

A few hours later the train stops again, Mrs. Brezhnev asks again, he opens the window again, puts out his hand, says again that no, my dear, we have not yet arrived. And the same thing happens yet another time. Finally, at the fourth stop of the train Brezhnev puts his hand out and exclaims to his wife: "Natasha, my darling, now have we arrived in Soviet Union."

"Oh, my clever husband, how did you find that out just by sticking your hand out of the window of the train?" she asks. And he replies: "It was easy. First time I put out my hand somebody spit on it, so I knew we were in Czechoslovakia. Second time somebody kissed it, so I knew we were in East Germany. Third time I stuck out my hand somebody bit it, so I knew we were in Poland. Just now somebody took off my wrist watch, so I know we are back in good old Soviet Union."

A corny joke, but illustrative of their problem—and where does Bulgaria, my country of assignment, come in? I think if the train had passed through Bulgaria and Brezhnev had stuck out his hand, someone would have shaken it. Yes, I apologize to those who might think me lacking in perspicacity or righteous anti-Communism, but we must not forget that Bulgaria has no Soviet occupation troops and that it has a tradition of friendship with Russia.

It is the country that the Soviet Union no doubt hopes to use as a model for its eventual relationship with other Eastern European countries, but the forces of history do not bend easily to the will of even a great power, as we ourselves have seen in other parts of the world.

16

Review of the Bulgarian press—and how it saw the 1976 U.S. elections. Carter stumbles again on Eastern Europe. Reflections on the changing of the guard. Credibility: We air our "July 4" broadcast to the Bulgarian people.

October 31. Recently there has been a Congress in Sofia of the Union of Bulgarian Writers, on the theme: "The Problems of the July Plenum (of the Central Committee of the BKP)—Problems of Literature." The Plenum had decreed that henceforth there should be more criticism in the press, but it had also warned that such criticism must be constructive and not stray beyond a certain level in the hierarchy. Academician Pantelei Zarev, President of the Writers' Union, called for "reinforcement of criticism in artistic creations as an integral part of the struggle for socialism and for socialist morality, etc. etc." Boilerplate.

But not everything that was said on that occasion was boilerplate. For instance, Bogomil Rainov, vice president of the institution, complained that the quantity of "junk" produced by the literary community exceeds the permissible minimum, "especially when one considers that that junk doesn't just remain on the shelves but goes into the minds of people." On the other hand, he said, one keeps re-issuing books (presumably of the propagandistic variety) which "nobody is willing to buy." There has come into existence, he complained, a sort of "assembly-line production of literature," but nobody is willing to talk about it. No writer, of course, he said, can be guaranteed success in the field of literature, "but one doesn't have to be very clever to figure out that many failures are due to arrogant fabrication, imitation, sterility and mindless versifying."

What is to be done? Mr. Rainov wasn't very precise about it—no wonder, since he was delivering his lecture under the watchful eye of Lyudmilla Zhivkova, the daughter of Number One and the appointed guardian of Communist orthodoxy in the arts and in

110

public information generally. "One of the troubles," he said, "is that frequently we show more enthusiasm for junk than for real creativity." Another difficulty is that in the business of writing there exists an atmosphere "where the number of cadres (writers in positions of authority), of people who cannot be criticized, is constantly growing and risks getting to the point where it will include every member of our Union."

Ah, but there's the rub. For the logic of his discourse had led Mr. Rainov almost to the point where he might seem to be calling for criticism of people in high places in the fraternity of writers or even above it. So he concluded his speech by saying that he didn't mean to exaggerate the existing weaknesses, that one mustn't promise the coming generation a sunny life without so much as a cloud, that indeed it must be the task of literature to prepare them for the hardships of reality. "The spirit of criticism mustn't be awakened by an excessive passion for details, but it must affirm, always and above all, the principles of our Communist life."

Another writer, Toncho Jetchev, went a little further, right up to the limit of what could be said in such a forum. Too often, he said, Bulgarian writers are like priests who bless something [meaning, of course, the system] with their writings and speak in such a general way about events that they do not convey much meaning, "while they do not express their veritable feelings." Bulgarian literary production has become a sort of cream, he said, which is rising above the mass of the people. What is needed, he concluded, is "the kind of criticism that is really political, but against which writers always react negatively, suspecting even that someone has been put up to criticizing them."

Clearly not everything is healthy in the Bulgarian literary establishment; and no wonder, for the Union of Bulgarian Writers consists of licensed sycophants of the regime and of a small minority of artists who chafe under the ideological restrictions placed upon their work. The latter can complain against those restrictions in more or less veiled form, but they cannot contradict the regime's basic premise that literature, indeed all art of any kind, must first and foremost serve the regime and help in the moulding of the new "socialist man."

—0—

And here, in connection with our forthcoming presidential elections, is a little item from the Bulgarian newspaper *Narodna Mladezh*, which tries to explain to its readers why a low turnout is predicted. Their correspondent Ivo Bozhkov reports that according to the U.S. Central Statistical Board, 70 million Americans will not vote in the elections. "There are different causes for the apathy among the voters. Some simply believe that voting would deprive them of precious time, and it is well known that 'time is money' for business. Others are prevented by illness, injuries, chronic state of intoxication, use of narcotics, and similar reasons. Another and more singular category are the 'outsiders' who cannot vote because they are criminals with false papers who are hiding from the authorities. Sociologists predict that the largest proportion of non-voters will be among young people, the Negro population, and the Indians. There will also be a large proportion of Americans who do not go to the ballot boxes because they understand that in actual fact problems like inflation, unemployment, recession etc. cannot be influenced by their vote. For the new President, whoever he may be, cannot solve problems that are inherent in the social and class contradictions of the so-called Free World."

Or here a little article from *Rabotnichesko Delo* entitled "In the South of the U.S.A." by Penka Karaivanova, datelined Atlanta, Georgia. She is standing in front of the grave of Martin Luther King and reports "I cannot shake myself free from the feeling that this epitaph has the meaning of a verdict: In this society only the grave can guarantee freedom for the colored man. Officially, of course, there is freedom, but actually it is being stalked from every corner. Cotton, poverty and the Negro issue have often been defined in the past as the common denominator of the southern states. This common denominator has now changed to some extent. The Negro issue has acquired primarily a socio-economic aspect, and has thereby become integrated into the general problem of poverty. Freedom is no longer persecuted by public outrages of the time of lynch law. The Ku Klux Klan crosses have disappeared, but the spirit of the Confederate disrupters of the Union lingers on.

"The heirs of the Ku Klux Klan operate meanly and surreptitiously by such means as placing small bombs under people's beds.

The Klan leaders now visit colleges and places of public assembly and try to convince people that the Klan, that 'vulture of America', has been reorganized into an organization of non-violence. Some of these leaders are even decent state employes. Many American publications look with irony on the efforts to revive the Klan's empire. They believe that it cannot any longer be a threat to the Negro population. They justify their view by pointing to the fact that in present-day America some official institutions can be no less dangerous (to the black man) than the 'reformed' racists."

After pointing to the industrialization of the South and the prevailing unemployment among the blacks, the article reports that "moderate Negro leaders" are working to do away with the remnants of segregation. "But politicians with a flair, like Jimmy Carter, are trying to win them (the moderate black leaders) to their side for their own ends. The presence of a substantial number of representatives of the Negro bourgeoisie in his pre-election team is being interpreted as one of the reasons for his ability to attract black votes in the South and in the North. But only people familiar with the traditional psychology of the southerner and his political affiliations can evaluate the claim that Carter can succeed in integrating the South with the rest of the country. It is true that this moderate Southern Democrat has won not only in his native Georgia but also in the North, due to his anti-racist position and his reserved conservatism, (but) Jimmy Carter has had to accommodate himself not only to the changing political picture in the South but also to the conflicting interests of different strata of voters . . . and by skillful balancing tricks he has also managed to . . . become the candidate favored by big business."

A number of interesting aspects of this article should be noted. (I have abbreviated the rather tortuous ending, but not in order to sharpen the point—which, as I will show, is rather less sharp than usual.) Leaving aside the propagandistic beginning about "only the grave" being able to guarantee freedom to the black man, or the bombs being placed under people's beds, there are some acknowledgments of true facts of our political situation—that industrialization has changed the South, that the Ku Klux Klan is no longer important, that there is such a thing as a "Negro bourgeoisie," that Carter has appeal both in the South and in the North, that he has taken an "anti-racist position and (one of) reserved conservatism," that he needed to accommodate conflicting interests in order to become the Democratic candidate, that there are different "strata" of voters and thus not only the exploiters and the exploited. In other words, while I do not like the insults to America that are strewn through the article, the fact that this lady journalist went there did possibly have the effect of making perceptive readers a little more aware of the realities, particularly when they discount, as many of them must surely do, the obligatory propaganda content of such articles.

And there is a little postscript to this item. At our staff meeting I asked whether we had any knowledge of Ms. Penka Karaivanova having gone to the United States to cover our presidential elections. In response our consul produced a record showing that she is not now in the U.S. nor has she been for almost a year. She was there approximately from October to December 1975.

There is nothing particularly reprehensible about date-lining her article Atlanta, Georgia and publishing it in 1976 even though it was written in 1975. Or is there? When I was in Frankfurt recently, I talked with our Consul General there about certain patterns of press reporting during the Vietnam war. He mentioned that in August, 1974, just before our Congress was to consider the Administration's request for assistance to South Vietnam and its armed forces, the *New York Times* published a spate of articles on alleged (and no doubt in many cases true) violations of civil rights in South Vietnam. Our embassy was startled to see these articles and made inquiries about when they had been written. It turned out that they had been written over quite a period of time, going back many months before, and had been "held" for publication at the time deemed most timely and opportune by the newspaper's editors.

So if *Rabdel* (as we call, for brevity's sake, the party organ *Rabotnichesko Delo*) uses Jimmy Carter's candidacy as a "peg" on which to hang an old article on the South, refurbished for the occasion, it is indulging in a practice that is also used by America's most prestigious newspaper.

—0—

November 3. Got up at six o'clock to hear the election returns, but since we are seven hours ahead of Washington it was still too early to know whether Carter had won as a number of races in key states were still undecided. We had a big scoreboard for the electoral votes set up in the show window of our Embassy, and when I got to the office at eight a.m. there were enormous crowds in front of them. One of our young men climbed into the window and posted returns as they came in. (Unfortunately, he posted the percentages of votes counted, and put them in the "Carter" and "Ford" columns according to who was ahead, which was a bit confusing—until we decided that he should just enter the electoral votes that seemed to be going to each candidate, according to the projections as they came in, and correct them if they turned out to be wrong.)

Later, when I was at a meeting with a number of other ambassadors, I was sent the AP ticker report that Carter had won and then the breakdown of electoral votes. I was asked to comment on what effects the Carter victory would have on American foreign policy, and naturally refused to comment on my own since we have to await guidance from Washington. In my own opinion, the Carter victory is a good thing for the country provided he does not adhere too closely to some of the things that he said during the election campaign. What had disturbed me especially, being stationed in the Balkans, was his statement that if he became President the United States would under no circumstances intervene if the Russians attacked Yugoslavia.

It may be a little parochial for me to worry about that statement, which was probably not reflective of Carter's general approach to foreign policy, but it is not only concern about the Balkans that makes me worry about any precise announcement of what we will and what we will not defend. On January 12, 1950 Dean Acheson—whom I have always very much admired—made what in my opinion was a disastrous mistake when in a speech to the National Press Club he drew a line of American security interests in Asia which excluded South Korea. Other factors than the Acheson speech, notably the withdrawal of our forces from South Korea, must have contributed to the decision of the Soviet Union to encourage or allow the North Koreans to invade South Korea in

June 1950, but surely that speech must have had a great deal to do with the decision.

Acheson himself, in his otherwise excellent book, *Present at the Creation*, claimed that he was only following what the Joint Chiefs of Staff and General MacArthur had said, but those military authorities were not official spokesmen for American foreign policy; and he claimed that he had not really excluded South Korea from our defensive perimeter because he had added: "So far as the military security of other areas in the Pacific is concerned, it must be clear that no person can guarantee these areas against military attack. . . Should such an attack occur . . . the initial reliance must be on the people attacked to resist it and then upon the commitments of the entire civilized world under the Charter of the United Nations. . ." But that made matters only worse.

It was a pure accident that the Soviet delegate was absent from the United Nations Security Council in mid-1950 when that body decided to put its cloak over the American military counter-actions in South Korea. And to place reliance on the "commitments of the entire civilized world under the Charter of the United Nations" to secure a given country is just another way of saying that we wash our hands of it. However, there are serious scholars of American foreign policy, for instance Hans J. Morgenthau, who even today hail the Acheson speech as an example of a prudent delimitation of American security interests and commitments— without mentioning, however, what its untoward consequences were.

My point, and that of other critics of the Carter statement (who include, of course, persons who voted for Carter) is that one cannot precisely foresee the circumstances that may lead to American involvement, and that it was imprudent to exclude Yugoslavia lest the Soviet Union be encouraged to think that it can invade that country—or some other country, such as perhaps Iran—without a military reaction from us. Whether we should in fact intervene militarily in Yugoslavia or Iran I do not know. But I do know from experience that when one is faced with a practical decision in a particular crisis, the situation and conditions surrounding it are usually different from what contingency planners, including very bright contingency planners, had envisaged.

It wasn't long before we got a telegram from the Secretary,

entitled "Transition to the next Administration," which contained the following key sentence: "During the transition period the President-elect will be formulating his own policies for implementation after his inauguration. I request everyone to remember that it would be a disservice to him and to the United States to speculate to foreign governments about the policies of the new Administration."

And one day afterwards, at his first post-electoral press conference, the President-elect prudently retreated from his campaign statement about Yugoslavia. He must be getting good advice.*

As far as my own future is concerned, every American ambassador submits his resignation after an election, and I should have been required to do so also if Ford had been reelected. Whether the resignation is accepted depends on many factors. In my own case, I will have been three years in Bulgaria next April and thus would not at all mind a change; and as noted in the introduction to this little book, I am a professional and not a "political appointee" like our ambassadors in London, Paris, Brussels, New Delhi, Tokyo, etc.

I am neither a Republican nor a Democrat, but whether I am offered another embassy so shortly before reaching the retirement age of 60 depends much more upon "peer judgment" and bureaucratic politics within the State Department than upon presidential politics. [Note: The mandatory retirement age was later raised to 65 by the Foreign Service Act of 1980, after the author's retirement.] It will also depend, of course, on what I want and what I will accept. The offer of an unattractive embassy sometimes makes

---

*But, alas, the advice apparently didn't "take": On May 2, 1977, the President in a press conference reiterated our security commitments to the NATO countries and Japan, which he said "are supported overwhelmingly by the American people," and then went on to say with dangerous precision: "The intrusion of American military forces into the internal affairs of other nations is highly unlikely and would not be supported by the American people or by me. The only exception would be if I felt that our nation's security was directly threatened." Directly? And what is meant by "intrusion into internal affairs"? This would seem, once more, to preclude even a plausible threat of American assistance to a beleaguered Yugoslav government if it had to combat a foreign-supported insurrection after Tito's death, or assistance against a foreign-supported guerilla movement in Iran or in South Korea. It is not wise to notify a potential adversary that he could act with impunity in such situations, whose ramifications one cannot predict—as the President himself had seemed to realize just after the elections.

it easier to decide whether one really prefers to retire, particularly since from the financial point of view every year that I have spent in the Service since 1969 has meant that my pension has become smaller, in *relative* terms, than the pensions of colleagues who retired then. This is due to the fact that since 1969 Congress has refused to increase executive-level salaries (even while increasing its own allowances), and during an election year has been especially loath to increase its own pay. Thus, even if the pay is now substantially increased, my pension will be relatively much smaller than if I had retired several years ago; and that situation will hardly get better unless I get a large embassy, which I consider on balance unlikely.

Whenever the time comes for me to leave Sofia, I know how the signal will be given from Washington: It will simply take the form of a telegram asking me to "request *agrément* of the host government for the appointment of (whoever it is) as your successor." Well, this kind of message will not—for me—come out of the blue. But there have been ambassadors who received this kind of insensitive "hint" that their services had come to an end, without previous notice whatsoever. The late G. Frederick Reinhardt, our ambassador to Italy, received that kind of message in a hospital where he was recovering after a serious operation. Walter Dowling, then in Bonn, and also one of our most meritorious ambassadors, was similarly told summarily that his services were at an end. More recently Nicholas Thacher, an able Arabist who was our ambassador to Saudi Arabia, received a telegram out of the blue to the effect that he was to ask for the appointment of James Akins as his successor. He was so outraged at the insensitivity of that message, the utter failure to explain anything let alone thank him for his services, that he didn't even inquire whether another embassy was available to him but put in immediately for his retirement. The "system" is not very effective in the niceties of human relationships, not even at the top, and sometimes especially not at the top.

—0—

Another political joke: What is the most neutral country in the world? Switzerland? Wrong. Sweden? Not at all. Well, which one then? Bulgaria! Why Bulgaria? Because the Bulgarians will not interfere even in the affairs of their *own* country!

—0—

November 4. The Soviet Foreign Minister is here, and we are trying to provide some grist for the State Department's mill, but it is impossible to find out anything beyond the fact that he was met at the airport by the entire Bulgarian Who's Who; that he was given a banquet at which both sides noted their complete agreement on all subjects; that he was given the Order of Georgi Dimitrov; and similar trivia.

His real purpose in coming here, of course, is to meet the Egyptian Foreign Minister, Ismael Fahmi. I was to have dinner at the Egyptian Ambassador's tonight, but he has, naturally enough, cancelled the dinner. All we have been able to provide Washington is some negative information on someone who apparently has *not* accompanied Gromyko here. But what information about the Gromyko-Fahmi meeting will become available to us will have to come from our embassies in Cairo and Moscow.

We have a drinking problem in the Embassy. One of our employes has lost control several times in a row, and most recently has been making abusive telephone calls to other members of the Embassy staff during the night. Since the same person has also made rather unseemly public advances to members of the opposite sex, it is clear that we must do something; and Washington is usually very helpful in cases of this sort—but does not necessarily believe that "exporting" them back home is the solution. Unfortunately our post is so small that it will be very difficult to take care of this situation without terminating the assignment. Harvey and I talked (in our secure room) about how to prepare for a further deterioration of this situation—and what we can do to prevent it happening.

At our staff meeting we discussed the Presidential transition arrangements; the Gromyko-Fahmi meeting; the cancellation of the Congressional visit (more below); arrangements for the Los Angeles Philharmonic Orchestra visit in December; the need to break the deadlock with respect to a pending export control matter, which is likely to result in the loss of a 3½ million dollar contract to the Japanese unless the U.S. Government will furnish us some information of a procedural nature that we requested two weeks ago; the economic growth targets of the Five Year Plan, which seem to have been scaled down from a 49.5% to a 45% increase in GNP; Zhivkov's visit to Byelorussia; negotiation of the program document for the Cultural/Technical/Scientific Agreement; the latest American-sponsored Eurodollar loan ($100 million) for Bulgaria, organized by the Bankers Trust Company on surprisingly favorable terms; new figures on the Bulgarian hard currency deficit in 1975, and projections for 1976 (which show a reduction from $740 million to $460 million); the possibility of a National Science Foundation visit; the presence of a Bulgarian TV team in the U.S. for the election campaign; our forthcoming photographic exhibit; Bulgarian automobile statistics and how reliable they are (there are now 220,000 passenger vehichles in the country and 50,000 trucks, plus 50,000 "specialized vehicles"); and the need to repair our roof, which can only be done by Bulgarian labor. Because the Embassy's roof contains our wireless transmitter, our transmission times will have to be adjusted since, according to our expert, the Bulgarian laborers would be "fried" if the transmitter is turned on while they are on the roof.

Things seem to be going well for the concert of the American harpsichord artist, Virginia Pleasants, who will be giving a small private performance at our residence next Monday before her concert at Bulgaria Hall in accordance with a contract with the agency "Sofiaconcert".—Our consul also reported on a welfare case which is rather poignant: A Bulgarian lady came to the embassy to report that her child, who had been hospitalized for a strange disease that involved excessive fluid pressure on the brain, could apparently only be saved if a certain piece of American medical equipment could be procured. The expense would not be very large, and we could probably raise the amount by just passing the hat in the embassy. But the question is whether the Bulgarian authorities would allow the equipment in, and whether her attempt to procure it from us wouldn't get the lady into trouble. While this is being clarified, we are trying to obtain specifications of the equipment.

The reason why the Bulgarian authorities might be unwilling to allow us to import the equipment to save the lady's child is essentially the same as the reason why Elisabeth, who is a skilled gynecologist, cannot do any work here even as a volunteer—the Bulgarian authorities do not wish it to appear that their medical problems require any kind of assistance from a foreign country, let alone a capitalist country, and least of all the United States. The Bulgarians could of course find the necessary money (about $100) to import the equipment, but their bureaucracy is so muscle-bound and doesn't permit any exceptions to be made to austerity rules laid down by higher authority, that it would be only sometime in 1977 before the lady could get the equipment, if then. And of course in the kind of society in which she lives, there are no private charities to which one can appeal and no possibilities of publicity for her predicament.

—0—

November 5. Well, we went to Bulgarian TV today and taped my introduction to the film about our Bicentennial which will be broadcast on prime time, as the Foreign Minister had offered exactly four months ago. Except for the fact that I stumbled twice over a Bulgarian word, the taping session went quite well. I had rehearsed my Bulgarian and had it honed to a fine point with the help of our Bulgarian teacher, but with the strong lights shining on me I was no longer as sure of knowing the text by heart as I had been before and therefore glanced down at it more than I should have, but it probably looked fairly spontaneous. There was both an introduction, which I modified by referring not just to our bicentennial (dvestagod*ish*ninata), but to the bicentennial of our *revolution*, since that word has such a favorable connotation here; and then a final expression of thanks to the Bulgarian government and BTV, and "greetings and good wishes to all Bulgarian television viewers from the American people."

As we went out, Mr. Vladelin Popov, who had been supervising this effort and very kindly provided the Bulgarian voice narration for the film, observed that it couldn't be shown on November 11 as we had originally believed, because it would now have to be looked at. By the censors? That was an embarrassing question, for Bulgaria doesn't acknowledge that it has such a thing as censorship. Well, it will be looked at by the people who look at taped programs to see that they are all right, in accordance with usual practice. We let it go at that. The censors, I hope, will be told that we were putting on the broadcast at the specific invitation of the Bulgarian government—but I wouldn't bet that some pieces of our tape might not yet be snipped out. I have a particular candidate for such snipping-out, not because I dislike it—I like it very much— but because I think that Bulgarians will wish to show it least of all.

The whole ten-minute program, which is a masterpiece of condensation of almost subliminal aspects of our people, is different in concept from what we had proposed, and suffers a little from trying to do too much. I had expressed the view that it would increase our credibility and certainly not do us any harm here, if some admission were made in the program that we have problems in the United States; that in fact by featuring at least a glimpse of those problems some useful points might be made about how we are coping with them; and that self-glorification should be held to a minimum. Well, the film is not exactly self-glorifying but it is totally lacking in self-criticism, and it has some passages so poetic that they border on bathos. Still, there are many scenes of the kind that we suggested—including one that is my candidate for excision by the Bulgarian censors.

That scene, which is just a five-second shot, accompanies some narrative about the fruits of the labors of the American working-man which have enabled him to attain a living standard not equaled anywhere; and the picture shows an American worker getting out of a big American car and walking across a lawn toward his nice, typical American one-family house. What shocked me, who am living here in Sofia, was the size of the car. Probably it was just a Chevrolet, but in comparison to the cars here it looks larger even than those driven by the Bulgarian oligarchs. If they take the scene out, we will have to complain, for a picture of an American worker with a typical American car is surely not "propaganda" but of a documentary nature. But if they leave it in, will it be credible? I'm not so sure. Just having a tiny Lada or Zhigouli car is beyond the dreams of a Bulgarian worker.

People here know that Americans are rich, but the question is whether they can really believe that an average American worker is *that* rich by Bulgarian standards. The situation reminds me of a propaganda leaflet that we dropped on German troops early during our involvement in World War II, probably in North Africa or Sicily. The leaflet described what German prisoners-of-war were getting for breakfast, probably because the amazement of the German POW's had suggested to our propagandists that this would be a suitable means of conveying the message that POW's were well treated. Well, when we interviewed German prisoners it turned out that they had been suitably impressed by the fact that POW's get "white bread" and "real coffee" for breakfast, but that they had guffawed at the suggestion that German POW's in American captivity were getting eggs for breakfast. Actually, of course, because of our strict application of the Geneva Convention, the Nazi POW's received the same breakfast as their American captors. But we soon found out that "white bread" and "real coffee" were sufficiently alluring and convincing about good treatment, so that we didn't need to refer to the eggs, and in fact were better off, from the point of view of credibility, by giving the German readers *less* than the full picture.

I'm just reading the book *The Americans: The Democratic Experience* by Daniel Boorstin, who will be visiting us later this month; and in it find rather the same thought expressed in an anecdote about an Irish immigrant to the United States which he attributes to Michel Chevalier. The immigrant had just written a letter to his family back in Ireland, which he was showing his employer. "But Patrick," the employer asked, "why do you say that you have meat three times a week, when you have it three times a day?" And Patrick replied, "It is because they wouldn't believe me if I told them so."

It is a truism, of course, that the whole truth can be incredible and many a falsehood can have the ring of plausibility. A simple rule to tell the whole truth and nothing but the truth in international communication may have the result, not of bringing people closer together, but of increasing suspicion between them. International communication can be true as well as plausible if it will select the facts according to what the listener or reader is likely to believe—and this doesn't mean "playing games with the truth." It is really what we do in everyday life, for you will constantly get into trouble if by telling the truth you are believed to be fibbing or to be some kind of a nut—or if by telling the truth you are getting people's backs up. Also, we don't particularly enjoy having people tell us how great they are, even if they are great, and that is the only fault that I can see in our little TV presentation.

The U. S. Information Agency, by the way, having been dragged kicking and screaming into this project, has offered the film to other posts in various parts of the world and has had enthusiastic acceptances from at least twenty embassies; so our effort, and their effort, and the investment of a few thousand dollars may have turned out to be worthwhile not only in Bulgaria but also, perhaps, in other countries where it hasn't been possible otherwise to get the American story across during our bicentennial year. It is true, of course, that considering the daily inundations of anti-American propaganda, our little drop will hardly act as antidote; but fortunately the anti-American propagandists overdo their thing to such an extent that a little pro-American information may go a certain way in helping to restore some balance.

17

Here is a sample of one of those glittering diplomatic occasions with champagne and eloquent speeches and toasts— an intense pain in the neck! An American harpsichord artist comes and has a minor translation problem.

This little chapter is entitled "A Touch of Class."

Feigning an admiration which is partly sincere, I managed to get the current Dean of the Diplomatic Corps, who is the Algerian Ambassador here, to let me have a copy of the remarks he made in the name of his colleagues on the occasion of the farewell champagne in honor of the departing Turkish Ambassador. The poor Dean has had to give about eight such cocktails in the space of only two months, but fortunately he was educated in the French tradition, and orotund phrases and polite pieties drop from his pen and lips with great facility. I do admire that facility; but it is not out of such admiration that I reproduce below his remarks on that occasion, but strictly from the well-known love of misery for company.

You have to imagine us foregathering for the eighth time in the space of two months, and perhaps for the twentieth time for me who has been here for 2½ years, in the Red Room of the Sofia Grand Hotel, shaking hands with the Dean and with the guests of honor as we enter, then standing around until we are asked to gather together to hear the speeches, and then having to hear the speeches once in French and then again in Bulgarian—and they always say virtually the same thing, that the Ambassador can look back with satisfaction, that he has won the esteem and affection, that he is moving on to more important things, and that he always will be. Here is the text of the speech given on that particular occasion:

"Excellencies, Mr. Ambassador of the Republic of Turkey and Madame Dinc, Monsieur Nikolay Minchev, Vice Minister of

Foreign Affairs, Monsieur Rangelov, Director of the 3rd Department of the Ministry of Foreign Affairs, Monsieur Malinikov, Deputy Director of State Protocol, dear colleagues, Mesdames and Messieurs,

"For some time, contrary to what is said in the old adage, the weeks pass and resemble each other; only one week has gone by and here we are again with the important mission entrusted to us of organizing the ceremony which is consecrated by diplomatic usage.

"That mission, while it is for me a signal honor, is nevertheless redoubtable, for it involves seeking and finding words that will be most appropriate, words that will permit the most faithful expression possible of the sentiments of all.

"Now, while seeking may seem quite easy, finding is an enterprise that is much more difficult, and in any case more uncertain.

"Every departure leaves an aftertaste of bitterness and of regret which at the same time is accompanied by a sentiment of consolation which is felt by everyone, realizing that his turn will come, too, ineluctably.

"Mr. Ambassador,

"Madame Dinc,

"You are leaving, certainly, but you are not leaving us entirely, for the impressions that you are leaving here, as well as those that you take along, appear to us as rich as they are imperishable.

"The brilliant results which you have obtained in all fields during your service in the People's Republic of Bulgaria will remain to testify to your incontestable human qualities, to your undeniable talent, to your impressive calm, which is accompanied by a dynamism capable of meeting every test.

"And not the least of these results, surely, indeed quite the contrary, is certainly the visit to your country of His Excellency Todor Zhivkov, President of the State Council of the People's Republic of Bulgaria, upon the invitation of His Excellency Monsieur Kuruturk, President of the Republic of Turkey.

"If I have allowed myself to mention that important fact, it is neither by accident, nor out of sentiment, but only because it has the objective of acknowledging that that fact is unique in the annals of the relations between the two countries, at least during recent centuries.

"Furthermore, and in order to be just, we must associate with your remarkable successes your charming wife who by her tact and her intelligence, her goodness and her sincerity, has known how to be for us at the same time a precious support and an indispensable ray of sunshine.

"Monsieur Ambassador,

"Madame Dinc,

"Our colleagues have wanted to manifest their sentiments of sympathy for you by giving you this modest souvenir of your stay in this magnificent country which is Bulgaria.

"And it is on this note of optimism and hope, that I ask all our colleagues, as well as our Bulgarian friends, to raise a toast to your health, to your happiness, and to your success."

Upon signal, two butlers advance with trays of champagne, and while the Dean hands to Ambassador Dinc the usual hideous Bulgarian cotton rug, and to his wife the usual bunch of standard "socialist" red carnations wrapped in cellophane, the assembled ambassadors and their spouses gather up the glasses and raise them to the health of their departing colleague—but that is not all. Thereupon the badly put-upon guest of honor is required to speak platitudinous lines of equal insincerity and to accept the best wishes of each and every one of the guests who come up to him to commiserate, to clink glasses and to shake his hands, and in some cases to kiss his wife.

I thought that I detected an ever so slight curling of the lip on the part of Nihat Dinc as he received encomiums for having arranged the visit of Mr. Zhivkov to Turkey, for many of his colleagues must be aware that that visit was long insisted upon by the Bulgarians and that they in fact maneuvered the Turks into a position where they couldn't refuse it—after a scenario of byzantine tactical moves too complicated to detail here. Nor can it have failed to startle the Turkish Ambassador to be told that that visit was "unprecedented . . . at least during recent centuries," for Bulgaria was a Turkish province for five hundred years until 1877 and certainly no Bulgarian president has made a trip to Turkey during that period because Bulgaria didn't exist.

There was also special piquancy, though probably not intentional irony, in the Dean's reference to the charm and tact of the Turkish Ambassador's wife; for while she certainly has charm she has been refreshingly direct in expressing her opinions and loved by all her friends for her unabashed sincerity. She made no bones, for instance, of the intense distaste she felt for the prison atmosphere in which her embassy residence was kept by the Bulgarians; for while the Americans may be under close surveillance here, certainly the Turks are even more closely hemmed in. And for good reason, for there is a minority of 800,000 Turks in Bulgaria of whom the government is highly suspicious because they have resisted assimilation and cannot be relied upon in case of trouble. (Thus, while for show purposes there are some Turkish deputies in the National Assembly and some Turkish officers in the armed forces, most Bulgarian Turks are immediately consigned to labor battalions when they come up for military service.)

—0—

November 9. We had a very successful evening last night when Virginia Pleasants, the American harpsichordist, performed at the Embassy residence after a buffet dinner. We had altogether 38 guests, including a number of Bulgarian cultural bureaucrats and also eight genuine and bona fide artists, as well as diplomats and Embassy staff. Mrs. Pleasants is a fine artist, and in my remarks to the guests I thanked the head of *Sofiaconcert*, the Bulgarian concert agency, for inviting her to perform publicly in Sofia (which she will do tomorrow). I also thanked Mr. Lyubomir Levchev, the deputy chairman of the Committee for Art and Culture, and Ambassador Chavdar Damyanov, the head of the Cultural Relations Department of the Foreign Ministry, for their cooperation "in the spirit of the soon-to-be-signed cultural relations agreement between our countries."

Actually, of course, laying on this visit had been a lot of work. Just getting a harpsichord lent to the Embassy required a number of visits and conversations with members of the cultural bureaucracy—I personally went to see the acting head of the Conservatory and the head of *Sofiaconcert*, and talked with officials of the Committee and of the Ministry. I did this because the visit of Mrs. Pleasants supports our cultural image in Bulgaria, and also because she and her husband have been close friends for many years. The evening was sufficiently successful that her concert will be recorded and rebroadcast over Radio Sofia; she has been invited to meet with Bulgarian musicians; and this afternoon she is meeting with the vice chairman of the Union of Bulgarian Composers.

There was one odd and totally unexpected moment of embarrassment at our musical evening, which had to do with translation. In order to help in the communication between Bulgarian artists (most of whom turned out to speak German) and Mrs. Pleasants, I had included among the guests our excellent language teacher who in addition to teaching us Bulgarian is teaching English at the university; and she dutifully rushed forward when Mrs. Pleasants asked for someone to interpret a few remarks before she sat down at the harpsichord. Because she had been traveling and was still not completely acclimated, Mrs. Pleasants said, she hoped the audience would forgive her if she "used music" in connection with the first two pieces that she would be playing. Only when she later put some sheet music on the rack did I myself realize what she had meant; but our interpreter gave every sign of distress and translated that Mrs. Pleasants begged the indulgence of her audience in connection with "the music" of the first two pieces she would be playing, because she had been traveling and was not yet completely acclimated.

This is a typical phenomenon which I have also noticed at the United Nations whose simultaneous interpreters are justly admired for their skill. When they come up against something they don't precisely understand—which actually is fairly often, especially when the discussions are technical—they are simply under too much time pressure to think very much about alternative renditions of the meaning, or about alternative meanings of what they are hearing, or about how to render a word they either didn't hear right or don't know; so they go right on without translating that particular term, which could be the key concept of an entire speech—which is why, at the Seabed Committee for instance, I usually made it a practice to pay a visit to the translators in their booths high up above the meeting hall to go over the technical terms that would be used by our principal speaker.

Mrs. Pleasants lives in London, and over lunch today we talked about the Crossman Diaries which have created a stir in England and elsewhere. Publication of those diaries, which revealed the inner workings of the British Labour Government, had been contested in the courts and questioned on ethical grounds. Should a member of a government keep a diary to which he confides his candid observations on internal, confidential dealings within the government to which he belongs? Naturally this is a question that concerns me also in connection with the present diary. But it concerns me, in addition, because I used to be a good friend of Dick Crossman, having worked directly under him in General Eisenhower's headquarters in London in 1944 and in Paris in 1945.

It was only during that luncheon conversation that, as often happens, my views became clarified as I was talking—about the question of the boundaries of morality and propriety that are involved when a public official keeps a private diary that he intends to publish. I said to her, and I now understand and believe, that I will have to stop writing this diary, or at least stop thinking of publishing it, if any confidential matters of high policy arise while I am writing it. Fortunately, I said to Virginia, the purpose of my little diary is not to bring out anything sensational, not to explain any inner workings, but just to describe the workaday tasks and joys and frustrations of an American ambassador in a relatively unimportant post. That, and not the revelation of any succulent matters that some people would wish to see concealed from the public, is my purpose in writing this book. It's just that I think my job interesting even when nothing of great moment is happening, and I address myself to readers who are interested in knowing what it is like to be the American Ambassador to a small Communist country.

I have mentioned Mr. Levchev as one of the guests at the dinner-concert. I wasn't going to raise with him the "subversive" American books in the Museum of Revolutionary Vigilance, but it was he who raised it with me—by asking whether I had noticed that the Kissinger book had been withdrawn from display. I said no, we hadn't noticed it, but once more sent Bill Black to have a look. It was still there. Apparently he tried and thought he had succeeded, but someone more important than he had taken a different view.

18

Washington raps ambassador's knuckles for having stepped out of line with his criticism of a "policy assessment." Can our Congress send a commission to Eastern Europe to investigate compliance with international agreements?

November 13. Oh, I forgot (forgot? or found it too embarrassing?) to mention that about two weeks ago I got my knuckles rapped by the State Department for having questioned, in a telegram (which also went to all other Eastern European posts) the so-called "policy assessment." You will recall that my quarrel had been not so much with the decisions that came out of Washington as with the totally bowdlerized account of a meeting that I had attended at which virtually everyone had agreed that one feature of our policy toward Czechoslovakia, Hungary and Bulgaria—waiting in one country until something had happened in another country— should be changed.

The reason Washington's response to my telegram came by letter was, obviously, that they had been unable to "clear" a telegram with all the major participants of that meeting, which had taken place in April but had been summarized only in August. The letter made the following points: The purpose of the telegram from the Department hadn't really been to summarize the meeting that I had attended, but "to make clear the continuing policy and program lines." However, this would still not have justified any "distortion of the sense of the meeting". But—and here the letter gets really tortuous—the arguments in favor of rank-ordering "had been articulated and made clear in the past, and the fact that much of the discussion (at the meeting) focussed on the arguments of the opposing view did not dictate the shape of our telegram. To do otherwise might have left readers bemused, if not amused, at a message which seemed to report one thing and conclude another."

There could not be a nicer way of acknowledging that the policy assessment meeting that I had attended was a charade, that it had no effect whatsoever on what was decided in Sonnenfeldt's office, and that it had been just for the purpose of letting people like me talk, giving them a sense that they had had their day in court—to the applause and with the active concurrence of others attending the meeting who were equally misled—while Sonnenfeldt, who didn't see fit to attend the meeting, just dictated what the conclusions of the meeting *should have been* and what the continuing policy was going to be. This is why people would have been bemused if the record of the meeting had accurately reflected what had been said. The current procedure, while not bemusing, is outrageous.

Then, after some discussions of detail, the letter concluded in a spirit of mock conciliation and perhaps veiled warning: "We appreciate your comments and are always ready to have exchange on any element of substantive policy. You do appreciate, I am sure, that the policy telegrams of the Department must and should reflect with reasonable clarity what the policy is." Who could disagree with such a general statement? My disagreement was not with the idea that telegrams should reflect policy, but with the fact that many arguments in favor of a change in policy (albeit a minor one) had been deformed in the process—and, what is worse, ignored by people who hadn't been present at the meeting and couldn't care less about what had been discussed there under the guise of "policy assessment."

A minor dispute, but a revealing one about the limits of an ambassador's influence. I wrote back a letter of thanks for the great courtesy of the letter; stressed that we had never questioned that policy is made in Washington, but wound up expressing the view that policy assessment meetings which are not attended by the people who will make the decisions are probably worthless. To have discussions in one place and decisions somewhere else was not, I said, a healthy situation. "The best solution would be for more authority to be delegated downward so that policy assessment meetings can really make decisions on such minor matters."

A few days after I had sent off this letter, feeling better about having lost the battle because I had told them what I thought of them, we received a general policy telegram on Bulgaria which substantially gave me what I wanted. The important thing, apparently, had been not to "yield under pressure" from an ambassador who complained that he had been misquoted or not properly understood. Once that had been made clear, namely that "the Department makes policy," apparently there had no longer been any difficulty in giving me what I had suggested. A somewhat Rube Goldbergian way of running a shop, but since it's the results that count I cannot complain any longer. I'm almost sorry I sent that letter. And I don't expect to hear what really happened—although perhaps now that Kissinger and Sonnenfeldt are lame ducks, some of their subordinates will discover that they have the courage to tell us in the field what is going on.

And perhaps, to return once more to the question about Crossman's book, I am after all disclosing secret things about the inner workings of the government. Only, these workings are disclosed in a microcosm, and not in connection with the larger foreign policy questions of our day.

—0—

On November 5 we received notification that a Congressional "Commission" to investigate East European compliance with the Final Act of Helsinki, would *not* be coming to Eastern Europe after all. I've not seen anything about this in the press yet, but it is highly unlikely that the rebuff suffered by that Commission can be kept out of the public record. At any rate, I think it may be interesting to set down how that enterprise looked from the vantage point of this embassy.

The so-called Commission had been a subject first of contention, and later of arm's-length cooperation, and finally of joint planning, between the legislative and executive branches in Washington. We in Sofia became aware of the new body only when the executive branch had reluctantly agreed to cooperate with the newly-established Commission last summer, even though the executive branch expressed doubts about the advisability of the Congress setting up such a body in the first place.

The Communist press immediately complained that creation of the Commission constituted "interference in the internal affairs" of the Eastern European countries, and thus was in contravention of the letter and spirit of Helsinki. In a rather polite and tentative way that was what a Vice Minister of Foreign Affairs implied to me when I saw him on other matters in August. He asked how our Congress could try to "control what other governments were doing" in the way of implementing the Helsinki agreement.

I said at that time that all our Congress can do is "control" what our own government is doing. I recalled that when I had first presented my credentials to President Zhivkov in 1974, I had remarked to him during the private conversation that usually follows that ceremony, that I had been greatly struck during my recent years in Washington by the increasing role that our Congress was playing in foreign affairs, and that foreign governments would have to take into account, in their dealings with us, not only the views of the executive branch but also of our legislature.

At that time, as I told the vice minister, President Zhivkov had responded that how our government organizes itself was an internal American matter on which he preferred not to comment. Did the vice minister now wish to depart from that position? Naturally, the vice minister did not wish to depart from the position enunciated by his chief, and the matter was left there. But it was clear that the Bulgarian government, in concert with the Soviet government, was getting uptight about the Commission and its purposes.

Well, in mid-October, just after I had left on my trip to Warsaw and East Berlin, all our embassies in Eastern Europe received a formal notification from the State Department that the Commission, consisting of six Senators, six Representatives, and members of the executive branch, was coming to Europe to "monitor" compliance of countries with the Final Act of Helsinki. The trip was described as a study trip, but the members wished to talk in each capital with the ranking political leaders and those who specifically were entrusted with the subject of CSCE (the Conference on Security and Cooperation in Europe, i.e. the Helsinki document). The group was to split up into five sub-groups, and we in Sofia had drawn Congressman Jonathan Bingham of New York who would be accompanied by several staff members.

It was clear that from the point of view of the executive branch, the major problem was in the arrogation by the Congress of what is known as the "primacy of the executive branch in the conduct of foreign affairs." Also, of course, a group of Congressmen and Senators does not always speak with one voice, and when in addition representatives of the executive branch might express views at variance with those of other commission members, there was a certain potential for confusion.

From our point of view in Sofia, the question was whether and how we might be able to get the "Commission" into Bulgaria. We had no illusions, of course, that the Bulgarians might make their own decision; but how they were approached might just conceivably make a difference. We noted that in one other Eastern European capital the Foreign Ministry had indicated that they would have no difficulty in issuing visas to Congressional visitors who came in a personal capacity but that they would have major difficulty in issuing visas to a Congressional investigating commission.

There was a great deal of telegraphing from Washington about the ground rules, as between the executive and the legislative sides of our government, which were to govern the visit; but not much evidence that the various members were aware that the whole enterprise was highly unlikely to take place because it had gotten off on the wrong foot; and it had gotten off on the wrong foot, in my opinion, not because of the executive-legislative problem but because the whole enterprise represented one colossal act of American arrogance.

As I pointed out to Washington (after the visit had to be cancelled because no Eastern European government—except Yugoslavia—was willing to admit the "Commission"), if the Congress had seen fit to invite the Eastern European parliaments to send "commissions" to the United States to inquire there into how *we* are abiding by the provisions of the Final Act of Helsinki, then they would have been practically unable to decline to receive a similar "commission" from the United States. But to expect to descend upon a foreign government to hold inquiries on how they abide by agreements (technically the Helsinki document isn't even an agreement) was unrealistic in the first place.

When I was in West Berlin I had dinner with a few Western newspapermen who were attending an East-West symposium, sponsored by the Aspen Institute, on the Helsinki Agreement and its aftermath. The points that were made at that symposium were well summarized by Peter Osnos in the *Washington Post* when he pointed out that "If the winner of the U.S. presidential elections pursues the pledge that both major candidates have made to demand greater compliance from the Soviet Union on the provisions of the Helsinki agreement, he is going to find the Russians and their allies very tough."

And Osnos enumerated the "preemptive attacks" that we could expect from the Russians and their allies when we might try to press for greater openness of their societies, more access to foreign information and ideas, etc., as provided rather sweepingly in the Final Act. The Communists would point to our refusal to admit Communist trade union delegations, they would claim technical inadequacies of invitations to observe certain NATO maneuvers, they would claim that their countries were showing more Western movies and translating and publishing more Western books than we were doing in the other direction, they would claim that we were more restrictive in issuing visas to their nations than they were in issuing visas to ours, etc. etc.

All these are matters that are well known in Washington for they have been reported by our various embassies in Moscow and in the Eastern European capitals. As far as Bulgarian compliance with the CSCE Final Act is concerned, I would have been delighted to discuss it with Representative Bingham, whom I have known for several years and who certainly is a fine gentleman, but it was always very unlikely that President Zhivkov, Foreign Minister Mladenov and other ranking Bulgarians would sit still for interrogations by an American Congressman.

As a matter of fact, we have embassies in foreign countries to provide precisely the information that the "commission" was seeking, or purported to be seeking; and the information is right in Washington where we have sent telegram after telegram for a year and a half in response to questionaires and other reporting requirements. There are certainly cases where visits by American legislators can be helpful to the conduct of our foreign relations, but the abortive "commission" visit was not one of them. It was a grandstanding operation for American domestic political purposes, and there was nothing the commission could have done and learned that could not have been done and learned for them by the men and women on the spot who represent the American government—and thus the legislative branch as well as the executive.

19

Discovery of a novel way to misquote a Secretary of State and other public officials. Visit of Daniel Boorstin, the Librarian of Congress. He says his institution "has no foreign policy," but can his hosts believe it?

I've had an exchange of correspondence with Alfred Atherton, the Assistant Secretary of State for Near Eastern Affairs, who a while ago was "severely reprimanded" by the Secretary of State for his alleged error of judgment in making available certain documents about the Kissinger Middle East peace missions of 1973 and 1974 to a scholar whom he was briefing. What gave rise to my letter to "Roy" Atherton was a brief note by the editors of the magazine *Foreign Policy* (Summer 1976—magazines always reach us with some delay) which had reviewed the affair.

The uproar had been over an article by Edward R. F. Sheehan in the Spring 1976 issue of *Foreign Policy* which the State Department had castigated because it contained details of the Kissinger negotiations that proved highly embarrassing not only to Kissinger himself—and to the United States—but also to Israeli Prime Minister Rabin, Egyptian President Anwar Sadat, and others. Kissinger had said that he had not authorized disclosure of the details that appeared in the article and that "those who did (disclose those details) committed a gross breach of confidence and a gross error of judgment."

"In all the noise," the Summer 1976 note in *Foreign Policy* said, "it was only occasionally remarked that no one was disputing the substance of Sheehan's article. We hope that now that the din has died down, the article will receive the attention that it deserves as a major original source for understanding how our present Mideast policy was forged, and what that policy is."

So far, so good. But what interested me was not the veracity *in substance* of the article, but the accuracy of the quotations of Kissinger and his interlocutors which had appeared in the article. The State Department had declared that "so far as the Department is concerned, the use of the word 'verbatim' to describe the conversation is inaccurate." *Foreign Policy* retorted, in a rather curious way, that the Department statement had referred "to our publishing the quoted material in indented form, rather than using quotation marks." Could this really have been the issue?

So I went back to the original article and found that Sheehan had written in his introduction: "The direct quotations of dialogue in the article are verbatim, *condensed from the actual conversations* between participants only when necessary for space reasons." (My italics.) Well, that really was interesting. When one condenses into a few paragraphs, for space reasons, an exchange that might have been covered by several pages of the record, can one still describe the "quotation" as verbatim? So I had written Atherton and asked him to comment.

His response was very precise, considering that he could have given me a lengthy obscurantist explanation in "State Departmentese" of what had happened. The indented paragraphs without quotation marks in the *Foreign Policy* article, he wrote, were derived for the most part from *paraphrases* of memoranda summarizing selected portions of memoranda of conversations. Now, I have been long enough in this business to know that MemCons, as we call them, contain both verbatim quotes of key sentences spoken and summarizations of portions of conversations. Even the most careful reader of a MemCon can usually not determine what precise words were actually used, and in this case Mr. Sheehan had had passages read to him so that he could not possibly have been able to tell which words had actually been spoken by Kissinger and by the foreign officials with whom he was negotiating.

Picking out a particularly pungent but not necessarily relevant phrase from a long statement is already a dubious practice in journalism, though it cannot be faulted on formal or legal grounds. A person may be interviewed at great length about Mr. X or Mr. Y and in the course of the interview may say something in passing about Mr. Z—and will then be furious to see that the latter quotation was the only one that was used. In that case, however, he has only himself to blame.

In the same way, if someone talks for an hour and finds that only one single sentence of what he said on a given subject is presented on television or in a news report, and he believes that that single sentence taken out of context doesn't do justice to his real thought or position, he has been sandbagged by the journalistic profession and has, again, maybe only himself to blame; for it is now accepted practice to truncate what people have said *as long as the truncated quotation is itself accurate.*

But neither of these things was involved in the Sheehan article, which is therefore a new departure in political journalism. There seems to be no argument that *in substance* what he reported was accurate; but when he had Kissinger speaking a short paragraph and Golda Meir responding with a short paragraph, the impression was created that those paragraphs, indented as they were, represented what was actually said; and since the dialogue thus presented had not taken place in the way it was presented, there was in effect a falsification of history.

Yet the general reader was provided a titillating glimpse which made it appear that the negotiating partners came to grips cleanly and clearly with key issues, and that Kissinger was direct (or devious, as the case may be) in a particular, crisp and easily understood way. Anyone who has witnessed actual negotiating sessions, however, appreciates that the joining of issues is rarely as crisp and direct as Mr. Sheehan made it appear to be; that the negotiators go around and around and around again before they come to the nub of the issue, that there are diversions and digressions and irrelevancies and interruptions and misunderstandings and many ways, including frontal, sideways and from the rear, of approaching issues.

So when Mr. Sheehan, who is a serious journalist, wrote the article on the Kissinger Middle East negotiations, he did the reader a service by simplifying those negotiations so that everyone could understand what had happened; but he did historians of that period and the journalistic profession in general a disservice because he invented a new journalistic technique, making paraphrased summaries appear as verbatim quotations. If the magazine *Foreign Policy* could get away with that technique once, there is no telling what they or others may be able to do with it next time; and unfortunately there is no procedure to adjudicate such questions of ethics of the journalistic profession.

—0—

November 23. We've had the visit of the Librarian of Congress, Daniel Boorstin, and it was a great success. Never have we had as many Bulgarian intellectuals—professors, librarians, deans and "cultural bureaucrats"—at our residence, and Mr. Boorstin greatly increased their interest by offering something to the Bulgarians that they want very much to have. He offered to put on an exhibit in Washington, timed to coincide with the opening of the Thracian Art exhibit at the Metropolitan Museum in New York, at which he would display the Bulgarian treasures in the Library of Congress.

This proposition obviously interested the Bulgarians very much, for they are looking for a "multiplier effect" of the exhibit in New York next June whose purpose is to make Americans more aware of Bulgaria. Mr. Boorstin almost got into hot water with his audience by seeming to denigrate the Thracian exhibit which deals, after all, as he put it, with a civilization that predates that of Bulgaria—and he was instantly corrected by some of the guests who pointed out (or claimed) that much of the Thracian culture of antiquity still lives on in the Slavic culture of contemporary Bulgaria.

Except for this, and an interesting byplay when Boorstin expressed some doubts about the missionary profession, his stay here was a pure love feast. He even was given an opportunity, during a visit to one of Bulgaria's leading historians, to have a colloquy with graduate students, which is unprecedented for an American intellectual visitor. Usually such visitors are carefully hedged in by phalanxes of Bulgarian cultural officials and establishment intellectuals and have no opportunity to meet even younger professors, let alone students.

A difference over missionaries, which was amusing but not at all important, arose when some reference (favorable) was made to the pre-1944 activities in Bulgaria of American missionaries. Boorstin perhaps thought that he would find special favor with his Communist listeners by deprecating the efforts of American missionaries to purvey American values to the denizens of other countries, but he met heated contradiction—probably because some of the popularity of prewar American missionaries in Bulgaria stemmed from their activities in publicizing Turkish atrocities during the liberation struggle.

Boorstin is a fascinating person, and his wife seems his intellectual equal. He is a brilliant conversationalist and in the course of half an hour can throw out more interesting and original ideas than another person might generate in a year. As a social scientist and historian he already occupies a secure place in the United States; but his interests go far beyond these areas, and I especially enjoyed discussing with him the interest of the Library of Congress in acquiring—if it is for sale—the only known copy extant of the Waldseemueller world map of 1507 which is the first map to carry the word AMERICA. (As a collector of old maps, I have a few of the less rare Waldseemueller maps of 1513.)

And we all learned a lot of interesting things about the Library of Congress, many of which have no place in this diary. But I must record my amazement to learn that over 850 professional staff members do nothing but perform research for members of our Congress—and that the results of those labors are not attributed to the Library of Congress. When I asked Dr. Boorstin how, then, the Library could obtain credit for what it was doing for the Congress, he replied that this depended largely on the good will of the staff members of the Senators and Congressmen.

In fact, the situation is even stranger: If one Senator or Congressman asks the Library to perform a particular job of research, which he may use in developing (or attacking or defending) legislation or otherwise in furthering his political position, the Library cannot give the same piece of work to another Senator or Congressman. It has to be rewritten, although of course some of the same research can be used and thus doesn't have to be done all over again. But it would never do to give the same report to two members—for, after all, one of them might be defending a particular piece of legislation (or line of policy, or personal position) and the other, on the basis of the same information, might be attacking the same piece of legislation (or line of policy, or personal position).

I did not think of raising the question with Dr. Boorstin when he was here, but it would be interesting to know whether unclassified information of this sort might not have to be made available to the press under the recently passed Freedom of Information Act. In that case one might have the interesting situation of the attackers, defenders and observers of a particular political battle having the same basic data—which doesn't mean, of course, that the speeches or reports or legislation produced on the basis of those data would be the same.

As it was explained to us, the Congressional staff can do with the information provided by the Library of Congress what they will— they can pick from it only the portions that support the position of their boss, they can also withhold from him information that might change his views about a particular issue or piece of legislation, and they can use the research of the Library of Congress to build up a case selectively—which, after all, is not very different from what journalists are doing when they practice what today is termed "advocacy journalism." (I thought a sterling example of that practice could be found in portions of the Church Committee report on the CIA, some of which read like lawyers' briefs.)

To come back to Dr. Boorstin's visit, one reason he was especially welcome here is because of the ongoing program of exchanges of books and periodicals with the Bulgarian National Library. The Librarian of Congress went to special pains to disclaim any political quality whatsoever of his visit. In fact, he stressed that "the Library of Congress has no foreign policy"—but I wonder whether the Bulgarian officials whom he met were able to believe this. The exchanges, after all, are of *mutual* benefit; and any American institution is suspected of furthering American "capitalist, imperialist" interests.

A strange moment at the dinner was when Mr. Levchev, perhaps to make conversation, asked Dr. Boorstin as a leading American intellectual to explain why there are only two large political parties in the United States. Dr. Boorstin mused for a while about the question, pointed out that the positions of political parties had shifted, recalled that at various times there had been a third party and that in fact there are many other small parties even now, and then ended his observations with an anecdote.

The anecdote was simply a reference to what P. T. Barnum had once said about American political parties. After explaining who P. T. Barnum was, Dr. Boorstin quoted him as having said that an American political party "is not really a party, it's a picnic." This, of course, is a play on words based on the fact that "party" in English has two meanings, and is thus untranslatable into Bulgarian. Some of us felt that the distinguished visitor, perhaps out of a concern not to appear "political," had missed an opportunity to point out that because most Americans consider themselves as belonging to the middle class, parties based on narrow class interests have no raison d'être in America; but that the existing parties do represent differing economic, social and regional interests and philosophies and that they appeal to different pressure groups and political outlooks.

20

Good judgment comes from experience, and experience comes from bad judgment: An ill-considered message results in the author getting slapped down personally by Dr. Kissinger. First reaction: What will my peers think?

December 1. Hardly had Boorstin left, when a blow descended upon me in the form of a personal message "From the Secretary to Ambassador Herz" taking me to task—very politely but quite firmly—for a recent telegram that I had sent to Washington in which I had severely criticized what seemed to me the absence of a well thought-through strategy for the Belgrade Conference in 1977—the conference where the results obtained since the Helsinki Conference of 1975 are to be reviewed. I must say, in retrospect, that my message had been unnecessarily abrasive. Perhaps what stung him most was my introductory remark that "maybe nothing much can be done during the present period of interregnum."

He always welcomed constructive comments from ambassadors in the field, Kissinger's message said, but they must not take the form of "indiscriminate" criticisms of policies that were carefully considered and "deserve at least a reasoned reply." There was no "interregnum" as far as he was concerned, he said. He continued to approve the Department's policies, which were developed on the basis of all foreign policy factors involved, bilateral and other.

And he was right. I should not have pretended that the inadequacy of the Department's preparations for the Belgrade Conference was due to there being an "interregnum." First of all, Kissinger is still very much in charge, and Sonnenfeldt still runs Eastern Europe. And besides, the inadequacy of preparations is surely due to other factors. Some of the things that I had advocated were then rebutted separately in another message, but in that other message a number of items of information were disclosed that we (and other recipients of the telegram) had never had before.

So, at the cost of some ruffling of feathers at home, perhaps my telegram did pry out of the State Department at least a more candid exposition of its position on the Helsinki agreement—including, I thought, a few rather weak rejoinders that indicated that they had still not quite pulled themselves together to do what needs to be done. Perhaps my message may yet help further in that process.

A second and unrelated message, addressed to all Chiefs of Mission from the Deputy Under Secretary, reminded us that "it is customary for all Chiefs of Mission to submit their resignations when a new President takes office." We are to send telegraphically messages to the Department, dated January 21, 1977, addressed to President Carter and containing the phrase, "In keeping with established custom, I hereby tender my resignation as (title to be inserted) to become effective at your pleasure." The signed letters are then to follow by diplomatic pouch, also dated January 21.

Well, there is little doubt that the political appointees among the ambassadors—such as the incumbents in London, Paris, Rome, New Delhi and Tokyo—will expect their resignations to be accepted almost instantly. My colleagues in Iran (Richard Helms) and in Belgrade (Laurence Silberman) have already seen the handwriting on the wall and tendered their resignations. Career officers will be at the very least shifted after they have been in their posts (like myself) for a sufficient length of time.

But what comes afterwards is impossible to predict. For every ambassadorial position there are at least a dozen candidates. The recent appointment of Anthony Lake—a 37-year-old ex-Foreign Service officer who had quit the service over the Cambodian incursion in 1970—to function as liaison between Carter and Kissinger, does not bode well for people like myself who are neither young nor of the opinion that the Cambodian incursion was all that misguided.

One of the specially piquant aspects of the Lake appointment is that he had sued Kissinger over the latter's role in placing his telephone under surveillance when Lake was suspected of passing information derogatory to the current policies to the press. The situation is analogous to that of Morton Halperin who is also suing Kissinger and who was also under suspicion of having passed classified information to the press.

Although they had "Exclusive Distribution" captions, I gave both the Kissinger knuckle-rapping message and the (presumably Sonnenfeldt-drafted) rebuttal message to Harvey to read and to Dan Simpson, our political-economic officer. (Our embassy is so small that it doesn't have separate political and economic officers, but Dan fulfills both functions splendidly.) Then I asked them to step into the conference room and said to them that both have bright futures ahead of them in the Foreign Service and I wanted them to learn from me and in this case they should try to profit from my mistake.

It had been a mistake, I said, to cast my points with respect to the Belgrade Conference in sloganeering terms, and especially wrong to use sarcasm in a message which dealt with an honest policy difference. Although my telegram had resulted in Washington giving us a little more information, I had failed to sell our main point and missed an opportunity perhaps to influence the policy-making process in Washington, because our points had not been taken seriously. If any good was to come from the episode, it would have to be in terms of these younger officers' education.

Since they had both seen my telegram before it was sent and had encouraged me to send it, Harvey and Dan dutifully said they shared any blame with me, but I said that I was not criticizing their judgment but my own. I am the ambassador, I drafted and signed the message, and I am the one who is supposed to have more experience and to be able to teach them how one gets things done in Washington. In this case, mainly because of the tone of my telegram, I had failed. They should profit from my experience. Unfortunately I had taught them in this case how *not* to do a thing.

Harvey then pointed out that another Eastern European post had sent in a much longer telegram which contained some of the same points that we had made. I looked at that message, but the points were tucked away in long paragraphs and didn't come through clearly enough to have made any impact on the upper levels of the State Department. Wryly we noted that if one disagrees too clearly one gets slapped down, whereas if one disagrees in a seven-page message in which the points of disagreement are muted and muffled, one isn't likely to get high-level attention.

Well, I said, the secret lies in phrasing one's questions or criticisms or recommendations succinctly and yet tactfully. There are a hundred ways of doing this, but the way I had phrased my telegram was not one of them. It is true that burying one's points in long discursive paragraphs or making them incidentally in the course of lengthy arguments doesn't really help the reader in Washington and may only make the writer feel better for having spoken his mind. In this case the effect was the same as if he hadn't spoken out at all. We were faced with two extremes. I wasn't recommending either of them.

Later that week, I spent an entire evening at the office looking through the original telegram from Washington which I had ridiculed, my own message, the telegrams from my colleagues in other Eastern European embassies, and the State Department's responses including of course the rebuttal message addressed to us and "repeated" to all other addressees of my message. I tried to keep down the sense of anger and humiliation which welled up in me, and to see what good could still be salvaged from this episode—not in terms of my own pride, but in terms of what could be done prior to the Belgrade Conference.

My point had been, in essence, that the State Department's approach to that conference was lacking in a sense of strategy; that we were being treated to a lot of generalities but would need to get down to specifics if any progress was to be achieved in Belgrade; that it would do no good to counter Communist accusations of our own shortcomings in implementing the Helsinki agreement by saying that "under our system" certain things couldn't be done, because that was exactly what the Communists would claim when charged with failures to observe the Final Act. We needed to agree with our allies where we would put our weight, because pushing all along the perimeter would result in no progress being made on any sector of the front. Also it was urgent for us to prepare certain responses to Communist propaganda about our own alleged failures in connection with Helsinki, and these responses would have to take the form of actions rather than words. I had cited some instances—a few of them rather weak ones—where things might be done or at least attempted during the months ahead.

As I read Washington's rebuttal message I was reminded of the term *ignoratio elenchi* which is a term in Logic meaning "the smashing refutation of an argument that hasn't been made." In some cases I was being demolished on counts that couldn't be found in my telegram. It would be easy to point this out—if it weren't for the fact that in one or two other cases I was being demolished rather accurately and precisely for things that I had indeed said in my telegram. The rebuttal message was thus a mixture of points that were on target and points that were wildly unfair—but in the blizzard of telegrams that descends upon all embassies every day I doubted that anyone would take the trouble to refer to my original message to see if all the rebuttals were justified.

And as I thought along these lines I began to realize that it really didn't matter to me very much what the drafters of the rebuttal message had thought when they wrote it—I was much more concerned with my standing with my peers, especially the ambassadors in the other Eastern European capitals. This was in itself interesting, for I had often taken the position in discussions with Foreign Service colleagues that the professionals in the field can always be relied upon to give loyal service to the political leadership in Washington, and that it is a tired old cliché that the Foreign Service is cliquish and clannish and more concerned with its own internal pecking order than with the policy officials on top of the pyramid.

Well, this situation was special, of course, because the political leadership at the top wasn't going to be around much longer—but that very fact troubled me because it might be thought by some readers of our exchange of telegrams that I was being sassy to Henry Kissinger because I knew he was on his way out—or that, perhaps, I was even trying opportunistically to play up to some of his critics. That was certainly not the case. I had given my frank opinions, intemperately and in questionable taste, because I had been frustrated with what I thought was a mealy-mouthed set of generalities in a policy message from Washington; and I would have done that at any time and not just after elections that had been lost by the party in power in Washington.

But things were even worse than that. I recalled that Harvey, in supporting the ill-fated message, had remarked dryly that if it didn't do any good with the present set of policy officials, it might yet do some good with their successors. Would he now perhaps think that I had deliberately provoked that outburst from Washington in order to attract the attention of the team that would be coming after Kissinger? That would have made no sense at all, because the team that will be coming after Kissinger will have to deal with the experts on the subject of Helsinki and Belgrade, and in the end the judgments of my professional colleagues—in the field as in Washington—will be much more important to them than the judgments of politicians. Having annoyed his predecessor is not likely to make any points for me with the new Secretary of State, whoever he may be, because he will still learn of my views only from the career professionals.

I can write about these things today, on December 1, because by the time this diary is in print—if it is ever printed—the Belgrade Conference assessing the results of Helsinki will be long past, and the position taken by the American Ambassador to Bulgaria in November 1976 will be of no consequence. As for me, and as of now, I am not very proud to have sent a badly worded and only half thought-out telegram to Washington which had an effect exactly contrary to that which had been intended. I had been less than professional. But aside from the matter of professionalism there is also the fact that I don't look very good with my "constituency," my colleagues in the Foreign Service. I do care about their opinion of me, even if I am close to retirement age and many of the younger readers of my telegram don't know me and will never meet me or hear of me again.

21

Death of The Great McClintock, and reflections on his dictum that diplomacy is most important in relation to one's colleagues. McClintock's performance in Cambodia in which he, too, may have learned from his mistakes.

Elisabeth and I have suffered a heavy blow through the death, in a car accident in France, of our old friend Robert McClintock, one of the most fascinating persons I have known. He was my ambassador in Cambodia twenty years ago when I was a second secretary, the first ambassador with whom I worked closely—since it was such a small embassy—and also the first ambassador whom I could observe at close quarters when the going got rough and from whom, therefore, I learned many things.

I once wrote a wise friend that a certain other ambassador for whom I had worked was able "but not a great man," and he replied that it is often a misfortune to be too closely associated with a great man. Well, it was no misfortune to be associated with a man as brilliant and mercurial as Rob McClintock, but it wasn't always easy. And perhaps because it hadn't always been easy for either of us, we emerged from that period as close friends for life. And now his life has been snuffed out through a stupid accident when he had so much left in him to give and to enjoy and to contribute even after his retirement.

An enormous vitality was, in fact, one of his characteristics, and he was untypical of the Foreign Service professional in that respect as in so many others. He had charm, wit, and a penetrating intelligence—a combination for which many of his colleagues never forgave him, especially since the wit could come quite unexpectedly. Elisabeth once observed how all the ladies at a party would straighten up and smile and seem more alive when he entered a room. Not because he made a "grand entrance," quite the contrary. He simply had the capacity of making everyone, but

150

perhaps especially women, think that they were especially interesting. As a result everyone, including myself, did become more interesting when touched with his magic wand.

Robert McClintock was ambassador to Cambodia, Lebanon, Argentina and Venezuela—but that statement conveys very little when it isn't realized that by general agreement among his peers his career was washed up several times, and yet he emerged Phoenix-like from its ashes, not because he had special connections in high places (he may have had those, too) but mainly because he was exceptionally able. He had the true gift of diplomacy, which consists of understanding how to find the best point of intersection between the interests of your own country and those of the country to which you are accredited. He had many accomplishments to his credit, but also some failures, and he made enemies for many reasons. The principal reason, in my opinion, was that he had *panache*, that indefinable combination of daring and style. And he was able to make instant calculations of risk/benefit ratios, which allowed him to carry off some coups as in 1958 when he drove General Chehab, the commander-in-chief of the Lebanese armed forces, right through the Lebanese front lines to the headquarters of the American Marines who had landed there and who might have been opposed by Chehab's forces.

He reminded me, in some respects, of Winston Churchill whose career was in ashes after Gallipoli and several times thereafter, but who was called back to power more than once because he was the best man available for the job, because it was obvious that his time had come, or because there just didn't seem to be any better alternative. Always debonair, Rob McClintock even during the times when his career seemed in the dumps never lost faith in himself or in his future. Neither did his wife, whose continued susceptibility to his charm must have been a source of great strength for him.

At one time we were in Washington together when he had just failed to obtain a position on which he had had his heart set—Deputy Director of the Policy Planning Council. As it turned out much later, his failure to get that promotion was a blessing in disguise, but at the time it was clear that he had missed out on something he had very much wanted. He poured champagne for himself and his guests and drank to *not* having become Deputy

Director of the Policy Planning Council. I never had much admiration for those colleagues in the Foreign Service who shunned him for a while as a has-been, as someone who was still around but would never again amount to anything. Afterwards he received perhaps the most important embassy of his career, in Venezuela where he served for five years with great distinction.

Rob McClintock often taught—or rather, admonished—me that diplomacy practiced toward a foreign government is the easier part of our job, and that diplomacy practiced toward one's colleagues is both more difficult and more important. He himself usually heeded this advice, but I have not been able to follow in his footsteps, and my career has suffered for it. When something completely outrageous happened, he would be *amused* while I would be angry. He had a light touch—I once attended one of his staff meetings in Venezuela, and he conducted it as the late Furtwaengler conducted the Berlin Philharmonic, with an imposing presence but seemingly without effort and with barely a visible motion of his hands.

In Cambodia, his first ambassadorial assignment, he got into trouble with Prince Sihanouk in the most unexpected way. Certainly I, as his political officer, did not anticipate that our press release on the occasion of George Washington's birthday in 1956 would call down upon him the Prince's wrath. There might have been some question whether the American Ambassador needed to release anything to the press on George Washington's birthday, but the text seemed quite reasonable—at least when read hurriedly. It was in fact a rather undistinguished statement prepared by our public affairs officer to which Rob McClintock had added a tiny sentence to the effect that "just as here" the Father of our country had not spurned foreign assistance in his struggle for independence.

There were ominous rumblings from the Palace after that release was made, and soon one of the local French-language newspapers attacked the propriety of the American Ambassador's statement. I well remember the term used by that paper since it was almost untranslatable. McClintock, it said, had been guilty of *une incartade*—something like an extravagant but ill-considered gesture, which is exactly what the inserted sentence had been. At any rate, Rob McClintock was not in the Prince's good books for quite a while because, as everyone was supposed to know, Sihanouk had *not* benefited from the help of foreigners in obtaining his country's independence. He had done it all by himself according to Cambodian historiography.

Well, Rob did not wait for things to settle down but went to work, quietly and not so quietly, to mend his fences in Cambodia—and also to place our (and his) situation in Cambodia into a larger context with his superiors in Washington. Those were the days when Prince Sihanouk was beginning to flirt with the Communists, when he invited Chou En-lai to visit, and when he was especially anxious to prove his neutrality between East and West. And of course those also were the days of John Foster Dulles when neutrality was regarded as immoral and cowardly and as something to be sternly dealt with, especially if it impinged upon American security interests as they were then perceived.

Deep in the jungles of Cambodia, near the provincial capital of Siemreap and not far from the fabled temples of Angkor, there lived at that time a local satrap by the name of Dap (for Corporal) Chhuon, an erstwhile resistance fighter against the French whom Sihanouk had rewarded with a fiefdom in that area. The fact that Dap Chhuon had fought against the French when the Prince (then King) had still been toasting them with champagne in the royal palace, was fairly immaterial. What was certain was that Dap Chhuon—don't ask me what the double h stands for, after two years in Cambodia I wasn't able to duplicate the sound—was an ambitious man with a slightly insane gleam in his eye, and he was not really well inclined toward his ruler. There were also other military figures who had made noises unfavorable to the new foreign policy orientation of the Prince.

To make a long story short, Rob McClintock never recommended that the United States should support any particular subversive or revolutionary activity against Prince Sihanouk, but neither did he completely exclude it as an "option," as something which the United States might hold in the back of its mind, to fall back upon if it proved necessary from a larger point of view. It was well known in the embassy that I thought that the idea of a coup was unrealistic and much too dangerous; that Prince Sihanouk was basically very popular in his country; that the would-be conspirators were amateurish and unreliable; that the Prince did have a certain justification in his strictures against the United States; and that our foremost task should be to swallow our pride and try to get back into his good graces since he was likely to be around for a very long time.

It was to his credit, especially in view of the atmosphere prevailing in Washington, that Rob McClintock, even while he ventilated the possibility of an "alternative solution" in Cambodia, never recommended that we should actively seek to bring it about; and in fact he worked through the Queen Mother and other Cambodian leaders to restore tolerably good relations with the Prince, which of course also meant an accommodation with his neutrality policy. To his even greater credit, he remarked to me wryly that "the chickens are coming home to roost" when suddenly a high-level mission of American military and CIA types descended on us in Phnom Penh to discuss with the ambassador ways and means of hastening or triggering the "alternative solution." I should emphasize, for the benefit of any reader who has not followed the diplomacy of that period, that we are talking here about 1956, not about the time several years later when the CIA was exposed as being actually involved in some highly dubious dealings with Dap Chhuon.

At the time of the meeting with the military and CIA types in 1956, I well recall that a certain chill had descended on my relations with the ambassador. Perhaps he vaguely thought me disloyal for not wishing Prince Sihanouk to get his comeuppance. Perhaps he resented the implication that if Prince Sihanouk was more sinned against than sinning, some of the sinning might have been done by Rob himself. At any rate I was not included in any of the preparations for the important visit, perhaps also because it was felt that my negative views were already well enough known.

However, when the chickens did come home to roost, I was suddenly summoned to the ambassadorial residence and, to my amazement, heard Ambassador McClintock say to the assembled visitors something like "Gentlemen, you have just heard about how Prince Sihanouk could be easily removed from power, and why the United States should support those in Cambodia who favor such a development. Now here is young Mr. Herz who will explain to you why in his opinion it wouldn't be at all easy to remove Prince Sihanouk from power, why the Cambodians who advocate it are ineffective and unreliable, and why the risks of such an enterprise would greatly outweigh the advantages to the United States." I don't recall exactly what I said, but the visitation passed and nothing was decided, which in my opinion was a very good thing. Also the chill between Rob McClintock and myself somehow thawed, and as he came to realize that perhaps I had saved him from a very risky adventure that might have wrecked his career, this possibly contributed to the more and more cordial and close and mutually trusting relationship that developed between us.

Many years later his wife said to Elisabeth, whom I had met and married only after that episode, that in Phnom Penh Rob would sometimes come home and say that he had to do something first thing the next morning because otherwise Martin Herz would do it first—which I found charming and a bit disconcerting for several reasons: It is always a little ridiculous to try to compete with a subordinate—and often it is dangerous to the subordinate. But in the case of Rob McClintock he could do in ten minutes what it would take me an hour to do. Often in Phnom Penh and afterwards I marveled at his ability to dictate long analyses or policy papers, well-organized with their chapter headings and subheadings, moving in an orderly way from premises to conclusions to recommendations, virtually each paragraph impregnated with his epigrammatic style. Among people I have known, only Dick Crossman, the British don and political figure for whom I worked during World War II, possessed a similarly disciplined mind coupled with personal flair, a gift for the apt turn of phrase, and the ability to jolt the reader with a sudden witticism. Both of them had more than a touch of genius and only one major weakness, which was a certain amount of vanity.

Lest anyone think that I did better than my ambassador in my own relations with Prince Sihanouk, let me add that I had in fact far worse relations with him—even though I was for a time (1967/68) in charge of the State Department's efforts to bring about a *modus vivendi*. In 1958 I had published a short summary of Cambodian history, largely because no book of that kind existed in the English language; and it wasn't long before I was subjected to worse treatment than that endured by Rob McClintock, and for a far better reason: My book, being a history, couldn't very well conceal the role of the man who actually did most to obtain

Cambodia's independence, someone named Son Ngoc Thanh who at that time was living obscurely in exile—and who would later, after the fall of Sihanouk, have again a brief moment in the sun. For even *mentioning* Son Ngoc Thanh I was severely castigated by the Cambodian press and by Prince Sihanouk himself—even though my references to that erstwhile rival hadn't been particularly favorable.

I am drifting away from my recollections of Rob McClintock but must recall one other lesson that I drew from that period when I was a second secretary. I actually journeyed to the headquarters of Dap Chhuon (whole real name was Chhuon Mochulpich) and had a lengthy conversation with him about the political situation. And I recall that I came away from that visit with the strong impression that many things that he had said about "the Free World," the dangers of Communism, and "democracy" had been said in order to please the Americans; and that naked ambition, and a certain mysticism and belief in his own star, were the driving forces of Dap Chhuon. The lesson was that it is necessary, when somebody claims to be sharing our ideals, to try to get him (or her) to explain why this is so. How the CIA could later have become mixed up with Dap Chhuon has always been a mystery to me. He knew nothing of politics. He neven even attempted a coup. Sihanouk's army one day descended upon him and killed him, and reportedly they found in his house not only an America radio transmitter but bars of gold, allegedly gifts from South Vietnam. That was long after Rob McClintock and I had left Cambodia.

—0—

Having just re-read what I have written above, I find once more that I cannot just leave it there, for the story didn't end when Rob McClintock left Cambodia, and like most people Prince Sihanouk changed considerably in the next twenty years. When he was ousted from power in 1970 he had become a very different man. He had long since made up his mind that the Communists were going to win the war in Vietnam and was therefore cooperating with them fairly openly—while denouncing the United States for any overt counter-measures and for instances of "aggression" which he trumped up against us. At the same time, when confronted by us with evidence of the violation of his country's sovereignty by the North Vietnamese, he would cynically tell us that he didn't mind if we bombed them as long as we didn't bomb any Cambodians. He was ousted, in my opinion, largely for the ironical reason that his compatriots, and especially the Cambodian army, didn't like his cooperation with the Vietnamese. The irony resides in the fact that eventually the ouster led to the Vietnamese becoming still more active and obnoxious in his country, which in turn led to the so-called American "incursion." So much nonsense has been written about that period in 1970 that many newspaper readers honestly got the mistaken impression that the Communist uprising in Cambodia and the North Vietnamese attack came *after* the American "incursion." It came before. We didn't cause them, we reacted to them, perhaps unwisely but certainly not against the wishes of the Cambodian government.

But this is a diary about my ambassadorship in Bulgaria, so I will not burden the reader with arguments about an obscure and complicated chapter of the recent history of Indochina. Suffice it to say, in conclusion, that I blame Prince Sihanouk for having gone over to the Communists of Pol Pot. It was a political blunder of the first magnitude, dwarfing any blunders committed by Lon Nol and the other non-communists. The prince has himself written in the magazine *Foreign Affairs* that he joined up with the Cambodian Communists out of hatred and a desire for revenge against the people who had ousted him. Had he not lent the prestige of his name to the Communist Khmer Rouge, his country might just possibly have successfully resisted the imposition of one of the most cruel dictatorships in the world.

22

*The Los Angeles Philharmonic casts its shadow before it.
Does one have to be wealthy to be an American ambassador?
The National Agrarian Union holds its Congress and demonstrates its "unshakable unity" with the Bulgarian Communists.*

December 3. It seems that every time another batch of telegrams is brought to my desk these days, at least several of them carry the caption LAPO and contain some kind of bad news. LAPO stands for the Los Angeles Philharmonic Orchestra which we are eagerly awaiting to hear perform here on December 6 and 7. They have scored smashing successes in Budapest, Warsaw, and Rome. Meanwhile, however, a host of administrative problems have arisen. For instance, at Budapest, where the contract with the local impresario agency (or with the one in Warsaw) called for the provision of adequate space on charter planes for both the 120-man orchestra and its bulky instruments, apparently everything went wrong with their departure. A sample from the escort officer's telegram following arrival in Warsaw, reporting only part of the disasters, went as follows:

"Cargo-loading delay, of course, caused passenger-loading delay. LAPO personnel sat in hotel lobby over one hour before buses departed for airport at 7:00 p.m. (Buses were available, but hotel departure delayed in effort to avoid long wait in dreary airport terminal.) Then there was further wait at terminal 8:00 to 10:00 p.m. before passenger-loading. Worst of all was claustrophobic three-and-quarter hours' wait aboard plane before take-off at 1:15 a.m. This last delay due to considerable snow-rain and icing conditions Budapest. De-icing equipment appeared primitive, slow. Despite LAPO's advance request, nets for lashing cargo not provided. Most of forward cabin was jumble of large and small musical instrument cases, trunks, etc., tied down by flimsy rope scrounged at Budapest airport—among which several LAPO musicians ob-

158

liged sit because of plane's remaining seating capacity. Much-traveled escort cannot recall ever being more apprehensive over take-off and flight. Fortunately, LOT crew did magnificent job and flight landed smoothly Warsaw at 2:35 a.m., six hours later than scheduled. Although musicians generally good-natured during this ordeal, they should not be expected to encore. (Manager) threatens to abort remainder of tour unless separate, adequate cargo plane made available. . ."

In Sofia, the difficulty concerns hotel rooms. The LAPO business manager was shown rooms in the Hotel Balkan, but according to the terms of the contract the orchestra will be housed in "First Class" accommodations, and the Hotel Balkan has meanwhile been up-graded to "De Luxe" which is a distinction without a difference but something which aroused considerable suspicion on the part of the business manager, particularly since he had not seen the Park Hotel Moskva into which the Bulgarian impresario agency proposed to put the orchestra. In my own opinion, which I sent along for what it was worth, the Park Moskva is actually a better hotel than the Balkan. But that was only the beginning of the problem, the end of which is not in sight.

The trouble is that the Park Moskva has two types of rooms, some of them classified De Luxe and some First Class; and the LAPO manager insisted, despite the terms of his contract, that the men and women of his orchestra had to be put into De Luxe rooms, which are supposed to be better than First Class. The State Department cultural affairs bureau, which subsidizes the tour, demurred. This produced an insulting telegram from manager Mr. Fleischmann and a thinly veiled threat to scrub the entire Sofia leg of the visit, particularly since new difficulties had arisen with the onward transportation of the instruments from here to Prague. It may seem a bit mundane for an ambassador to concern himself with the question of hotel rooms, but we had a number of discussions of the LAPO visit in my office, and various officers of the embassy were given assignments to make sure that as little as possible goes wrong.

For instance, I have drafted and personally signed welcoming letters to all 120 members of the orchestra, and we are informing them of special attractions (a mass on Sunday afternoon, a Mexican art exhibit) which can be seen here in Sofia during their stay. Buses have been laid on to take them to the center of town whenever they want. I've had flowers ordered for the premiere, and we are planning a large reception after it. Getting tickets for the embassy and its guests was in itself a major operation; and then came the cliff-hanging period of sweating out acceptances or declinations from the Bulgarian dignitaries whom we had invited, for such things are not simple in this society. Finally I found myself personally allocating seats for the premiere and making last-minute telephone calls to members of the diplomatic community to whom we gave seats that could not be used for Bulgarian dignitaries.

A minor note, but one that has very much to do with the life of an American ambassador: We will have the "fringe benefit" of being able to have Maestro Zubin Mehta and his wife for a quiet dinner on Sunday, to which we look forward very much. But my wife and I will be paying out of our own pocket for 72 tickets for the two performances to which we have invited guests, and we will by paying out of our own pocket for the flowers and for the reception in honor of the Mehtas and members of the Los Angeles Philharmonic. This will be so because the embassy has already exceeded its quarterly allotment of representation (i.e., entertainment) funds, and I make it a practice to assume the deficit, or the lion's share of it, since we have no children and my salary and fringe benefits are after all better than those of others in the embassy. As was stated initially, I'm not a wealthy man, I'm a career officer, and any savings we have were slowly accumulated over many years (and, Elisabeth would add, we would have more of them if I didn't have such an expensive hobby as collecting ancient maps).

Actually, the situation with respect to representation funds has greatly improved during the last year or two (apparently after the retirement of Representative Rooney), and we no longer go into the hole as much as we used to do. At the end of the last fiscal year I had a deficit of only $29. But I can remember years when "unreimbursed representation expenditures" made up about 5 percent of my salary, at a time when Foreign Service salaries were quite low. (My present salary is $41,800 per year.) For many years the idea was deeply rooted in Washington that "only a wealthy man" could afford to become ambassador to London, Paris, Rome and similar world capitals with great requirements for entertaining. I have never agreed with that, and in fact wrote (under a pseudonym, of course) a letter that was published in *The Economist* a while ago when that respectable British journal had lamented that only a wealthy man like Mr. Annenberg could afford to be ambassador to Great Britain.

"What is there about the British ruling classes," the letter began provocatively, "that requires an American ambassador to dispose of personal wealth in order to communicate effectively with them? . . . None of the expensive things that Mr. Annenberg did and which you list in your article seemed essential for the functions of an ambassador, unless you regard his giving of expensive gifts and his lavish entertaining as necessary for the conduct of diplomacy with your leadership. I cannot imagine why an American ambassador needs to prove to his guests by the opulence of his table or the number of footmen that the United States is a wealthy country.

"Suppose an American ambassador invited only 12 people to a dinner instead of 74—perhaps that would give him more of a chance to talk with his guests; and as for the maintenance of Winfield House I suppose if the Government had its choice for [sic] an ambassador who is an amateur but who keeps the grounds impeccably, or an experienced professional who allows them to run down a little, perhaps it would not follow your implied advice and would opt for the man of intellectual and professional substance, rather than pecuniary substance."

The Economist added "Yours faithfully," which had not been in my letter, but I was pleased that they did not correct the awkwardness of syntax in the last sentence which was supposed to make the letter more plausible as having come from someone in Vienna (from where we can mail letters, with Austrian stamps, when we do not want mail to European destinations to pass through Bulgarian censorship).

Actually, I am not categorical about politically-appointed ambassadors. During my 30 years in the Foreign Service I have worked under three—David K. E. Bruce, Douglas Dillon, Ellsworth Bunker—who were, and are, as good as anyone in the service; but I have also observed the antics of some of the amateurs and have shuddered about the damage they must be doing to the interests of our country—damage which their subordinates cannot report to Washington because the professionals are supposed to uphold and support and if necessary cover up the shortcomings of their chiefs or at least minimize the damage. Only the gravest cases of malfeasance would cause a Foreign Service officer to blow the whistle on a dangerously incompetent chief.

In this respect President-elect Carter has made it very clear that he wants to make a new beginning. He did not say, nor is there any reason why he should, that he would appoint only professional diplomats to ambassadorial positions, although most countries do exactly that; but he did say that he would put a stop to the awarding of embassies as political plums or as pay-offs for services rendered, that he would only appoint highly qualified ambassadors, and that his criterion would be merit. He said: "I want these (diplomatic appointments) to depend firmly on merit. I am not under obligation to anyone, and I don't believe people should be paid off for helping elect a president by getting embassies." We shall see.

—0—

December 4. I have just read the daily USIA Wireless Bulletin which contains news items especially from Washington and am amazed to find in it that the Congressional Commission on Security and Cooperation in Europe—the very body which wasn't permitted to visit any Eastern European capital except Belgrade— has come out with a statement that comes very close to the position I had taken in my telegram to the Department of State which had been "rebutted" so strenuously.

"The United States should take a more energetic role in follow- ing up the gains made possible by the 35-nation Helsinki Agree- ment and in assuring that American practices conform to its principles and provisions," the statement begins; and later, with reference to the very point on which I had been unfairly rebutted, the report went on to say: "The group also recommended Execu- tive branch 'mechanisms' to review American compliance with the Final Act, *in particular U.S. visa laws and regulations.*"

So perhaps I wasn't all that far removed from what it will soon be safe to say in Washington, but that may make my aggressive talking out of turn all the more unforgivable. Nothing is more hateful in a big bureaucracy than for someone to come out with a controversial statement and to get involved in controversy about it, when a few months later it turns out not to have been so controversial after all but just a plain statement of the existing situation or problem, unwelcome though its enunciation may have been initially.

—0—

The National Agrarian Union is having a congress and international conference in Sofia, and it is amazing how many foreign non-communist delegations dignify with their presence an event organized by the Communist satellite of a Communist satellite. The purpose of the exercise is baldly stated in the *Sofia News*, a publication issued for the sole consumption of foreign diplomats and visitors to Bulgaria, which featured the heavy headline: *"The Unity Between Communists and Agrarians Has Proved: Socialism Can Be Built With the Participation of Other Democratic Parties, Too."*

In other words, Western European and other democratic—i.e., truly democratic—parties are supposed to find the existence of the Agrarian Union in Bulgaria as proof that when the Communists come to power, they share it with "other democratic parties." It is hard to see how even naive delegates to the Congress can have failed to note that there exists not even the slightest difference in policy, approach, tone or style between the BKP and what today passes for the descendant of that doughty old democratic party, the National Agrarian Union.

According to the *Sofia News*, the Congress was attended by delegations from over 80 "peasant and kindred parties and organizations from 65 countries throughout the world, as well as by three international organizations—the World Peace Council, the International Trade Union Confederation of Farm, Agriculture, Forestry and Plantation Workers, and the International Trade Union Confederations of the Food and Kindred Industries [all Communist front organizations] with which the BAP maintains active contacts."

I was invited to attend a portion of the Conference but decided not to go, as did most of my Western colleagues; but some of them, especially those who had delegations here from parties or groups that supported their governments, felt that they had to go, and of course this lent additional *cachet* to the proceedings. The lesson for the foreign visitors, which was in no way subtle but was driven home with a sledgehammer, was stated by Petur Tanchev in his report when he said:

"The experience of Bulgaria and the other socialist countries emphatically refutes the slanders propagated by reactionary circles that, having seized power, the Communists failed their allies. The relations of friendship and cooperation between the Bulgarian Communist Party and the Bulgarian Agrarian Party are an indicative example of the unity of view and action of progressive forces in the building of socialism in a country and in the struggle for peace and cooperation in the world." Tweedledum and Tweedledee do indeed display unity of view and action.

It isn't clear whether the organizers of this kind of charade realize how unintentionally revealing are some of the pronouncements made by Agrarian spokesmen—they may be "inadvertent" because individual spokesmen no longer are able to differentiate between things that they must say to please the ruling Communist Party at home and things that they are supposed to play down, at least during such a Congress, because they may not seem altogether reassuring to those delegations that do not themselves represent front organizations of the Communists in other countries.

Thus Mr. Lalyu Ganchev, Secretary of the Bulgarian Agrarian Union's Standing Committee (and we should note that during the conference the BAU suddenly was referred to as the Bulgarian Agrarian *Party* BAP), was quoted as saying the following in answer to a planted question: "In the framework of socialist construction the Bulgarian Agrarian Party has undergone profound ideological, organizational and political developments, by far outstripping the aims and tasks which the founders had posed for it. While preserving its peculiarities, structural and political independence and distinct image, the BAP has moved to an important place in the country's life. This is corroborated by our Constitution whose Article One reads: 'The BKP leads in building a developed socialist society in the People's Republic of Bulgaria in close fraternal cooperation with the BAP.' "

Translated into English, this means that the democratic character and emphasis on individual land holdings of the original

BAU has been completely turned upside down ("undergone pro-found ideological . . . and political developments") and that now the BAU (or, as it is now billed, the BAP) is a loyal stooge of the Bulgarian Communist Party (BKP) whose leadership in all matters it accepts unquestioningly. And this is supposed to prove to foreign non-Communist parties that are inclined to cooperate with their national Communist parties that "socialism can be built with the cooperation of other democratic parties."

23

The Los Angeles Philharmonic brings down the house with John Philip Sousa's "Stars and Stripes Forever." An artistic triumph, but the visit is beclouded by a political incident—unplanned, perhaps inevitable, but quite unfortunate.

December 8. LAPO has come and conquered, and departed. The visit of Zubin Mehta and the Los Angeles Philharmonic Orchestra was an artistic triumph. It also provided us with several supremely interesting and enjoyable evenings plus a lot of hard work, a certain number of headaches—and one political incident. They arrived on Sunday, and we had virtually the entire embassy out at the airport to smooth their way through customs and to the hotel. Zubin Mehta and his lovely wife were charming, indeed stunning. My wife and I shook hands with all the members of the orchestra as they filed in, thanking them for coming to Sofia. They got through the passport controls in fairly quick time, but then things began to jam up.

Unfortunately, despite our prior arrangements the customs officials insisted on spot-checking the baggage of the orchestra—and as there were 118 people with their baggage in a narrow space, a few tempers flared for a moment. The Mehtas decided to wait until everyone had cleared customs before going off with us to their hotel. With 118 people to take care of, there simply weren't enough porters, and so most of the members of the orchestra had to lug their baggage about 15 yards to the customs desk and then past it to an assembly area where the bags were picked up by porters and people of our embassy and taken to a truck.

"So you are the ambassador," said one of the orchestra members, a very distinguished looking man. Yes, I said. "Well, I want you to know that I consider the arrangements here very inadequate." We had done all we could, I said. "Yes, but why do we have to be checked by customs?" Well, I replied, we had thought we had

166

it arranged that they would not be subject to any checking, but this was Bulgaria, and the American Embassy really couldn't control such things. "Well, I think the arrangements made by your embassy are entirely inadequate," the man said, "and I intend to write a letter about it as soon as we get back."

At the hotel there was more confusion because the orchestra had insisted on having as many of its rooms as possible upgraded from "First Class" to "De Luxe"—which, according to our information, amounted to having precisely one more square meter per room. Unfortunately the hotel had not placed all the right keys in the right envelopes, and because of the shifts from one class of rooms to another they lost track of which rooms were empty and which were occupied, and it took a couple of hours before the last member of the orchestra was assigned to his room. As it happened, Elisabeth and I were in the same hotel later that morning as we had attended the Finnish national day reception there, and as fate would have it we encountered the same hypercritical artist in the lobby as we came out. I asked him if he was satisfied with his room, and he immediately began to berate me for "inadequate arrangements." I said we really were in no position to control the room assignment process, but he wouldn't hear my explanation and just said something like, "I hold you personally responsible, you are the American Ambassador here, you should have seen to it that everything was properly arranged."

At that point something boiled over, and I took the man by his lapels and said something like: Listen here, now, I think you people are doing a fine thing for our country by coming here, but I also think you haven't a clue about how much we in the embassy have worried and worked and prepared and all we have done to try to make your visit here more agreeable. We are breaking our ass for you, and all I get out of you is complaints. Who do you think is running this country? I'll tell you a secret, the Bulgarians are running this country, and it is they who control the arrangements in the hotel. We've been up since early in the morning, we've had virtually everyone out at the airport, we are trying to help you here at the hotel, I'm having a large number of you to the residence at my own expense, and I am glad to do all this, all of us are glad to do what we can for you—but we don't appreciate being attacked in this way, we don't appreciate it one bit! (Or words to that effect.)

Whereupon the man, who was really a lovable old gent who apparently had gotten into the habit of venting his frustrations at embassies and ambassadors, took me and Elisabeth—who had visibly winced during this contretemps—and embraced us. He said that was the spirit he liked, and he was proud that the United States was represented here by people who would stand up on their hind legs, that he appreciated our problems, and that he had not intended to criticize us. As things quieted down, we found that we rather liked each other. I still don't know his name, but when we met next we embraced again. When the orchestra was on stage on Monday, I noticed him looking down on us and he winked at us; and we waved back to him. He played like an angel, as did all his colleagues; and later at the residence, after the premiere, it was as if we had known each other for ages. Each of us knew that the other had problems; and having had a go at each other I think we became something like friends.

Very selfishly, we asked the Mehtas for dinner alone on Sunday evening and only asked two couples from the embassy to join us afterwards for coffee. Mehta is a great artist, but what we had not expected was that our conversation would cover such a large number of subjects, on all of which he seemed knowledgeable and sophisticated. Mrs. Mehta discovered a book about Angkor in our library, and this led to an interesting conversation about Cambodia and its vicissitudes. It even turned out that we had known Mrs. Mehta some ten years ago when she had spent some time in Teheran, and that we had mutual friends. It was a relaxed and charming and interesting evening, and I record that fact because we were so unprepared for what happened two days later.

The first concert was a triumph. The Bulgarians, as I had noted in my letter of welcome to the orchestra, are not demonstrative people; they cannot be compared, for instance, with the more romantic and temperamental Hungarians and Poles, and often they do not applaud at great length even their own most celebrated artists. But the applause for LAPO and Zubin Mehta was unbelievable. We had been totally unprepared for such an outburst of enthusiasm, partly also because we hadn't been sure that the tickets had really gone to the most musically conscious people in Sofia. Both the first concert and the big reception we gave at the residence afterwards were great successes, not just for the Mehtas and the orchestra but for the United States and its cultural relations with Bulgaria. But then came the incident.

We were in our seats after the intermission of the second concert on December 7. The hall was packed, and even additional chairs had been put in front of the first row, and some people—in defiance of the strict fire regulations—were standing along one wall. The orchestra, or at any rate most of them, were in their seats, but some seemed to be missing. Minutes passed, and nothing happened. Then there was some whispering among orchestra members, and gradually more and more of them got up and walked off the stage. Now only about one-third of the orchestra members were sitting there. Since the concert was being broadcast over Sofia radio, the delay was becoming more and more embarrassing, mysterious, and disquieting. After about ten minutes of waiting, Elisabeth urged me to go backstage to see what was happening.

"Now, let's not panic," I said. "Perhaps they have some disagreement about union rules. How could I help with things like that? Besides, if they need me I am sure they will send for me." And I turned to my neighbor on the right, Mr. Aleksandrov, the head of the Department of Cultural Relations with Foreign Countries at the Committee of Art and Culture, and mumbled something about the unions being very strong in American orchestras.

More minutes passed, and still nothing happened. The audience was visibly uncomfortable. About twenty minutes after people had resumed their seats our press and cultural officer, John Karch, came down the aisle and motioned to me. As we stood together in the central aisle, in full view of over 1,200 people, he whispered to me that the orchestra were refusing to go on stage because "some students" had been roughly treated by the police. It seemed that some students had made a nuisance of themselves at the rear entrance, where the orchestra had been resting and smoking during the intermission, and the management had called the police who had unceremoniously ejected them from the rear entrance. Now the orchestra, the business manager and the conductor had taken the position that unless the young people were allowed into the hall they would not resume the concert.

What does an American ambassador do when confronted with a situation like that? My own opinion was quite clear—that the orchestra had a contract with *Sofiaconcert* to perform on that evening, and that they were creating an incident that could do no good for the cultural relations between the United States and Bulgaria that they were supposed to be promoting. But as usual the situation turned out to be more complicated the more one heard of it. It was not just a case of people pleading to get in after they had been unable to get tickets, as generally happens when there are foreign artistic offerings. What had apparently happened was that members of the orchestra had first been told that no standees were allowed—but had then noticed people standing along the walls during the first part of the concert. So they had "invited" the young people in as their "guests"—and were horrified to see their young protégés not only ejected from the rear entrance area but also hustled into a black maria by the police.

Zubin Mehta and Mr. Fleischmann had early taken the side of the orchestra members, despite the pleadings of the concert management. There had been a great deal of shouting, though when I arrived it was deathly still. Miss Khinova, the English-speaking official of *Sofiaconcert* who had done so much to smooth the arrangements for the orchestra, was in tears, white-faced and trembling as she came up to me and asked: "Mr. Ambassador, what are you going to do?" I said I first needed the facts of the situation. Mr. Mehta began to explain them, but was interrupted by Miss Khinova shouting "*Mr. Mehta, I am talking with your ambassador!*" Another LAPO official told me that the concert hall management had behaved as any concert hall management would behave in Paris, London or New York when people come in who have no tickets and whom it is proposed to let into the hall in contravention of fire regulations.

I was about to make a solomonic judgment when to everyone's amazement the rear doors opened and the students—nobody knows if they were students or just young music lovers—streamed in and were hustled into the hall. There was applause from the orchestra members, Mr. Mehta got ready to return to the stage, and within one minute everything was back to normal. I had trouble, in fact, returning to my seat in time for the resumption of the concert. As I looked back, I saw a small knot of young people clustered against the rear door of the hall. I wondered what would happen to them after the concert. I also wondered what could have made the police relinquish control of students whom they had put under temporary arrest, or at any rate under restraint. In fact, I marveled how utterly wrong I could have been in my expectations of what was going to happen.

As I looked back on the incident then, and as I look back upon it now while writing these lines, it is quite obvious that I would have bet one hundred to one that in a contest between the management of a concert hall in Sofia and the dreaded *Militzia*, the latter was bound to win; and that particularly in a situation involving "students," of whom the authorities are apt to be especially suspicious, there wasn't the slightest chance of the young people being released, let alone allowed into the hall, and still less so when capitalist imperialist "provocateurs" were demanding it. Quite aside from being the most hidebound and reactionary Communist state in Eastern Europe, the Bulgarians have a deserved reputation for being the "Prussians of the Balkans." Yet—perhaps because the concert was on the air and the holdup was creating a public embarrassment—the police had yielded to an ultimatum laid down by foreigners in their own country.

Well, as I have often said, good political judgment on the part of a diplomat is a matter of batting averages. If he is always concerned, as some of us are, with covering himself by giving the "on-the-one-hand-on-the-other hand" kind of judgment, then he will rarely be wrong but will also rarely be right. In my own career I have often stuck my neck out. Over the years, while I have sometimes been wrong I have been right more of the time and have thus acquired a certain reputation for making sound political judgments and predictions. But in this instance I must confess that I would have been proved utterly wrong if I had had to make a prediction—which, in the event, I didn't have to do. In fact, I never even got to the point of pleading with Mehta and Fleischmann to send the orchestra back on stage; but rather doubt that even if I had persuaded those two gentlemen, they would have had the power to make the LAPO members, who were up in arms about what had happened, resume the performance.

Not knowing what had happened during the intermission, the audience—including some distinguished Bulgarian officials—applauded heartily at the end of the concert, which was even more of a success than the first one. Zubin Mehta led the orchestra in one encore, the overture to the "Marriage of Figaro", and then, when the applause wouldn't die down, in a smashing finale of "Stars and Stripes Forever," which brought down the house. The Bulgarians and other non-Americans in the audience didn't know about the patriotic American connotations of that stirring Sousa march, but the rest of us felt a swelling in our chests, and some of us choked up. As we left the concert hall, there wasn't a policeman to be seen; and as far as we know, the students whose admission had been forced by the American visitors, did not suffer for it—which once more is contrary to what I would have expected.

What did happen in accordance with our expectations was a rather frosty departure from Sofia airport. Actually the physical arrangements in Bulgaria compared very favorably with those in other Eastern European capitals, but the Bulgarian officials present at the airport were, shall we say, highly reserved. When I told Miss Khinova that I was sorry about what had happened the previous night, she responded curtly, "I am sorry, Mr. Ambassador, but I cannot accept that." But she consented to pass my expression of regret along to her superiors. The Mehtas, too, seemed a bit melancholy. I do not know at this writing how widespread the knowledge of the "incident" will be in Sofia, but of course not a word of it appeared in the press. Nor have I, a week after writing the foregoing, heard anything about the incident from any Bulgarian official.

An amusing and slightly irrelevant footnote to the "incident" is that the State Department escort officer of the Los Angeles Philharmonic pleaded with the lone American newspaperman who had accompanied them to Sofia (and who had been barred from accompanying them to Prague, their next stop) not to report the "incident" in a way that could harm the chances of further such cultural exchanges in Eastern Europe. Naturally the man reported the story just as he had witnessed it. The story (in a London paper that was sent to me) carried the headline "U.S. Orchestra In Strike For Sofia Students" and began, not inaccurately: "The Los Angeles Philharmonic Orchestra refused to play the second half of a concert in Sofia, Bulgaria, until police released 15 students arrested at the stage door and let them attend. The strike was led by Zubin Mehta, the orchestra's forceful conductor, according to reports reaching Los Angeles yesterday."

24

Visit of Bill Macomber—a friend now, but a disconcerting superior in days past. How some people have the "whammy" on others in large organizations. Just as there is no free lunch, so nobody in government can be his own boss.

December 10. We have had a two-day visit by our colleagues in Ankara, Ambassador William Macomber and his wife Phyllis; and this has allowed us, who sometimes feel pretty isolated way out here in Bulgaria, to exchange notes with a real pro. One of the things that I discussed with him was the proposed visit of a high official of a Washington Department who insisted on coming to Bulgaria for a total of two working hours, in the course of a swing through the Balkans, and who seemed to be engaged in a last fling before going out of office with the Ford Administration. How does one cope with the importunings of such people?

Bill Macomber said he had had a similar case and had been able to turn it off by sending a personal appeal to the Secretary of the particular department involved, pointing out the sensitivity of our relations with Turkey and the apparently uncoordinated, free-lancing character of the proposed visit by a very high official of that department. As a result the visit was cancelled altogether, perhaps also because of an implied threat that if its junket character became public knowledge it would do the person concerned no good. We weren't so lucky in our case.

While I was traveling with the Macombers in Eastern Bulgaria, Harvey hosted the visiting dignitary, for whom we had requested three appointments—even though he was going to be here less than half a day. None of the appointments came through, but Harvey and our economic-political and commercial officers briefed the visitor as best they could about the opportunities and problems in his line of work in Bulgaria. The man seemed satisfied enough, but when he reached the capital where a close relative was ambassador, either he or one of his minions let loose a blast at our embassy for the alleged inadequacy of the arrangements, of which I quote one paragraph: "We had hoped the visit would provide an opportunity for the embassy to expand its contacts with the leaders of the . . . sector in Bulgaria. We learned therefore with incredulity and disappointment that appointments could not be made by the embassy. They frankly admitted that persons were perhaps better off making arrangements directly with the Bulgarians, rather than through the embassy. Had we known of the poor relations existing in Sofia we would have coordinated appointments through good contacts here [in that other capital] and in other [European] capitals."

Now, that poison-pen paragraph was erroneous from start to finish. Nobody ever said that an official visitor would be better off making his own arrangements—that would get him precisely nowhere. The Bulgarian government cannot be dictated to (by the United States, at any rate) regarding whom they will see and whom they will not see. The visitor had specified people whom he wanted to visit, some of them very high-ranking, and those people—quite understandably—experienced no urgent desire to talk with him because they had more important things to do and suspected that the gentleman in question, whose very title showed that his appointment was temporary so that he wasn't likely to be around much longer, would be of little use to them. No matter how good our contacts are in Bulgarian ministries—and it is true that they aren't very close, except in a few instances—we could not force this visitor upon them; and even less, of course, could he have forced himself upon them by his own devices.

It is these short-termers, who want to squeeze foreign travel into their last weeks in office, who contribute to giving our political system a bad name in foreign countries. (Congressmen and Senators are actually worse, but Bulgaria isn't a favored country for their investigations—London, Paris, Rome, Tokyo, and Hong Kong rank at the top of their list.) Whether relations with the U.S. are good or bad or indifferent, however, foreign public officials just like our own have only limited time available, they have work to do and will naturally judge the requests of foreigners to see them in light of the benefit they will receive from the prospective discussions. In the case of defeated members of Congress or someone, however eminent, who is a "special assistant" to a cabinet member who will be out of office in a few weeks, they may be forgiven for harboring doubts that the visit would really be useful to them.

We had expressed doubts before about the visit; had communicated them to the person himself and to his department and also to the Department of State; but nobody—including myself—had had the courage simply to say "no" to the visit on the grounds that it served no useful purpose and was a waste of the taxpayers' money. In our own case we had hoped that the threat that the visit might be misinterpreted as involving a conflict of interest—for the man in question was about to return to private business—would scare him off. However, when a political appointee is intent on wringing the last drop of perquisites from his position before relinquishing the political scene, it is very difficult to shame him or scare him off his contemplated final fling.

I have referred to William Macomber as "my colleague" in Ankara. Our relationship during the last few years really has become one of colleagues who enjoy discussing their problems, who discuss the Service and the foreign policy-making mechanism, examine history together and gossip about other colleagues and about the profession of diplomacy (about which he has written an excellent book). It is, in other words, an easy relationship *now*, and it is based, I think, on mutual respect. Bill Macomber is doing a good job in Ankara under exceedingly trying circumstances, and there is irony in the fact that he, whose job was made so much harder by the Congressional decision to cut off aid to Turkey, used to be in charge of the State Department's relations with the Congress.

My relationship with him started when he was Deputy Under Secretary of State for Management and I was a fledgling Deputy Assistant Secretary of State for International Organization Affairs. To the layman, both positions may seem pretty high on the totem pole; but in actual fact the man in Macomber's position has *power* over *people*, whereas a Deputy Assistant Secretary has *influence* on a small part of the foreign policy picture. In other words, Macomber was a man who could get people promoted or fired, who could recommend (or block) their appointment to ambassadorships, whereas I could at best make recommendations—through my boss, the Assistant Secretary—to the Secretary of State about such things as our strategy toward China in the United Nations.

In all frankness—as I told Bill Macomber when raising my glass to him at the dinner party we gave for him here in Sofia—I must acknowledge that when I first knew him, I was afraid of him. This was not only because of his position but also because of the way he handled people. In Joseph Heller's book, *Something Happened*, the narrator describes his relationship with various people in a big organization whom he calls Mr. White, Mr. Brown, Mr. Green, etc. And he describes one individual as "having the whammy on him." Bill Macomber had the whammy on lots of people in the Department of State when he was riding high there as Deputy Under Secretary.

I got on the wrong side of him almost immediately upon arriving in my new position in Washington, because I had the ambition of wanting to see the U.S. delegation to the United Nations General Assembly sworn in before the beginning of that General Assembly. First the Secretary of State hadn't been able to make up his mind whom to recommend to the White House, then the White House couldn't make up its mind whom to nominate, and then two things happened that seemed to spell disaster. First, one of the prospective nominees called us up and made it known that she wasn't in the slightest interested in becoming a member of the U.S. Delegation to the UN General Assembly. (That lady was appropriately sat upon by somebody in the Nixon White House and suddenly discovered that she actually wanted very much to become part of the delegation.) The other problem, however, seemed insoluble—it took a minimum of x weeks (I think it was six) to obtain the requisite security clearances from the FBI, and the General Assembly was going to open in x minus one weeks.

As best I can recall the incident, I got into Bill Macomber's bad books after trying to speed up the security clearance process by calling up the White House and explaining to somebody there how embarrassing it would be to the President and the country if the General Assembly opened and we didn't have a delegation ready to take its seat. How did that problem arise in the first place, I was asked. Well, I said, there simply had been too much horsing around in getting a decision on the composition of the delegation. The whole process was preposterous; everyone thought he had a part of the action but in the end it would be we, in my Bureau, who would be responsible when the United States had egg on its face—

but the professionals in our Bureau had the least influence on the choice of the delegation. In future there ought to be a firm deadline by which the White House would be obliged to make a decision, and clearances should be started on people not when they were chosen but even earlier, while they were under consideration, to avoid that last-minute rush.

Somehow those remarks got back to Macomber in a form which seemed to cast discredit on his own organization (for everything having to do with top-level appointments was part of his job), and he blew a gasket. At a meeting of Bureau heads he came up to me and made it clear that he thought we—or, more specifically, I—had "mishandled" the appointment of the delegation, and he said he wanted to talk with my boss, the Assistant Secretary, about the responsibility for that mishandling. I was naive enough to ask whether I could be present during that meeting. He of course cut me off right there, saying "in the first instance" he wanted to talk with the Assistant Secretary alone—in order to complain about me, of course.

That was not the first time I had a run-in with Macomber. Etched in my memory is a meeting in his office when we had proposed that a member of the U.S. Mission to the United Nations be given a certain rank because most of the people with whom he was meeting in committees had that rank, and Macomber dismissed the idea with the words "Everyone wants to keep up with the Joneses in these matters of rank. *We are the Joneses*, let the others keep up with us." To which I replied, rather injudiciously of course, that the days were long since gone when the United States were the Joneses in the United Nations and we were quite unable to set the tone or the level of ranks or anything else because we simply didn't have the working majority that we had had years before. To which he had replied, "Well, then maybe we ought to pull out of that outfit altogether." (Not that he believed in doing that, but he hated to have anyone contradict him at a meeting.)

But worse was yet to come. When a man whose appointment as ambassador to a small African country was encountering trouble in the Senate Foreign Relations Committee, Macomber had sent word down in the State Department that "the Foreign Service" ought to rally to the man's defense since he was one of us. However, since the man's unpopularity stemmed from the ad-

ministrative policies which he had carried out, I wrote a memo to
Bill Macomber saying, in effect, that it was all very well to ask the
Foreign Service to rally in support of a man who was in trouble in
the Senate, but that the first thing that ought to be done was for
"the political leadership," whose decisions he had carried out, to
go up to the Hill and explain that it was they, the political
leadership, who were responsible for those policies and not the
hapless nominee—in other words, that Macomber himself should
assume his responsibilities. As I put it in my memorandum, the
Service would watch very closely to see whether this was done,
because while there had been a great deal of talk about loyalty
lately, there were really two kinds, loyalty-up and also, sometimes,
"loyalty-down."

And then I had made a mistake. I had sent a copy of that
memorandum to the American Foreign Service Association, and
they had made a mistake by circulating my memorandum to all the
members of their Board of Directors. Somehow a copy of that
memorandum was fed to someone on Capitol Hill and its full text
was inserted into the Congressional Record. Bill Macomber
wasn't amused one bit. Yet he was big enough to recognize that I
had had a point, and actually did come out and defend his
nominee—not so much on the ground that he had carried out
policies of the political leadership but at least as a nominee whom
he personally supported. When I met Bill in the dining room on the
seventh floor of the State Department (called, euphemistically,
"the Secretary's dining room" although the Secretary of State is
never seen there), he acknowledged to me that I had had a point
although, as he put it, "I didn't particularly care for the way you
expressed it."

That Bill Macomber nevertheless supported me for an ambassadorship was a miracle; and as it turned out I obtained it only a
year after he had departed for Turkey. Somehow we developed a
relationship of mutual respect, and so it was especially gratifying for
Elisabeth and me to have spent two days hosting him and his wife in
Bulgaria, one day traveling (we visited the Shipka Pass, and its
monument to the Russians who died in the battle against the Turks
which resulted in the liberation of Bulgaria in 1977), and a day here
in Sofia reminscing about old times and talking about the Foreign

Service and its future. He was especially pleased when some of the younger officers here told him that however controversial his tenure as Deputy Under Secretary had been, he would be remembered as someone who tried to improve the professionalism of the Foreign Service.

During the first night that Bill and Phyllis were here, we were all up at three o'clock in the morning because a NIACT (Night Action) IMMEDIATE telegram had come in from Ankara; and while he was sitting in his dressing gown in our living room two more such urgent messages arrived, in connection with the American relief effort in the eastern area of Turkey which had been hit by a bad earthquake some weeks ago. Elisabeth made coffee, and the duty officer hovered discreetly in the background while Bill Macomber very carefully drafted a telegram that addressed one of those "insoluble" dilemmas that confront diplomats and that one hears about only when their decisions turn out to be wrong. (The problem was whether to authorize further aid when, due to the dispositions of the Turkish authorities, the aid already supplied was in place *but not yet used*, because the Turks were waiting for the distressed population to come to specially established camps, rather than bringing the aid directly to them.) I confess that I was a bit envious of Bill that he had urgent problems of that sort at night. In the over 2½ years that I have been here, we've received only one NIACT IMMEDIATE and have not sent a single one.

As I think back on their visit there rises to the surface another, earlier memory of Bill Macomber, which perhaps he will be less delighted to read about, but which left a very strong mark in my memory some five years ago. We—a group of senior officers of the State Department—had had one of those meetings with Secretary Rogers which seem to have been a hallmark of his stewardship at the head of the State Department, discussing a complicated problem and coming out with only half a decision, with the other half postponed, perhaps in order to give him time to consult the political leadership in the White House. In the course of that meeting, which was excruciating because it usually was very difficult to keep Rogers focussed on the unpleasant decision at hand, the Secretary had flared up against Bill Macomber. After we had left his office, Bill excused himself and said he had to go back into the Secretary's office "in order to explain to him" that he had not meant to contradict him, or that he had not been properly understood, or something of that kind.

It was only then that I realized, at any rate more sharply than before, that the people near the top are just as insecure about their relationship with the man at the top as we, further down, were insecure about our relationships with men like Macomber, who were only one step removed from the top. If Macomber "had the whammy" on someone like Herz, it was entirely possible for someone like Rogers to "have the whammy" on a seemingly mighty man like Macomber. Everyone likes to speak out for what he believes to be right, but everyone also has to worry lest his speaking-out be misinterpreted as somehow lacking in loyalty to the boss. I have seen ambassadors, even men like the great McClintock, assuming what the Japanese call "the low posture" in the presence of men higher on the totem pole. It is a disconcerting and humbling experience. More important, it is also a lesson in the realities of power.

There is no position in our government, except to some extent that of the Presidency, which really represents "the top," no matter how much authority may be vested in a particular office. The Secretary of State has to be constantly concerned about his credit with the President, the Under Secretary even more so; and of course a mere Deputy Assistant Secretary like myself, who seemed to occupy an impregnable position of "power and influence" in the eyes of those 175 people who served (to some extent) under his orders, wasn't anywhere near the top and had to worry about his standing with at least a dozen people whose loss of confidence could be fatal to his career. And of course, if one has a propensity to speak unpopular "truths" or express unpopular opinions, he has good reason to worry.

Winston Churchill put this beautifully in the volume *Their Finest Hour* of his series on World War II. At the top, he said, there are great simplifications. "In any sphere of action there can be no comparison between the positions of number one and number two, three or four. The duties and the problems of all persons other than number one are quite different and in many ways more difficult. It is always a misfortune when number two or three has to initiate a dominant plan or policy. He has to consider not only the merits of the policy, but the mind of his chief; not only what to advise, but what it is proper for him in his station to advise; not only what to do, but how to get it agreed, and how to get it done. Moreover, number two or three will have to reckon with numbers four, five, and six, or maybe some bright outsider, number twenty."

There is no escaping, in other words, the fact that everyone in government always has a hierarchy of bosses sitting on top of him, unless he is at the very top; and this means that even when you attain the exalted rank of Assistant Secretary in a major department, you aren't the boss. You are that to your subordinates, of course, but you are also still very much a subordinate. And even though, seen from Washington, it seemed such a blessing to be one's own man as ambassador, to run one's own shop, to make recommendations from an unassailable platform as the man on the spot who knows better than anyone else what needs to be done in the country to which he is accredited, in actual fact an ambassador still has the problem of knowing not only what to advise, "but what it is proper for him in his station to advise; not only what to do, but how to get it agreed." I have not learned those lessons well enough. Macomber, who is not a career officer but has worked in top government positions for over a dozen years, knows it a great deal better.

25

How George Kennan's pessimism about Western society looks from Sofia. Sequel to the Los Angeles Philharmonic incident. The Chilean Communist leader Luis Corvalan is released, and Bulgarians get exactly half of that story.

December 18. Surprisingly little attention has been paid in the American press to a debate precipitated by George Kennan in Great Britain by an interview he gave to George Urban in the pages of the intellectual magazine *Encounter.* In that lengthy interview of 34 pages in September he took the position, not for the first time but more sharply articulated than before, that in view of the inherent limitations on foreign policy in our democratic society, the United States "ought to follow a policy of minding its own business to the extent that it can. When I say that I am an 'isolationist', which in a sense I am, I do not advocate that we suddenly rat on NATO and abandon our West European allies. . . But I do feel that we should not accept new commitments, that we should gradually reduce our existing commitments to a minimum, even in the Middle East, and *get back to a policy of leaving other people alone and expect to be largely left alone by them.*" (Italics supplied by this chronicler.)

Asked by his horrified interviewer whether such a policy wouldn't "leave the world wide open to Soviet territorial and political expansionism," Kennan replied that he was only in favor of "a gradual American withdrawal" and eventually delivered himself of this key passage, which he himself termed extreme for the purpose of sharpening his argument: "Show me first an America which has successfully coped with the problems of crime, drugs, deteriorating educational standards, urban decay, pornography, and decadence of one sort of another—show me an America that has pulled itself together and is what it ought to be, then I will tell you how we are going to defend ourselves from the Russians."

Encounter itself carried in its November, 1976 issue a lengthy refutation of Kennan by Hugh Seton-Watson, in which that British historian tried to explain why the defense of Europe is in the American national interest even though, as he put it, "the political class" in his own country is in a state of decay (as indeed the American "political class" may have lost a sense of faith in itself). But most pungent, I thought, was a leading article in *The Times* of London which first acknowledged the correctness of many of Kennan's strictures: "He is right to stress the limits on both American and Soviet power, the importance of other issues facing mankind, the dangers of relying too much on military power for the defence of democracy, and the absence of any really coherent western policy towards eastern Europe, where Soviet hegemony is both a tragedy and a potential danger to peace, since it is not accepted by the people of the area. . ." But then the writer came to grips with the basic pessimism of Kennan's analysis.

"He must, however, be challenged on a number of points," *The Times* continued. "His pessimism is too facile, too fashionable and perhaps already out of date. Nobody can be sure at the moment whether western democracies are on the way up or down but they are changing in ways that are at least as likely to bring renewal as collapse, particularly in the United States. . . Secondly, even the most acute awareness of our internal defects is not a reason for being too casual about external defence against a system with infinitely worse defects. It is certainly true, as Mr. Kennan suggests, that there are many obstacles to Soviet expansionism other than western arms. They include not only the Soviet Union's internal troubles but also local nationalism, rival forms of communism, and the difficulty which the Soviet Union has in exerting its influence over different cultures. But the balance of military power remains one of the essential foundations of peace. Mr. Kennan briefly acknowledges the need for stronger conventional troops, but otherwise seems rather more sceptical than is necessary about the continuing validity of his own doctrine of containment."

A fair criticism, but Kennan has always taken the position that people are worrying about the wrong kind of danger. When he expounded the doctrine of containment immediately after World War II, he took the position that there was no need to fear Soviet attack if the West only took the necessary trouble to prevent a vacuum of power from arising into which Soviet power could flow unopposed. When that policy (containment) was pushed to extremes that he had not foreseen, he began to expound the need for a disengagement of forces in Central Europe; and later, when the United States applied the policy of containment in areas other than Europe, he protested that that was not what he had had in mind. More recently, however, he has taken a position of deep pessimism about our own society and the way in which it governs itself, which has led him to rate the internal dangers to our society as overbalancing the external dangers—as if the two were commensurable.

Nowhere did he write this more pungently than in a letter to the editor of the West German newspaper *Die Zeit*, which was reprinted (without comment so far) by the American publication *Freedom at Issue*: "Poor old West: succumbing feebly, day by day, to its own indulgent permissiveness: its drugs, its crime, its pornography, its pampering of the youth, its addiction to its bodily comforts, its rampant materialism and consumerism—and then trembling before the menace of the wicked Russians, all pictured as supermen, eight feet tall, their internal problems essentially solved, and with nothing else now to think about except how to bring damage and destruction to Western Europe." This persistent "externalization of the sense of danger," he concluded that letter, "this persistent exaggeration of the threat from without and blindness to the threat from within: this is the symptom of some deep failure to come to terms with reality—and with one's self."

How true, but how strangely put, as if it weren't possible to have a realistic appreciation of *both* threats, the one from within *as well as* the one from without. While it is certainly true that the Russians aren't eight feet tall, it still seems as true as it was when Kennan enunciated the doctrine of containment that they will be driven by their internal dynamics to take advantage of power vacuums into which they can flow at little risk to themselves. Kennan concluded his letter to *Die Zeit* by saying: "If Western Europe could bring itself to think a little less about how defenseless it is in the face of the Russians, and a little more about what it is that it has to defend, I would feel more comfortable about its prospects for the future." But wouldn't we all feel still more "comfortable about the future" if

Western Europe—and the United States—were able to think *both* about what they have to defend and about the means to defend it?

I am aware that I am writing this from the vantage point of Sofia, which is an atypical capital of an Eastern European country; but precisely because it is atypical of Eastern Europe, what one learns here about the belief system of orthodox Communist leaders who are in tune with the thinking of their betters in Moscow, has great educational value. One can learn here, as one can learn anywhere else in Eastern Europe, that the Russians aren't eight feet tall. But one can also learn here that they are very self-confident in their ability to overbalance the West, that they truly believe that they are riding the wave of the future, and that they see our society in precisely the terms that Kennan sees it—rotten to the core. And because they see it in such terms, they also see it as capable of being manipulated so that the balance of power will shift further to the East, whereupon they will be able to work their will—not all of a sudden, of course, but gradually—toward the greater glory of the Communist world revolution.

When one considers what the victory of that "revolution" would mean in terms of the everyday lives of people in the West, Kennan's strictures against their permissiveness, devotion to creature comforts, and lax moral values pale into insignificance. As a letter to *Encounter* put it, Kennan's views have something in common not only with the puritans of old but also with "the 20th century puritans (also called Hippies and New Left)." It is that "America must first 'green' herself before she can rejoin the world. . . The similarity between Kennan and America's other self-flagellants is striking." The difference between Kennan and Solzhenitsyn, it seems to me, is that Kennan, coming from the West, worries whether the West is worth saving; whereas Solzhenitsyn, coming from the East, *knows* that it is. Because, while our democracy may be the worst form of government, it is still "better than all the others."

—0—

December 21. Here are some of the things that have occupied my time at the office lately. First of all, there came the expected

Bulgarian reaction to the "incident" during the second concert of the Los Angeles Philharmonic: I was summoned to the Foreign Ministry and given a talking-to by Ambassador Damyanov, the head of the Cultural Relations Department. He also handed me a Note Verbale, which said just about what one might have expected, except for two points about which I will comment further below.—I also had to call on a Deputy Foreign Minister in connection with the currently most vexing "divided family" case, involving two children in Bulgaria who are not receiving permission to join their parents in America. This case, like almost every one of its kind that we have handled here, turns out to be considerably more complicated than one might believe at first; and I placed my emphasis on the overall relations between the United States and Bulgaria, and President Zhivkov's promise ("statesman-like decision") to clean up the divided families issue between our countries, rather than on the particularities of the case.

I also called on the Vice Premier who deals with economic relations with the "capitalist" world and had a long and interesting conversation which consisted to a large extent of sparring but yielded also a little useful information on the current hard-currency trade and payments balances of Bulgaria (which of course are state secrets but about which one can find out certain things in the course of such a conversation) and about the prospects for certain American exports to Bulgaria.—Telegrams have now come in from the State Department commenting on the views of the various embassies in Eastern Europe about the forthcoming Belgrade Conference (the follow-up to Helsinki), and I was of course especially interested to see how Washington reacted to the telegram from the other post in Eastern Europe which had made two points similar to the ones that had gotten me into trouble, but had made them in a "muted and muffled" manner, burying them in long paragraphs. Well, the outcome is pretty clear: The Department found it very easy to overlook those points, and they weren't addressed at all in the generally friendly message that was sent to that other embassy—as if they had never made those critical points at all.

We have also had a number of "housekeeping" and "family" problems in the embassy lately, one of them quite serious and the other funny. The serious one concerns the wife of our army attaché who has been hospitalized in Greece and Germany for several weeks now, and nobody seems to be able to determine what causes the numbness and tingling in her extremities, which came after an onset of intense and rather generalized pain. Most recently she has had a liver biopsy, and that resulted in internal bleeding. We are all very worried, and some of us are wondering if this is the first case of several peculiar to this post.—On the more humorous side, our Marine detachment held a terrorist alarm drill two weeks ago. I happened to be away at the time, so I didn't witness the confusion when the sirens sounded and everyone rushed to put away classified papers, lock doors, "break out" arms, etc. while those Marines who were off duty plunged down the stairs to their duty stations—and "plunged" quite literally with the result that we have two men with their legs in casts, one with a broken and the other with a sprained ankle. However, all their missions were accomplished, the Bostwick gate was closed in time, the elevator stopped dead in its tracks, the steel door locked, so any miscreant trying to penetrate to the ambassador's office would have been foiled.

I am very skeptical about the subject of terrorism in a place like Bulgaria because to kidnap an American ambassador here would be exceedingly difficult for terrorists—unless the government were to wink at their activities, which is exceedingly unlikely (if only because all Communist governments depend on our law enforcement agencies to protect *their* diplomats). If anyone tried to kidnap me, where would he take me? Certainly any foreigners would find it almost impossible to find quarters here in Sofia, let alone outside of Sofia, without instantly coming under surveillance of the *Militzia*. Terrorists might hold me, of course, at gun point in some public place; but if they decided to do that it is hard to see why they would do so in our own embassy, which is next to a police station and under constant Bulgarian security surveillance. Although my official car is armor-plated, it has no bulletproof glass; and besides, I have to travel the same route every day because there simply is no other way for a good part of the trip between the Embassy chancery and the residence. It would be a lot easier to waylay me in front of the residence or on a weekend or while returning from some social occasion, than to try to capture and/or hold me in the embassy itself. It could happen, of course, but it would involve a rather unpromising risk/benefit ratio for the terrorists. Still, I am grateful for the solicitude of our Marines whose job, of course, is to guard the entire embassy against intrusions of any kind, and not just against attempts directed at the ambassador.

Now let me return to my session with Ambassador Damyanov about the incident at the Los Angeles Philharmonic concert. It was clear from the beginning that the interview was going to be more formal than usual because Damyanov had asked an interpreter to translate his remarks, which he read from a piece of paper, even though he himself speaks perfect English. He went over the progress that we had achieved during the last year or so in developing cultural relations between our countries, and expressed the "concern and anxiety" of the Ministry of Foreign Affairs over the incident which it found highly improper and "inexplicable". The fact that some people had been unable to obtain tickets was no reason to disrupt the performance and cause the delay of a live radio broadcast. The Note Verbale said, among other things, that "the Ministry of Foreign Affairs are of the opinion that the behavior and actions of the conductor and director of the orchestra are absolutely contrary to generally accepted norms for guest-performers and can only be characterized as an act of improper behavior and disrespect for both the Bulgarian audience in the concert hall and the established regulations for organizing cultural events in this country."

I had to take strong exception to the statement that neither the Embassy nor the State Department representative accompanying the orchestra had exerted themselves to get the orchestra to resume its performance, for I knew that John Karch had done what he could—and I myself had come onto the scene only when the issue was just being resolved. But I acknowledged that the incident was regrettable, expressed personal regrets (though making it clear that I could not speak for the Orchestra), and attributed the whole business to the temperamental outburst of high-strung artists. Damyanov and I agreed that the incident had had no political character, which was important since some Bulgarian hotheads could have termed it a "provocation." We even agreed after some verbal sparring that perhaps the word "incident" was a little too formal in describing what had happened and that we should talk about a "happening" instead. I also gave some other explanations, which went into more detail than is interesting here; but Damyanov on his part then said something which I do think interesting.

He said that the Bulgarians had been particularly stung by the claim, which he attributed to Mr. Fleischmann and which apparently had been broadcast on the BBC, that the authorities here had carefully selected the audience for the concerts and had thus excluded some of the musically interested public. This, he said, was completely contrary to the truth and very damaging to Bulgaria's reputation. It was true that only a limited number of tickets had been available at the box office, but that had been due precisely to the efforts of the Bulgarian organizers to make sure that tickets would be available to such musically interested persons as members of the Sofia Philharmonic, the State Radio Orchestra, and other artistic organizations. Now, I must confess that I had been skeptical on that score before the concert, knowing that the political bureaucracy can swallow up a large number of tickets to such an event; but in retrospect, having seen the audience and especially having heard its frenetic applause, which was quite unprecedented, I must agree that the suspicions had been unfounded. That is not to say that every musically interested person in Sofia could find tickets, but that situation prevails also in other places when there are exceptional attractions.

There was only one significant change in the facts as presented in the Note Verbale, for obvious reasons. That document said: "It was only after the interpreter had taken the orchestra director Mr. Fleischmann to the entrance to convince himself that no one had been arrested and only after he had announced that to the orchestra members did they come on stage and continue with Part II of the concert." No mention, in other words, that the students (or young music-lovers) who had created the commotion were let into the hall at the insistence of LAPO and its music director and business manager. But then, how could the Bulgarians admit in such a document that they had in fact knuckled under to the threat of a body of foreigners? The lone American journalist who had witnessed the incident (or happening) had of course placed special emphasis on that aspect. We now have all the clippings from the *Los Angeles Times* and the story by Murray Seeger included this paragraph which of course was entirely accurate:

"The only visible sign of the incident came as the house lights dimmed and Mehta turned to begin the first movement of Bartok's 'Concerto for Orchestra.' At that moment, the rear door of the hall opened and 15 students quietly entered and stood at the end of the main aisle. The audience was never told why the intermission was nearly 30 minutes longer than usual. A national radio audience was also left in the dark. 'Nothing like this ever happened here before,' one young Bulgarian musician said. 'Most of us did not know the orchestra was coming. And then, after we found out, there were no tickets to be had. To take care of the people who wanted to come they would have had to have two more concerts at least, or one just for students.'"

It will not have escaped the reader that I am especially interested in the question of accuracy of press (and other media) reporting; and so I must note with regret that Mr. Seeger gave me credit that I didn't deserve when he wrote, in the same story, that "U.S. Embassy officials, fearful that the incident would abort the slow development of normal relations with Bulgaria, considered the most loyal ally of the Soviet Union in the East Bloc, successfully mediated the dispute." Alas, I wish it had been so. But I give Mr. Seeger high marks for having, for once, pictured the role of an American diplomat abroad in more favorable terms than he deserved, for it is usually the other way around. He also correctly quoted Zubin Mehta as saying: "I hope this incident does not mean that another American orchestra won't be able to come to visit Sofia." Well, that is precisely what I have to try for now.

Seeger also wrote a fairly objective if not entirely flattering article on the situation in Bulgaria, making sure—perhaps as a result of advice we gave him—not to use the unfortunate phrase "slavish" in describing Zhivkov's following the lead of the Soviet Union, for it was that word which had resulted in a Bulgarian protest when it had been used by the ever-helpful Malcolm Browne of the *New York Times*. (I understand it was also the reason why Browne later had trouble being admitted to Czechoslovakia.) Seeger instead wrote, I think accurately: "Bulgarian government and party officials resent the suggestions of outsiders that their country is a 'slavish' or 'docile' follower of the Kremlin. The Bulgarians insist that their association with the Soviet Union is voluntary and of great benefit to Sofia." This formulation has the virtue of being both accurate and not preventing Mr. Seeger from being allowed back into the country on another visit.

One strange thing happened in the same story, as it was featured in the *International Herald Tribune*. In describing the various monuments of Bulgarian-Russian friendship, Seeger wrote the following paragraph: "Most impressive of all, the most beautiful structure in the city is a church named in honor of Alexander Nevsky, the Russian admiral whose victory over the Turkish Empire assured Bulgarian independence." I had laid that article aside to become part of my treasury of journalistic howlers, for apparently Seeger—perhaps working with the benefit of clipping files—had picked up the same historical error that had been committed a few months ago by a correspondent of the *Wall Street Journal*. I must record my admiration either to Seeger or to his editors, however, that when the same article appeared in the *Los Angeles Times* the passage had been rectified to read: "The most beautiful building in the city is a church named in honor of Alexander Nevsky, a 12th century saint of the Russian Orthodox Church famed as the defender of the country's northern border." It is not often that a correction catches up so quickly with an original news story.

Actually, Alexander Nevsky was the patron saint of Czar Alexander II whose troops liberated Bulgaria. He had distinguished himself as the general in the 12th century who defeated an invasion of Russia by the Teutonic Knights. Sergei Eisenstein, the great Russian director, has immortalized the feats of arms of Alexander Nevsky in a film, made just before World War II, which pictured the victory of the light Russian infantry in a battle on the frozen Lake Peipus, not far from today's Leningrad. The film showed how the warrior-saint lured the heavily armored Teutonic Knights on their heavy mounts onto the ice where they crashed to their deaths in a scene of cinematic grandeur rivalling D. W. Griffith's battle of Gettysburg in his "Birth of a Nation."

While we're on the subject of media, I would like to record two events: First, our ten-minute film on the occasion of the bicentennial was shown on BTV at prime time day before yesterday. It wasn't shown just after the evening news broadcast, as the Foreign Minister had offered, and the reason Harvey was given was amusing: Whereas Mladenov had told me that they would give us the distinction of having our message to Bulgaria featured at the time that is normally given only to the Soviet Ambassador, Harvey was told by his contact in BTV that the reason our little program was shown just *before* the evening news broadcast was that the later spot "is only given to the Soviet ambassador." But I would not cavil at such a small matter. The ten-minute film came off very well, with only minimal cuts—not for censorship purposes, apparently, but to fit it into the ten-minute format. (What was lost was the midnight ride of Paul Revere at the beginning, whose significance would have been lost on the Bulgarians anyway.) And my introduction and sign-off appearances were so convincing that some friends have commented that they had not realized I was so fluent in Bulgarian.

The other media event, just before Christmas, is the celebration in the Bulgarian Communist press of the release of Chile's Communist leader, Luis Corvalan. Next to Brezhnev's 70th birthday, this event has generated most pictures and congratulatory comment—but one rather important detail is missing: Nowhere are Bulgarians told how it came about that the Chilean "fascist" government had released that Communist leader and allowed him to return to Moscow. The fact that the Russians had been required to release the dissident Vladimir Bukovsky as a condition for Corvalan's release is a well-kept secret in Bulgaria although the facts of the case must be seeping in through BBC, the Voice of America, *Deutsche Welle* and, to the extent that it can be heard through the jamming, Radio Free Europe. Corvalan, who is supposed to have languished in the Chilean jails under inhuman conditions, looks remarkably fit in the pictures; whereas the 33-year-old Bukovsky, who spent ten of his last 13 years in prison camps and insane asylums for "anti-Soviet activities," is in poor physical shape. But of course a Bulgarian was in no position to make a comparison since his TV screen showed only pictures of Brezhnev genially embracing his equally beaming and ebullient Chilean friend.

Postscript: Finding that they cannot leave Bukovsky entirely unmentioned, the Bulgarian newspapers—following the Soviet example—finally did come out with a report about this "criminal who is now being celebrated as a hero." Bukovsky, according to a Tass report, is a man "who prepared acts of terrorism, who is a paid agent of the fascist scum, a criminal three times convicted for criminal acts in accordance with the penal code of the Soviet Union, and who has now been expelled outside the Soviet frontiers". That he is allegedly celebrated as a hero by "fascist Chile" is taken as confirmation of his fascist convictions—without any mention, still, that this Russian dissident had to be released by the Soviets in order to procure the release of Corvalan.

26

Why it is unwise for the Congress to try to look into who advocated what policy in internal State Department discussions—because this could have a chilling effect on the advocacy of implausible or unpopular policy moves.

December 27. Tom Boyatt, a former President of the Foreign Service Association and a close friend, has written an article for the *Foreign Service Journal* to which I found it necessary to send a rejoinder. Because the issue concerns the role of the professional Foreign Service officer vis-a-vis the President and the Congress, it is, I think, of general interest. I will therefore first summarize Boyatt's position, as fairly as possible, and then explain why I think it is untenable; and I do so with great respect for him, for he has played an important role in strengthening the career principle, the idea to which most of us in the Foreign Service are devoted, namely that a service of professionals (rather than politicians) is desirable for the first line of defense of our country, and that that service should be protected from arbitrariness and manipulation by the political leadership.

Boyatt's article goes back to his experience when, as director for Cyprus Affairs in the State Department, he was summoned to Capitol Hill by the Pike Committee which was investigating (along with the Church Committee) "intelligence failures and, by extension, foreign policy failures"—as part of the trend in our Congress to press for a greater role not only in oversight of the executive but in the foreign policy formulation process. Tom Boyatt points out, quite accurately I think, that when a Foreign Service officer swears his oath to "support and defend the Constitution of the United States," he does not swear loyalty just to the President and the Executive but also assumes obligations toward the co-equal Legislative branch of our government.

We are now coming out of a period, Boyatt says, when it seemed normal for Foreign Service officers to be directly responsible only to the President. A generation of essential bipartisanship in foreign affairs and a "code" of absolute loyalty to the hierarchical Executive, he writes, had limited internal debate and excluded "external debate" (i.e., the public airing of policy differences within the State Department). "Issues were discussed with greater or lesser openness within the Executive Branch, and a monolithic facade was presented to the public, the press and the Congress. Dissent on any issue became insubordination at best and treason at worst; most FSO's thought McCarthy demonstrated the costs of even internal dissent. Soon conformity, caution, more or less slavish obedience within the system and total isolation from outside elements (particularly the Congress and the people) were the hallmarks of the prevailing code of conduct." Boyatt acknowledges that this description may be overdrawn. His point is that in any case such a situation represents an anachronism in today's world when Vietnam, Watergate and other events have shown that increased openness is insisted upon by the Congress and the American public; and he welcomes that openness as likely to contribute to a healthier atmosphere and the formulation of better foreign policies.

The State Department first tried to prevent Boyatt from appearing before the Pike Committee, but it soon became clear that refusal to testify would have opened him to charges of contempt of Congress—and that, in the view of his legal counsel, "the Secretary of State could not legally order a Foreign Service officer to refrain from responding to a summons, much less a subpoena, by the Congress of the United States to appear before it." The question whether a subordinate officer of the State Department should be required to testify on policies which were the ultimate responsibility of the political leadership soon became a major issue within the Foreign Service on the grounds that it could rekindle McCarthyism and stifle freedom of expression within the Foreign Service. Boyatt considers that these fears were unfounded. "The McCarthyism charge was simply not borne out by events. I appeared before the Pike Committee and staff under oath six or eight times. Never was there any activity by any person on or connected with the Committee that could even remotely be construed as an effort to 'get' me, the Foreign Service, or anyone. . .

The Pike Committee was trying to find out what happened in Cyprus and why. How else could they perform an oversight function?"

After conceding that he could appear before the Committee, the State Department originally instructed Boyatt to testify only on matters that weren't confidential (classified), but it soon had to abandon that position and allowed him to "deal with classified subjects in Executive Session but only as they related to facts and not analysis and policy; then I was ordered to respond to every question asked me except those relating to policy advice." Finally Pike and Kissinger got to the nub of the controversy—Pike's interest in seeing a "dissent memorandum" written by Boyatt, which he threatened to obtain by subpoena. In the end, a compromise was worked out whereby the State Department agreed to send the memorandum to the Committee "but to intersperse comments and policy recommendations from other officials"—in other words, to obscure what the position of Boyatt had been and what the positions of others in the Department had been during the controversy. It should be noted that Boyatt considered that compromise "sensible and serviceable"—but in view of his position that it is a healthy thing to have subordinate officers questioned about their views by Congressional committees he did not get around to explaining *why* such a compromise was sensible. The position of his article was that there really cannot be any harm, indeed that there is a great deal of good, in having the "experts" down the line summoned before Congressional committees.

Far from stifling controversy and healthy dissent within the foreign policy-making machinery, Boyatt states, "the knowledge that the Congress under appropriate safeguards has access to testimony by officers at all levels will encourage rather than inhibit dissent. The officer who has had the courage to express dissent against prevailing orthodoxy within the Executive Branch, which can harm him, will not be concerned that the Congress, which cannot hurt him, also has access to his views. On the contrary, knowledge of real Congressional oversight will encourage working-level officers to express dissenting views because such views will necessarily be taken more seriously and will be more likely to influence policy." I must say, the argument was presented very plausibly and eloquently. Nevertheless I think it is quite wrong, and I wrote so, citing the following countervailing considerations.

The Pike Committee, in my opinion, behaved in a very unusual fashion in not trying to 'get' anyone, and this certainly is a credit to its chairman; but things have not always worked that way—and people like myself who have a longer memory owe it to their colleagues to warn that what happened in the fifties and sixties could very well happen again. I remember for instance the subcommittee headed by the late Senator Dodd which browbeat junior State Department officers and wanted to know who, precisely, had "thought up" a particular policy line or recommendation in connection with curbing the activities of the Katanga lobby. The questioning of that subcommittee was clearly not so much concerned with finding out how a particular policy had been made but with *influencing the people who were carrying it out*—influencing them, by public castigation, to let up on the attempts of the U.S. Government to control the activities of Mr. Streulens, the "representative" of Katanga in New York.

It is also not true, as Boyatt assumed from his more limited experience, that a Congressional investigating committee "cannot hurt" a person in Boyatt's position. Technically, of course, it was John Foster Dulles who got rid of Foreign Service officers who had incurred the displeasure of Senator McCarthy but, as I pointed out in my letter, "it is all very well to say that the actual blade was that of Dulles, but the instrumentality that triggered the descent of that blade was Senator McCarthy and his committee." And even some time after McCarthy, right during the Kennedy Administration, Congressman Porter Hardy "investigated" the origins of our policy toward Angola not so much with the idea in mind of finding out how the policy had been arrived at but in order to discredit it—or at least so it seemed to the people down the line who were responsible for carrying it out.

Certainly it is true that an officer of our Foreign Service owes an obligation not only to his superiors in the executive branch but also to the legislature; and it is hard to see how he can refuse to cooperate with an investigating committee—and in fact the Senate Foreign Relations Committee makes it a practice to ask every nominee for an ambassadorial position to confirm that he will make available to the Committee any information that it may require from him in the future; and the State Department instructs ambassadors-designate to promise that they will do so. But it has happened that ambassadors have been summoned before committees and subcommittees of the Congress in order to divulge information embarrassing to the administration, which means that they can have difficult problems of conscience about the extent to which they can fulfill their constitutional obligation without involving themselves in acrimonious partisan attacks against those responsible for the policies they carried out.

The problem is that there simply isn't an issue of foreign policy debated within the State Department and elsewhere in the executive branch which could not be transformed into a public donnybrook by politicians who wish to pry into the question of how and by whom that particular policy was proposed—or opposed. The very point made by Boyatt, that "the officer who has had the courage to express dissent against prevailing orthodoxy within the executive branch . . . will not be concerned that the Congress . . . also has access to his views" could be interpreted to mean that anyone with a dissent should be free to run to the Congress—and perhaps the press—for a public airing of his dissenting opinion. If this happens, partisan politics will have entered the career service, something that the Congress itself has tried to avoid when it passed the Foreign Service Act.

Boyatt in his article reported that "a savvy Washington reporter responded to Secretary Kissinger's assertion that the bureaucracy must be 'protected' from Congress by asking in print, 'Why? So they (the career professionals) can go on making mistakes at the expense of the American people?'" This sounds fair enough until one starts thinking about the implications. There is no issue in our foreign policy where *someone* doesn't feel that "mistakes are being made at the expense of the American people," and if everyone who feels that way can run (or leak) to Capitol Hill we will not have a better foreign policy but utter confusion.

In actual fact there is no lack of divergence of opinions within the Foreign Service and the State Department. There is an adversary process of policy formulation which sees to it (most of the time, at any rate) that real alternatives or "options" are presented to the political leadership; and where this doesn't work there is now a dissent mechanism that makes sure that any views that may have been overlooked (or given short shrift) will come to the surface within the Department. The trouble is that many a policy recommendation may be very sensible and in the public interest but may, if presented or interpreted in a partisan fashion, look nefarious or idiotic. The criterion of a sound decision in foreign policy cannot always be its popularity. The best course of action is not always the one that is superficially the most plausible. Sometimes risks have to be taken which, with the benefit of hindsight, can look—or be made to appear—like egregious blunders.

In short, it is my opinion that the executive and legislative branches were very wise in the Boyatt case to have refrained from forcing the issue whether confidential memoranda by subordinate officers should be disclosed upon demand of a congressional committee; for if such a practice had been sanctioned the result would not be better policies and more willingness to dissent but, on the contrary, a rush by all subordinate officers to "cover their ass," to take the most plausible, the most popular, the least attackable position in the papers they send to their superiors. What might appear as daring dissent would in fact be a playing to the galleries, and actions which might make the person recommending them subject to public "investigation" would have a smaller chance of being proposed or adopted.

Boyatt was handled with kid gloves because the subcommittee wasn't after Boyatt but after bigger game; but in the future such a subcommittee might well—as happened in the past—go not after the bigger game but precisely after people like Boyatt. It is not so terribly long since a fairly senior officer of the Foreign Service failed to obtain a top position because he was suspected by some vociferous Congressmen of having "lost" Cuba. We don't need anything that might possibly lead to that kind of investigation, which did tremendous harm to the China experts of the career service and thus to the national security of our country.

27

Special treats for the populace on the occasion of Bulgaria's equivalent of Christmas. How affordable are these goodies? Holiday blues. The political elite doesn't flaunt its wealth, but they live very comfortably, thank you.

January 2, 1977. Yesterday was the Bulgarian equivalent of Christmas Day, and New Year's eve was the evening when gifts are given and families get together, sometimes around a "New Year's tree." Of course, there must be substantial numbers of Bulgarians who still celebrate Christmas on Christmas Day, but the government takes no notice of them. A bit of Christmas spirit is still evidenced by decorations in shop windows, some of them featuring not only tinsel and silver balls but even decorated trees, but the whole business is pretty perfunctory; and given the generally drab appearance of stores and the absence of advertising, somehow everything looks a bit like going through the motions. However, more things are available in the stores during this season, and reportedly some 94 items have been reduced in price for the occasion. Elisabeth and I went for a stroll downtown on Friday, the 30th to observe what was going on.

The first thing we were struck by was that oranges were available—all in two-kilo net bags priced at 1.96 Leva a bag (down from 2 Leva). When we tried to count the number of oranges in one such bag and remarked that there were seven—which comes to 28 stotinki (about 29 cents) an orange—a salesman proudly produced another bag weighing the same that contained 11 smaller oranges. The exchange rate is of course highly artificial, so it is not entirely accurate to say that 1.18 Leva a kilo for lemons comes to about 50¢ a pound, but an idea of purchasing power can be gained from the fact that the average *monthly* wage of an industrial worker in Bulgaria is 150 Leva.

There were also large quantities of meat at prices ranging from

200

2.40 Leva a kilo to 3.20 Leva, which is less than we pay at the Diplomatic Store, but at that store they sell the better cuts that aren't available to the general population. We also noticed frozen fish, in large blocks that are chopped into smaller blocks for the customers, ranging from 80 stotinki to 1.50 Leva a kilo. Sausage cost 4.60 a kilo, and a kind of paté was 1.80. There were also tiny grapefruit at 1.76 for a two-kilo bag. They are supposed to be very juicy and are a rarity here. Most amazing, we saw several well-known brands of imported scotch whisky at only 12 Leva, but they seemed to have been sold out. The silver balls that people hang on New Year's trees cost 60 stotinki.

It is quite unfair, of course, to note only the average wage of Bulgarian workers without also noting the benefits they enjoy. Such people pay only a pittance for rent, get free education and medical care, and usually have vacations at institutional resorts for nominal amounts. A telephone call costs 2 cents, and postage for a letter inside Sofia is 1 cent, to destinations elsewhere in Bulgaria 2 cents. A streetcar ride costs 4 cents, and a bus ride 6 cents. It would take a great deal of sophisticated analysis to work out real comparisons with the West, but two things are clear: Consumer goods are in very short supply, of poor quality and expensive; but the lot of the average Bulgarian is certainly better today than it was a few years ago. Moreover, *some* people have lots of money and can thus take advantage of the announced reduction of Uher tape recorders from 1,650 Leva to 1,400 Leva.

Over the long holiday weekend we had the visit of an American professor who has spent three months here. He was very circumspect in his judgments about anything political, but felt that he could talk with greater assurance about the social and economic aspects of his academic colleagues at Sofia University. (When I remarked to him that I had the impression that there couldn't be widespread opposition to the regime since if it were widespread it would have come to our attention, he only noted that in his contacts at the university "there might very well be widespread opposition without it having come to my attention since people simply don't discuss such subjects with a visiting American.")

He said a full professor at the university has a basic salary of 320 Leva (nominally $310) a month, but then there are extras: If he has a Ph.D. degree, which would be normal for a professor, then he has an additional 80 Leva a month, and if he is chairman of a department he gets another 15 a month. An associate professor would have a basic salary of 260, a lecturer 205, and a teaching assistant 165 a month. Added to this, however, would be increments for longevity: 4 percent more after five years, 8 percent after 10 years, etc. If he (or anyone else) has one child, he gets another 5 Leva a month; if two children, 20 Leva a month; and if three children, 80 Leva a month—Bulgaria encourages larger families. In addition to the salary and allowances, he would also get paid for his academic publications—an article of 75 pages would yield 600 Leva. In addition, a professor would get extra pay for extra work, for instance for giving courses during periods between terms. Most important, chances are that in a professor's family three members would be bringing home wages or salaries. One professor whom he knows, and whose apartment he described as attractive by Bulgarian standards, pays 19 Leva rent per month.

Incidentally, the university has recently revised its system of incentives to students who, in addition to free tuition, can also draw certain "stipends" depending on their grades and their political activity. Thus a student with an A average will get 65 Leva a month, one with a B average 50 Leva, and with a C average 40 Leva. Extra sums will be paid for participation in Komsomol (party youth) activities, brigade work, etc. Since Komsomol leaders at the university tend to be the children of party bigwigs, a certain proportion of the stipends will thus wind up in the hands of Sofia's gilded youth. I am told on good authority that a C student who is active in the Komsomol could now receive more than an A student who isn't. Married students, incidentally, get 80 Leva a month for every child—a strong incentive to have children, but also an incentive to stay at the university as long as possible since these special benefits cease upon graduation.

—0—

One of the burdens of being at this relatively isolated post is that we are cut off from mail from home during this holiday season—this year longer than usual. Because a pouch from Washington missed the connection at Frankfurt, and because Lufthansa suspends its flight over the New Year holiday and Balkan Air (the only other airline flying in from Frankfurt) also does not fly on New Year's day, the earliest we can get mail will be on Tuesday, more than a week since the last mail bag arrived; and due to the pile-up of mail in the post offices and in the sorting room in the State Department, the mail we received last week was dated early December. By the time we get the next mail, it will be three to four weeks old; and what is maddening is that we now have a three-day holiday during which we could be answering such mail and attending to personal business. And if Monday is foggy in Frankfurt or in Sofia, we may have to wait still longer for a still larger accumulation of personal mail. Well, at any rate the mail is something to look forward to.

—0—

I've said earlier that some people here have a lot of money. This is a puzzling subject, for it isn't clear how some young people, in particular, can have their own cars and can display the latest sporting equipment from the West when they go skiing on Mount Vitosha. That there is a "new class" is obvious, but the size of it is less clear. Altogether there are about 100,000 privately owned automobiles in Sofia (a city of about a million). Anybody can get a car if he has the money—some 5,000 Leva for a small Zhiguli—but to get a high place on the waiting list and to get the car under favorable payment conditions clearly depends on a person's political status and connections; but the ownership itself is indeed private, just as apartments and country houses can be owned by those with the right connections.

The political elite does not flaunt its wealth, however. Zhivkov himself lives in an apartment—the official "residence" in Boyana is for ceremonial purposes, as are the government "residences" at Losenets and Vrana. But some of the bigwigs of the government have fantastic private villas with swimming pools and beautifully manicured gardens in a section near Boyana which isn't accessible to the general public. We know this because Elisabeth was invited to one such house a year ago. Wanting to make sure that she would arrive in time, she asked our chauffeur to take her to the street ahead of time. It was impossible to penetrate into the area because all streets have one-way signs coming in your direction, plus

Militzia to see to it that no one enters them. When it was time for Elisabeth to keep her appointment, the police had set up a circuitous route which all the visitors had to take, with frequent checks of their identities along the way.

Another, minor and unsurprising note about "Christmas," or rather New Year, is the news that "schoolboys and schoolgirls have come to the government residence 'Boyana' to congratulate on the coming New Year Messrs. Todor Zhivkov, Stanko Todorov (the Prime Minister), Aleksandur Lilov (the party ideologue), Grisha Filipov, etc. etc. (giving a long list of party and government leaders). . . Attending has also been the Ambassador Extraordinary and Plenipotentiary of the Union of Socialist Soviet Republics to our country, Vladimir Bazovskii." And in another paper: "The traditional meeting of officials of the Foreign Ministry and of the Embassy of the USSR in Bulgaria, took place yesterday at the 'Boyana' residence." The meeting was also attended by "leaders of the artistic and intellectual community."

The annual meeting of Zhivkov with the heads of the diplomatic missions takes place tomorrow, Monday at 11:30. All ambassadors line up in a semi-circle in order of protocol rank, which is according to the date when they presented their credentials; and the dean will read an address in which he will, in his usual mellifluous prose, pay tribute to the beauty of Bulgaria and the hard-working virtues of its people. Then Zhivkov will make some equally trite and friendly remarks in his more folksy style, whereupon champagne will be served and everyone will clink glasses with the chief of state. If anything out of the ordinary occurs, I shall note it separately.

28

"Divided families," a humanitarian issue with political over-
tones. The Bulgarians are reluctant to "reward" people who
left their country illegally. We are reluctant to "force" children
to leave our country against their will.

January 5. We have had some unusually interesting and complicated consular problems lately. One occurred yesterday when a
man came to see our consular officer in order to present demands
for compensation for the injury he said he suffered at the hands of
our embassy three years ago when he was allegedly turned over
against his will to Bulgarian hospital attendants, who took him to
the insane asylum where he had been kept because of his political
convictions and from where he had managed to escape. The person
with whom he said he had talked, and whom he held responsible
for notifying the Bulgarian authorities (who are supposed to have
beaten him up on our premises) is now in Washington, so we
immediately sent a telegram asking him to search his memory since
we want to know whether we are dealing with a madman or with a
genuine dissident.

My own impression is that we may be dealing with a bit of both,
for our receptionist (a Bulgarian) recalls that we had indeed
notified the authorities, perhaps because the man refused to leave the
embassy, but she recalls nothing about any beating, which would
have had to take place right in front of her, as the consul's office
opens up to the reception area. On the other hand, the man handed
us some publications in English, from which it would appear that
he must be taken seriously as a physicist at least by some colleagues
in the West. We are in no position to evaluate those publications,
which are highly technical, but are a bit taken aback that the
author purports to have advanced beyond Einstein's theory of
relativity to a theory of "time-space absoluteness."

About half a year ago we did have a case of a man who arrived in a highly excited state, declared that the satchel he was carrying contained explosives with which he would blow up our embassy and himself if he wasn't given an opportunity to leave the country, and delivered himself of a stream of incoherences that raised serious doubts about his state of mind, particularly since he, too, claimed to have been held in an insane asylum for political reasons. One of our officers, Joe Lee, talked with him for almost an hour and finally succeeded in persuading him to part with his satchel. Later examination showed it to contain not explosives but fuzes which, had he set them off, could still have done considerable damage to himself and those around him. Our officer, after talking with the man for an hour, came to the conclusion that he was dealing with a very sick person, and after careful consultation I authorized my deputy to ask the Bulgarian psychiatric clinic to come and pick the man up. But that case involved a man who was not nearly as rational as the visitor yesterday seemed to be. Also, while we have a careful record of the event of six months ago, there seems to be no record of the earlier event that is supposed to have taken place in April, 1974.

I was asked by the head of the Foreign Ministry's consular department to call on him today, and he raised with me the "humanitarian" case of three children in the United States whose father, allegedly a Bulgarian citizen, had killed his wife, his mother-in-law, and then himself last April. The maternal grandfather of the children, who is their nearest relative in America, now wants to return to Bulgaria where other members of the family are prepared to take care of him and the three children. A court in Chicago is supposedly making objections, and a hearing is to take place in ten days. The Bulgarian government doesn't know whether the deceased parents of the children had taken out American citizenship, but considers that question to be immaterial since one child was born in Bulgaria and the other two were born (in America) of Bulgarian parents. Yes, I said, but since two of the children were born in the United States they are American citizens. Not in the eyes of the Bulgarian government, said the head of the consular department, for a Bulgarian can only lose his citizenship if he formally renounces it before duly constituted Bulgarian authority, and any children that we consider Americans are also Bulgarians.

There ensued some sparring about the validity of the American-

Bulgarian naturalization treaty of 1923, which was reaffirmed by both governments in 1947, and according to which each government will recognize the naturalization of its citizens by the other country. The Bulgarian government does not recognize the validity of that treaty in cases where the Bulgarian citizen "committed a crime against Bulgaria," and if he left the country illegally they would consider him not entitled to the benefits of the treaty; but the head of the consular department did not know whether the deceased parents of the children had left Bulgaria illegally and considered the question irrelevant since his government's appeal for our cooperation was based on humanitarian grounds.

Now, it so happens that we have a case of Bulgarian children in Bulgaria whose parents are in the United States and are petitioning for assistance from our government to have them join them in America. In that case the Bulgarian government takes the position that if the parents, who had left the country illegally, wish to be reunited with their children, they should return to Bulgaria and benefit from an amnesty law which was passed with such cases specifically in mind. To which we respond that the case is a humanitarian one of precisely the kind that President Zhivkov had promised to get cleared up; that the parents are unquestionably American citizens now; that the humanitarian elements—and Bulgaria's obligations under the Final Act of Helsinki—should override all other considerations; and that in any case the naturalization treaty invalidates the Bulgarian claim that the parents are still Bulgarians.

Logically, the Bulgarian contention that in the case of the three children in America humanitarian considerations should override the legalities, should enable us to argue with greater force that the two children in Bulgaria should benefit from the same attitude on the part of the Bulgarian authorities, i.e. that they should be allowed to go regardless of the dispute over nationality and applicability of treaties. The only trouble is that it is far from certain that a court-appointed guardian in Chicago will regard the children's travel to Bulgaria as being necessarily in their best interests; and besides, arguing about logic and consistency is not necessarily the best way of making headway with Bulgarian authorities in a matter that they regard as essentially political. The issue is in fact highly political, if only because the naturalized

American father is picketing the State Department and has enlisted the interest of five Senators and one member of the House of Representatives.

As if these matters were not complicated enough, there is another pending case which complicates the situation still further. There is in America another child whose parents left Bulgaria illegally but then decided to return to Bulgaria, from where they are supposedly petitioning to have the child returned to them. The court-appointed guardian has a role to play, and the child himself not only does not wish to return to Bulgaria but even refuses to see anyone from Bulgaria; and there is reason to suspect that his father and mother aren't married any longer and that the father in fact is in jail. But the Bulgarian authorities take the position—in that case, as well as in the one discussed today—that the wishes of small children are of little consequence in comparison with the desire of parents to be reunited with them. To which I usually respond by asking whether the Bulgarians would really expect to see a child "forced on a plane against his will" and whether they don't realize that such an event, even if it were countenanced by an American court, would result in a tremendous outcry against anyone who had anything to do with it. We have expelled criminals from our country, I said, for instance when we deported Lucky Luciano, but to "expel" a child who wants to stay in America would hardly be seen as an act of humanitarianism.

One thing has become clearer to me as I wrote this—why the Bulgarian government has never raised the most obvious question about the two children whose naturalized American parents are petitioning to get them to America. The question is "obvious" because the children were one and three years old respectively when the parents defected, and more than nine years have elapsed since that time. If the wishes of children are immaterial in the cases of children in America whom the Bulgarian government wants to see "repatriated," then that government cannot look into the question whether the children in Bulgaria want to go to the United States. From a humanitarian point of view, that question would seem quite relevant, but apparently it isn't going to be brought up by the consular section of the Foreign Ministry. And as long as there is no reason to believe that the children would prefer to stay in Bulgaria, we have an excellent case to insist, as we are doing, that they be permitted to join their parents. I am hopeful that the case will be resolved, and we have been taking it to successively higher levels of the government here.

29

The appointments of Anthony Lake and Richard Moose to senior positions in the State Department: Is it wise, is it fair to reward people with high office for having quit a career service because they didn't like a policy?

January 8. More appointments in the State Department have become known, or confirmed. Mr. Warren M. Christopher will be Deputy Secretary of State. He is a fine lawyer but doesn't seem to have had much exposure to foreign affairs. (Mr. Vance is also a fine lawyer, but he has demonstrated ability in foreign affairs in a multiplicity of very difficult assignments.) Philip Habib is to remain as Under Secretary for Political Affairs. This is excellent not just because continuity in having a career man in this position near the top is useful to the new Administration, but also because Habib is a "political animal" in addition to being a seasoned career officer—he is a good man to have at the interface between the political leadership and the professionals. Professor Richard N. Cooper is to become Under Secretary for Economic Affairs, and Lucy Benson Under Secretary for Security Assistance. I don't know enough about these people to comment.

But I have very strong feelings about two other appointments— Anthony Lake, who is to become Director of the Planning and Coordination Staff, and Richard Moose who is to become Deputy Under Secretary for Management, the position that Macomber used to hold. [Note: Moose later became Assistant Secretary for African Affairs.] These are both one-time career officers who quit when they were fairly junior in the Service, and they now come back into very senior positions. It's a little as if two Majors had left the military service, had worked in freelance capacities or on Capitol Hill in connection with military matters, and then returned to the Army as Lieutenant Generals, having skipped Lieutenant

210

Colonel, Colonel, Brigadier General and Major General. The question immediately arises whether such people are really so much better than more plausible claimants to such positions.

Well, Lake and Moose may of course be exceptionally able people to whom the rules and customs that apply to a career service are simply not applicable because they are so exceptional; but I see nothing in their records to indicate this. I do see some things in their records, or in my own experience, that cast serious doubt on the wisdom of their appointments, quite aside from what these appointments do to the morale of the career Foreign Service. I am aware that the morale of the career service cannot be the first consideration of the political leadership; but equity and fair dealing with a corps of people who devote their lives to foreign affairs and to service in dangerous and unhealthful posts, and who accept the discipline of step-by-step advancement in the belief that merit will be rewarded impartially, are not negligible factors.

Let us take Anthony Lake, who at 37 steps into the shoes once filled by the likes of George Kennan, Paul Nitze, George McGhee, Walt Rostow, and Henry Owen. Lake entered the Foreign Service by examination in 1962, served in Vietnam, then in the State Department, had two years of academic sabbatical (one of them at government expense) at Princeton, and then was working for Kissinger in the White House when the decision to invade Cambodia in 1970 made him quit over an issue of conscience. I congratulate people who have the moral courage to quit over an issue of conscience, but unfortunately Lake has written an autobiographic essay, in cooperation with his wife, which appeared in the *New York Times Magazine* of July 20, 1975; and as the self-portrait of a man of conscience it is very unimpressive. After leaving the Service he made a career of attacking the foreign policy of his erstwhile superiors, and now he will be in a position of authority over the people who loyally served those whom he attacked.

In their article, "Coming of Age Through Vietnam," the Lakes described how they were first impressed by the cruelty they saw during their service in Saigon and Hue. Mrs. Lake described the physical fear she experienced from the threat of terrorist attacks: "After we had been in Saigon over a year, I went to the gate of our garden to admit a cycle driver. In his hand I saw a round object, with a pin protruding from it. I fled, screaming hysterically. It was the only time I lost control. The object was his pipe." Lake became progressively more skeptical, as many of his colleagues did, about the military reports and forecasts about the war, and he described his position as "increasingly suspicious, then cynical, about claims of progress." He was also depressed by the moral decay of a society racked by incessant civil war. He got involved with the Buddhist demonstrations in Hué and, contrary to the impression of more dispassionate observers, concluded that the demonstrators represented "the people."

Returning to the United States in 1965, Mrs. Lake described her position as uneasy about the American role in Vietnam but still on the whole believing that we were at least trying to do the right thing. But then "I felt very defensive before critical liberal Americans who questioned me closely." Gradually she came to sympathize with opponents of the war and came to think that "we were creating an enemy which was not really ours. And we were forcing Vietnamese to choose sides among their own people"—as if that didn't happen in any civil war. Her influence on her husband was unmistakable from a revealing paragraph which was couched in the odd format of her addressing herself to Anthony Lake in the *New York Times Magazine* article:

"Increasingly appalled by the killing and the lying, I put a ban on the television evening news; the horrors shown there nightly were too painful for me and certainly for our 3-year-old son who had no way of understanding what kind of reality he was seeing. The workings of our Government, which formerly I had trusted, were now the object of distrust and disillusionment. Your loyalty to the Department of State in the face of inhuman working hours and inhuman policies increased the strain. And your work seemed consistently to have precedence over personal and family matters. So my resistance to the Vietnam involvement became one of personal resentment as well as one based on convictions."

How well those of us who did *not* quit under such circumstances know that situation! With the wife resenting the hard work required of her husband, he finds it necessary to justify the neglect of his family obligations by pointing to the supposed importance of what he is doing, and the resentment against the claims on the husband's time becomes intermingled with resentment against the policies and programs with which he is dealing. Elisabeth went through a similar period in connection with the Congo crisis, and later in connection with the status bill in Iran, the Laos crisis, land reform in Vietnam, the China representation issue in the United Nations, and other problems. But Mrs. Lake was demonstrating against our Vietnam policy outside the White House at the very time when her husband was inside working for Henry Kissinger! One can imagine the tensions under which he was operating.

"My growing despair about the war," Lake himself wrote in the same article, "was undoubtedly fueled by the way it dominated personal relationships, literally separating me from you and the children as work dominated my life, figuratively separating me from friends whose views on politics and foreign policy I generally shared." Gradually, the issue became simplified in his mind—for instance he referred to the American negotiating position on Vietnam as clearly unacceptable to the North Vietnamese, and therefore unrealistic. "It called," he wrote quite erroneously, "for their surrender." Mr. Cyrus Vance, if he has read that article, must have been somewhat surprised, for he was in Paris trying to negotiate with the North Vietnamese and got the impression, as the rest of us did, that it was they who wanted us to surrender South Vietnam to them. When issues became that much simplified, the choices and the personal relations must also have become simpler. "And television," he wrote, "which blows up a particular event until it looks like a general condition, made the human suffering I could recall from my own experience still less tolerable."

In the end, Lake came to believe that what we were really fighting for in Vietnam were "abstract notions of national prestige." When he quit over the incursion into Cambodia in 1970, he had apparently become convinced of a kind of primacy of moral considerations in foreign policy. "I was trained," he wrote, "to think of foreign policy as a bloodless, intellectual exercise. Identify national interests, formulate policies to serve them, manage them. Find the Aristotelian mean between extreme alternatives. The smartest official will do his best. I still find such kinds of analysis interesting, and am attracted to 'middle options.' But I am as interested, now, in the values held by our foreign policy makers as I am in how intelligent they are."

One does not have the impression that this man will find it in him to recommend policies which speak more to the mind than to the heart. And since the world is a hard place in which good intentions and the avoidance of bloodshed do not always suffice to maintain and assure peace, I am troubled that this immature ex-career officer will be in charge of planning and coordinating policy papers in the Department of State—quite aside from the grave doubts that I have of the wisdom of promoting to such a senior position a man who left the service in protest when he could have asked to be transferred to a position where he did not have to deal with the Vietnam war. Diversified experience and maturity count for something in diplomacy, and this man has had a very one-sided and limited kind of experience.

Richard Moose's is an entirely different sort of case, but it has something in common with that of Anthony Lake. Whether he quit the Service for reasons of conscience I do not know, but he also worked directly for Kissinger in the National Security Council and apparently did not like it, transferring instead to the staff of the Senate Foreign Relations Committee. The team of Lowenstein and Moose then played a role for Senator Fulbright analogous to the role played by the team of Cohn and Schine for Senator Joseph McCarthy—being sent out to bring back reports that would support the positions of their superiors, which they apparently did without any violence to their personal convictions. In the case of Vietnam, the Lowenstein/Moose report was a superficial piece of work that did little credit to its authors and was promptly used for partisan political purposes.

Now this man, who is probably honest and hard-working but cannot be imbued with much sympathy for the dilemmas of officers who stayed behind to serve their country under the duly constituted authority of the executive branch, will sit in judgment over those erstwhile colleagues. It is, to my mind, a worse case than the millionaire career officer (Angier Biddle Duke) who left the Service as a Class 4 officer, roughly the equivalent of a Major, and returned—after having made a substantial contribution to the 1952 election campaign—as an ambassador. Even if by talent and general ability such men might deserve senior positions, which is not always certain, there is considerable doubt whether this serves as a good example to people who accepted the discipline and hardships of step-by-step advancement for merit in competition with their peers.

—0—

Had an interesting discussion with Harvey, my deputy, and with Dan Simpson, the politico-economic officer, about a matter of interpretation of a recent announcement here about the "Committee for State and People's Control." This is an organ of the government which is supposed to oversee performance not only within the government structure in Sofia but all down the line to units of production (factories, collective farms, etc.)—and it was severely castigated in the government announcement.

So far, so good. The new decree declares, first, that "the work of the controlling organs is not yet . . . in keeping with the strategic task of the Party for effectiveness and quality." The control committee's work is marked by a "high degree of formalism" and it is "still not using its delegated rights to control, coordinate and direct the work of the specialized controlling organs." Ministers and department heads "do not pay enough attention to the controls and checks on performance."

After these strictures, the decree strengthens the authority of the Committee for State and People's Control, which is headed by a venerable Vice Premier and "candidate member" of the Politburo who had recently been moved into the cabinet presumably for the specific purpose of strengthening its control mechanism. The question was how to interpret the announcement, which criticized the performance of the control mechanism and at the same time strengthened its hand within the government.

On one thing we all agreed, namely that there must be serious shortcomings in the economy to have given rise to this blast. The economy of a Communist country is, after all, one vast bureaucratic structure. Lack of motivation of the working force has been a perennial problem, and exhortations to them to "fulfill and overfulfill the plan" as part of their devotion to the Party simply don't yield adequate results. For a long time the regime has been complaining about low work morale, bureaucratic inefficiency, "formalism," low quality of production, etc.

Where I parted company with my colleagues was when their telegram, which was submitted to me in draft, concluded: "Once again, the problem is seen as one of individuals rather than as a systemic one, and once again the remedy is seen as further increasing coercive powers of state and party." I found this too pat. Are inspection and control "coercive"? I maintained that by "coercive" we usually mean something stronger than having inspectors descend upon you to find out whether you are doing what you are supposed to be doing.

My colleagues argued against this. They said—and I agreed— that what is missing in the government's prescription is something like an *incentive* to the working force. Yes, I said, but I'm not arguing about that—if you put that in our telegram to Washington I will be glad to sign it. It's the characterization of the control mechanism as one of coercion that bothers me. Well, they said, isn't an inspection a coercive measure? Perhaps, I said, but the U.S. Government also conducts inspections and so does General Motors. Any large organization must have means of assuring that its decisions are carried out and that its goals are being attained. Besides, the Bulgarian economy isn't doing all that badly—we in the United States might not be unhappy with a growth rate of 8 per cent, no unemployment, and a 4 per cent a year improvement in the standard of living. Yes, the *regime* is coercive, but in my opinion the new decree doesn't add to the coercion.

In the end we compromised and the telegram went out with a final sentence which read that "the focus has been entirely on criticism and tightening of control procedures, without mention of incentives to either managerial or working staff for greater efficiency." I'm as convinced an anti-Communist as anyone, but don't want to see the Bulgarian regime accused of "increased coerciveness" where it is simply tightening up administrative procedures. And I don't accept that an inspection mechanism—which can, of course, have someone fired for inefficiency—is an instrument of coercion. Perhaps it's a matter of semantics, I said, but the word coercion when applied to a Communist regime usually means something different.

30

More State Department appointments. A conversation about CSCE with the Foreign Minister, which finds him exceptionally well-prepared in depth. More on the vexing "divided family" case involving two children in Bulgaria.

January 13. Several more State Department appointments are out: The Bureaus of European, Near Eastern and African affairs will continue to be headed by professionals who are experts in those fields. The East Asian Bureau, however, will be headed by Richard Holbrooke, 35, a former Foreign Service officer who for the last few years has edited the magazine *Foreign Policy*. His case is much more difficult to comment upon, for I think that Holbrooke acquired considerable breadth during recent years when his magazine was in effect a rallying-point for intellectual opposition to all kinds of foreign policies of the Nixon/Ford/Kissinger administrations. He has really managed to attract some first-rate people to debate in his pages. That the magazine has pretty systematically criticized the Administration's foreign policies isn't particularly damning if one looks upon Holbrooke as the opposition politician whose party has now come to power. Of course, that also means that he should not be reintegrated into the Foreign Service, any more than Lake or Moose.

Now, I happen to think that some of the articles published by Holbrooke were scurrilous—like the recent one which "proves" that the United States encouraged the Arabs to raise their oil prices in 1973; or a lengthy article some time ago, by an expert in internal American politics, which purported to "prove" that the United States could have headed off the coup in Cyprus which triggered the Turkish invasion of that island. This is also the magazine which featured the indented "verbatim quotes" of Kissinger which the author—but not the editor—later acknowledged as not having been verbatim. *Foreign Policy* also has the dubious distinction of being the first serious magazine on foreign affairs in recent years which published an article (by Paul C. Warnke) favoring *unilateral* disarmament—on a "trial" basis, to encourage the Soviets to do the same, an idea which some people regard as naive in the extreme. But *Foreign Policy* was certainly not a narrow activity, and it rendered a public service in stimulating debate on serious issues of foreign policy, furnishing a platform to some important thinkers in that field.

I think where I come out is that Holbrooke would have been a great deal better placed in the job that has now been given to Anthony Lake. Both men have strong records of opposition to the Vietnam war; but Holbrooke has a great deal more depth as well as breadth—only, he doesn't have it in East Asian affairs. One only has to compare Holbrooke with the present incumbent as Assistant Secretary for East Asian Affairs, Arthur Hummel, to see what Holbrooke is lacking. Hummel was born in China, the son of a scholar on Chinese affairs; he was educated in China and taught in China; he was interned there by the Japanese, escaped, and joined Chinese guerillas. In the Foreign Service he has served in Hong Kong, Tokyo, Rangoon, Taipei, in USIA, in several positions in the State Department dealing with Far Eastern affairs, and as ambassador to Burma (as well as Ethiopia). The Department is fortunate to have such experienced experts, including of course some who are younger than Hummel (though still older than Holbrooke). How will such men and women feel working for this young and aggressive man who quit the Foreign Service and then comes vaulting back into a top position that is usually only earned by devoted and meritorious service in positions of increasing responsibility over a period of years?

Let it not be thought that men like Hummel lack courage in expressing their opinions. The Assistant Secretaries of East Asian Affairs whom I have known—Bill Bundy, Marshall Green, Phil Habib and Art Hummel—are all tough customers. Bundy, who was not a career man, is now editing the other major magazine in foreign policy, *Foreign Affairs*. There is irony in the fact that Holbrooke was one of the editors of the Pentagon Papers, which helped to discredit Bundy—at least in the eyes of men like David Halberstam, who took Bundy apart in the book *The Best and the Brightest*. But Green, Habib and Hummel are men who worked their way up to senior positions by proven merit, and that merit did not consist in making a secret of their opinions, even when those opinions differed from those of their superiors. Courage is not a monopoly of young and brash outsiders; it is also found among those who stayed in the service.

—0—

January 28. Two weeks ago I had a two-hour conversation with Foreign Minister Mladenov. This was supposed to have taken place three weeks before. It was the longest wait I had had to see him, but he explained that he had been ill. Actually, he had been ill for a brief while and then very busy, but the delay in the appointment may also have had to do with the subject of our discussion—Helsinki and the Belgrade Conference—on which, perhaps, he had been awaiting new instructions. If I had had to do a lot of homework for that conversation, it is not unreasonable to suppose that he, too, had needed to spend some time briefing himself on present and potential issues.

It was a very professional kind of discussion. I had detailed instructions from Washington, some just confirming what we had proposed to say; and I had spent two evenings going through the Act of Helsinki and extracting from it the passages that seemed especially important for our conversation. Mladenov, on his side, had "defenses in depth" on certain subjects, such as the non-availability of foreign non-Communist newspapers and magazines in Sofia: First, he had thought they were available, was I really sure they weren't? (I was.) Second, such things take time; the Act of Helsinki did not prescribe a specific time for compliance. Third, it costs foreign currency to import such papers and the Bulgarian government was short on such currency. Fourth, Bulgaria was already importing more Western publications than the West was importing Bulgarian publications. And so on.

I commented on a number of aspects of the Final Act on which Bulgarian performance had been less than complete, but each of us made it clear that we were just reviewing together what might be done at Belgrade, and that ours was a routine conversation of the kind that we had had before—in other words, we weren't negotiating, nor were we "institutionalizing" the consultations on CSCE

(which is how we refer to the Final Act of Helsinki. The initials, as noted earlier, refer to the conclave which produced the Helsinki document, the Conference on Security and Cooperation in Europe.)

Neither side was willing (or authorized) to push issues very far, but the discussion was on the whole constructive, with two exceptions: A long harangue by Mladenov on the subject of Radio Free Europe (RFE), and some "explanations" he gave about a divided family case which we simply couldn't accept. On both subjects it took some time to sort out what could and could not be done, and I believe the conversation was worth the preparations that had preceded it. I made a proposal to Mladenov about RFE which seemed to surprise both him and Washington, and which in my opinion put the Bulgarians on the defensive, where they belong on that issue—unless it turns out that the station has been grossly violating its charter, which I do not expect to see. There need be no secret about what I proposed when the Minister claimed that Radio Free Europe was attacking the person of the Bulgarian chief of state. I invited him to give me the dates and verbatim quotes and said I would be able to put a stop to it, since I happened to know that RFE's internal directives prohibit *ad personam* attacks against East European leaders.

The position we simply couldn't accept had again to do with the divided family case where the parents, who had left Bulgaria illegally, were now American citizens and wished their children, whom they had left behind at very young ages nine years ago, to join them. The Foreign Minister read to me from a long brief prepared by his lawyers, and half of it was clearly in contravention of every basic principle of international law, while the other half was irrelevant.

In such situations it may be profitable to try to bowl over the charging opponent by letting him push against an open door—in this case it meant that I accepted without question one-half of Mr. Mladenov's legal brief which tried to prove (and did indeed prove conclusively) that the children in Bulgaria couldn't possibly have become American citizens at the time of their parents' naturalization because they had been here in Bulgaria. I said we absolutely agree, but we had never claimed that the children were American citizens. We had only requested the issuance of travel documents so that they could join their parents in America. As for the Bulgarian contention that the parents had to be considered Bulgarians despite their naturalization as American citizens, because they had left Bulgaria illegally, this was of course something we couldn't accept. The legalities are on our side, but legal arguments tend to be very drawn-out, so I pleaded that legal considerations be laid aside and that the case be viewed from a higher political and humanitarian perspective.

Then he raised the case of the allegedly Bulgarian children in the U.S. whose parents had died under such tragic circumstances. A brief discussion confirmed what I had suspected, namely that Mr. Mladenov took it for granted that the wishes of minors were of no consequence. When I told him that we don't "deport" children who want to stay in the U.S., Mladenov's eyes lit up and he asked me whether we would consider relevant whether the Bulgarian children whose parents are in America want to join their parents there. I said yes, and by that fact a link was established, at least in Mladenov's mind, between the children in America whom the Bulgarians want to bring here and the children in Bulgaria whom we want to bring to America.

Fortunately, we then had a lucky break. We learned a few days ago that the court in Chicago had entrusted the three orphans to the custody of their Bulgarian grandfather, and that the latter with court permission had already left the United States accompanied by the children. What was too bad was that it took the State Department one week to get that news to us. And even then, because they promised us "comments on what might be said to the Bulgarians" we lost yet another day. Meanwhile perhaps the Bulgarian Embassy in Washington was claiming credit for having gotten the children to Bulgaria. None of these cases is simple: The court, for instance, still requires proof that the children are actually in the custody of relatives in Bulgaria and that their needs are well looked after; and, as it happens, all three are indeed American citizens—although they seem to have gone (in the case of the eldest, returned) to Bulgaria with Bulgarian travel documents.

When I called today on the acting head of the consular department of the Foreign Ministry, I found him grateful that the children in America had been allowed to depart, but rather unyielding on the children in Bulgaria. He claimed that the simplest way to reunify the family was for the parents to profit from the Bulgarian amnesty and to return to Bulgaria, even if only for a visit. And then he added: "After all, the children do not know their parents since they were one and three years old when the parents left here nine years ago." I broke the conversation off at this point because I didn't want the question to arise whether the children are now willing to leave. Possibly, just possibly, we were being told that if the parents could persuade the kids to go to America with them, the Ministry would cooperate; but the parents, who left the country illegally, would have to make their obeisance to the Bulgarian state first, "since they are still Bulgarian citizens as long as they have not formally renounced that citizenship at a Bulgarian embassy or consulate."

I said I did not wish to go into the question of nationality, which would lead to endless legal arguments—although it does seem to us that the Bulgarian position on the non-applicability of our naturalization treaty is contrary to established international law—and that it was fruitless to have any discussion of the case on the level of the consular department because the issue, essentially, was humanitarian and political—and I pointed at the enormous portrait of Todor Zhivkov which hangs in the official's office, just behind his desk.

Did this mean, he asked, that I wished to discuss that case only with the Foreign Minister? Not necessarily, I answered, for it was conceivable that the Foreign Minister wanted to help but was unable to do so because the head of another ministry (I had in mind, of course, the Ministry of Interior) held a differing opinion. So I might be forced to take it higher yet, perhaps to the level of the Prime Minister. This seemed to have a little effect on my interlocutor. As of this writing I don't know whether I will get instructions to take the case up to the PM level, for there are still things that the parents can do, and I recognize that there are factors which make this case an especially difficult one for the Bulgarians to approve. But there are also political factors which make it very desirable, in the interest of the normalization and development of relations between the U.S. and Bulgaria, to settle this issue without any further bureaucratic pettifoggery.

Even though it happened subsequent to the cut-off date of this chronicle, I think the reader is entitled to know that the case was in fact settled eventually. My own contribution was mainly in seeking new ways of presenting the issue—and resisting the inclination of lawyers to argue our case in legal terms. I was convinced that that would get us nowhere. In diplomacy there is no tribunal which decides issues on the basis of their merits—results are obtained by pointing out that it is in the interest of the other party to do what you want it to do. Pointing this out can take the form of more or less veiled "disincentives" or inducements. Only rarely, where national interests conflict, are arguments alone sufficient. In the end this case, the Marev case, was resolved by oral communications in Washington and Sofia, very subtly and almost subliminally enunciated, that led to a realization somewhere in the Bulgarian hierarchy that the regime had more to lose by stonewalling than by giving in. The children are now happily re-united with their parents and getting rapidly adjusted to their new surroundings.

[A wry footnote to this episode is that the signal that the Bulgarians were giving in came through in the form of a remark by an official of the consular department that "the Bulgarian side has of course never interposed any obstacle to the departure of the children" but that they could not leave unless tickets were sent for their air transportation to America. . . Since this was at one time a controversial subject involving the State Department, Congress, the press and of course the parents of the children, I also want to state here that the parents were their own worst enemies in this business and their actions almost resulted in the whole operation being aborted. Furthermore, instead of showing gratitude to the State Department for having helped to re-unite their family, they resorted to accusations bordering on the slanderous—but then, nobody expects gratitude in such situations in which emotions run very high, and there is much praise or blame that can be distributed among many actors in that little drama.

[The case was brought to conclusion only after additional complications had arisen and had to be overcome. One of those complications will be found in a further entry on February 17. For a while things went downhill as the Bulgarians seemed to be digging themselves in further and further, but then we had some good talks on the subject of the two children both in Washington and in Sofia, and the forthcoming visit of a high Bulgarian dignitary to Washington may have contributed to the Bulgarian decision to wipe the case off the books.]

31

Rootlessness in the Foreign Service. Discovering why our routine handling of certain inquiries is bound to send some people at home through the roof. "Charter 77" and the question of human rights in Communist countries.

January 21. I recorded a few pages ago the perplexing case of the Bulgarian who claimed that our embassy had turned him over against his will to a psychiatric clinic from which he had escaped and where he had been held for political reasons. There has been a tremendous amount of telegraphing all over the world to piece together from the memories of people who have long since left this embassy what might have happened. Lawyers considered whether he might have a claim, assuming that the facts were as he had stated them. It turned out that he had not only a theory that supposedly disproves (or "goes beyond") Einstein's theory of relativity, but that he had also been involved in the development of a *perpetuum mobile* machine. Our consul had two more interviews with him and found him calm and collected, but the facts simply did not add up to a valid claim, and it was decided that we could do nothing for him. He is no longer under psychiatric care, nor under any other constraint, but we wouldn't be surprised if he got into trouble with the Bulgarian authorities, for reasons that would be preposterous to an American but plausible to a Bulgarian. He seems an innocent idealist who, however, might be mistaken for a political zealot. My heart goes out to people like him—whether or not he is to be taken seriously as a scientist. But there is nothing we can do to help him. On the other hand, we do not refuse to see people who come into the embassy and want to talk to someone. Perhaps in his case, however, it would be better for all concerned if we did discourage him from coming to see us anymore.

A number of people in our embassy are suffering from depression, insomnia, headaches and other possibly psychosomatic disorders—and the question has arisen whether perhaps there may be some microwave radiation directed against us which could cause such symptoms. One of our officers is circulating two articles in *The New Yorker* which describe the subjective and hard-to-diagnose symptoms allegedly caused by a bombardment of microwaves—headache, eye pain, weariness, dizziness, irritability, emotional instability, depression, diminished intellectual capacity, partial loss of memory, loss of hair, hypochondria, loss of appetite—and some certainly seem to correspond with problems that are found among our personnel and some of their family members. It is my own belief, however, that this is a seasonal matter, as I have noted a high incidence of all kinds of disorders during the winter months when the skies are grey, the mails are slow, the city seems more inhospitable, and the loneliness is harder to bear. Yet, since the local representative of the American Foreign Service Association has formally asked that a check be made for microwave radiation, I have passed this along to Washington with a strong endorsement by our embassy.

In my own family both Elisabeth and I might have some of the symptoms, particularly since we are fretting about the question of when to retire—the mandatory retirement age of 60 is only half a year away—and what to do afterwards. We have made certain plans for retirement in Vienna, but there are also good reasons why we might retire elsewhere, notably the fact that there is little that I could usefully do in Austria. On the other hand, Elisabeth has roots there, and I also know a certain number of people since I went to school in Vienna and my first post in the Foreign Service was Vienna. There is involved here a question of identity—where do we belong, where do we feel at home, where do we have roots, where do we have opportunities for self-realization? These are not easy questions to answer when one has lived a life of representing the United States abroad. My home town is New York, but I hardly know anyone there anymore, even though I went to college there, entered the army from there, entered the Foreign Service from there, and for many years had my "home leave" address there.

The essential tragedy of the end of a Foreign Service career is that one's "home town" is the Service itself—our friends are scattered all over the world, and there is even a question whether many of them qualify for the appellation of friends; and the same goes with the people we left behind when we entered the Service—one's roots tend to wither when one has been away so long and appears only periodically for short visits with friends (or rather, acquaintances) with whom one has less and less in common. As a result, we are the truly *déracinés*, as we have been uprooted not once but every few years over many years—I myself have moved eleven times in my 30 years in the Service—and the friends that one made for instance 12 years ago in Iran will not be the same people any more if by any remote chance we try to visit them there. Being uprooted in America is bad enough, as Vance Packard has demonstrated in his book, *A Nation of Strangers*. But being uprooted and replanted from one culture to another, time and again, makes the need for some stability in one's life seem all the more urgent when the "final" move is imminent, but even now there is little prospect for wholesome stability in our lives.

—0—

Even in a small organization, the top executive can only do so much; and even if he were able to do more, it wouldn't be desirable for him to give too much supervision to subordinates. Yet he is responsible for the mistakes made by his organization. There are standard ways out of this dilemma, and they are delegation of authority, good communication up and down, motivation of the staff so that they will want to do a good and conscientious job, rewards for good performance—and an occasional kick in the behind when the top executive discovers that something is being, and probably has been for a long time, mishandled *routinely*.

I had a shock in connection with a letter from a lady in the U.S. who had been born in Bulgaria and addressed me personally with a request to procure for her a copy of her birth certificate. I took the envelope home with my other mail, discovered there that it was really for our consular section to handle, and sent it along to them with a short draft of a response in which I proposed to tell the lady that we had received her letter, that we would do what she had asked us to do, but that it might take a little time since we were dependent on the good will of the Bulgarian authorities. I might add that the lady's letter had stated both her present name and her maiden name, and her birth place and birth date.

When the letter came from the Consular Section for my signature, it had been modified to include five questions which that section routinely requires in order to be able to process such requests: (1) full name, including maiden name; (2) birth date; (3) birth place; (4) name of father; (5) name of mother. They also needed to know the purpose for which the copy of the birth certificate was required (for reasons having to do with the fee charged by the Bulgarians). Naturally I sent the letter back with the question why it was necessary to ask again questions 1, 2 and 3 when they had already been answered in the incoming letter.

That is where I got my shock. We *always* go back and ask for all the information in one letter, I was told, because we file such incoming letters under "Miscellaneous" and often cannot find them again, especially if several months elapse between their original receipt and the arrival of the supplementary information. I called in Harvey and told him that surely there must be something awfully wrong if our consular section sends such letters routinely to correspondents. If I were the lady who had asked for help, I would be furious to receive a response which asked me for information that I had already furnished.

Well, this is only a tiny matter—although it does, in its small way, reflect the larger problem of the image of the U.S. Government in the eyes of the American people if bureaucrats down the line can keep sending letters of this kind; for one has to imagine this situation multiplied ten thousand times. It wasn't at all easy to get the Bulgarian clerk who had drafted the original letter to accept that things would henceforth have to be done differently. She pointed out, no doubt truthfully, that an inspector from Washington had criticized the amount of "inactive" files maintained by that section, and ever since that time they are maintaining files only on cases where a particular action requirement already exists. From now on they will have files also for cases such as the one of the lady who had written me.

—0—

January 29. The really exciting thing that is happening in Eastern Europe at this time is the "Charter 77" document issued by 300 Czechoslovak artists and intellectuals, how the Czech authorities are dealing with them, and what the reaction to all that is among the Communist parties in the West and also in other

Every American embassy receives a daily "wireless bulletin" from Washington which contains teletyped summaries of the news, of White House and State Department press briefings, and the texts of important government statements and selected press editorials. From the bulletin and from the telegrams we received from other Eastern European posts we had a pretty good idea of what was happening, but it was only today that the bulletin carried (with some inevitable garbled lines) the full text of the original "Charter 77" document. It raises the fundamental question whether a line can be drawn between sweeping humanitarian concerns and internal politics. I know there are many people who believe that the Czechs in 1968 were only looking for "socialism with a human face;" but when one raises fundamental questions of human rights in a Communist context, there is a real question whether one isn't really raising fundamental questions about Communism.

The Bulgarians, incidentally, have had nothing original to say about the controversy. Silent for almost two weeks, they finally came out with the routine bluster that one hears from Moscow about people who are in the pay of imperialist agents, who cloak their subversive designs with the appearance of humanitarian concerns, and the like. There is nothing important I can contribute as ambassador to Bulgaria, and for that reason this embassy has reported very little on the controversy; but I can and must record here privately what my views are after having read the text of Charter 77.

As I understand that document, it really calls for the establishment of what the philosopher Karl Popper termed an "open society" in Czechoslovakia (and elsewhere). Referring to the UN Covenant on Human Rights and other documents including the Final Act of Helsinki, the signatories call for "freedom guaranteed to individuals" which exists "only on paper" and castigate the repressive actions and organization of the Czechoslovak state. "The right of free expression guaranteed by Article 19 of the first act, for example (is being violated . . . and people are) prevented from working in their professions for the sole reason that their views differ from the official ones. . . Any attempt to exercise the right to 'seek, receive and impart information regardless of frontiers and of whether it is oral, written or printed' or 'imparted through art'—point 2, Article 13 of the first pact—can result in persecution not only outside the courts but also inside. . . . No political, philosophical, scientific, or artistic work that deviates in the slightest from the narrow framework of official ideology or esthetics is permitted to be produced. Public criticism of social conditions is prohibited. Public defense against . . . defamatory charges by official propaganda organs is impossible, despite the legal protection against attacks on one's reputation and honor (being) unequivocally afforded by Article 17 of the first pact. False accusations cannot be refuted, and it is futile to attempt rectification or to seek legal redress. Open discussion . . . is out of the question. Many scientific and cultural workers, as well as other citizens, have been discriminated against simply because some years ago (they) articulated views condemned by the current political power." This is an excellent description of the situation that prevails in every Communist country, whether it be Czechoslovakia, Russia, Bulgaria, East Germany, Cuba, or Vietnam.

"A whole range of civil rights is severely restricted or completely suppressed by the effective method of subordinating all institutions and organizations of the state to the political directives of the ruling party's apparatuses and the pronouncements of highly influential individuals. Neither the constitution of the CSSR nor any of the country's other legal procedures (are observed). The authors (of governmental directives) are responsible only to themselves and their own hierarchy, yet they have a decisive influence on the activity of the legislative as well as executive bodies of the state administration (etc.). . . . If some organizations or citizens in the interpretation of their rights and duties, become involved in a conflict with the directives, they cannot turn to a neutral authority, for none exists. Consequently, the right of assembly and the prohibition of its restraint, stemming from Articles 21 and 22 of the first pact; the right to participate in public affairs, in Article 25; and the right to equality before the law, in Article 26—all have been seriously violated. These conditions prevent working people from freely establishing labor and other organizations for the protection of their economic and social interests, and from freely using their right to strike as provided in point 1, Article 8 of the second pact."

And so it goes, with magnificent eloquence, and to the cheers of decent like-minded people inside and outside of Eastern Europe. But the issue is so broadly drawn, the implication is so clear that the signatories wish to substitute an open society for the closed system of their Communist regime, that the outcome of the controversy is a foregone conclusion; for which Communist country can afford to give free scope to internal criticism and debate, to the open expression of differing views (and sometimes even of artistic tastes), to the rights of people to assemble peacefully, to the rights of workers to assert their interests against the effective owners of the means of production in their countries, the 'new class' of Communist officials? Reading this deeply moving but patently futile declaration sent me back to a book by Romain Gary, the French novelist, who had witnessed the Communist takeover in Bulgaria when he was a member of the French diplomatic service just after World War II. Deeply disillusioned by his experiences in the service, he quit a few years later and ridiculed in a passage of his book, *La Nuit Sera Calme*, the tendency of some diplomats to be excessively clever in their interpretations when sometimes it is sufficient to draw obvious conclusions from obvious events.

"Diplomats are often able to kid themselves," he wrote. "I recall once being in the presence of a great French ambassador at an important post some ten years ago, who tried to explain to me that the break between China and the USSR was a particularly clever and diabolical maneuver which the Chinese and the Russians had mounted together in order to deceive the United States. . . He was simply too intelligent. There is nothing more frustrating for a great mind than to be obliged to stop after adding two and two to make four. That is why Olivier Wormser, who was our ambassador in Moscow before he became governor of the Bank of France, was the only ambassador there who predicted three weeks beforehand that the USSR would occupy Czechoslovakia. He had stopped after adding two and two, which requires great strength of character."

In the same book, incidentally, Gary describes how the Bulgarian police tried to compromise him by taking pictures of an intimate encounter with a young Bulgarian lady who had declared her love for him. A few days after their tryst Gary was accosted by two men who asked him to accompany them to a coffee house where they showed the pictures to him. He was appalled, he reports—not by the attempted blackmail but by the poor figure he cut in the pictures, which had been taken on a day when he "was not at his best" and the lady had really done nothing to inspire him. The two policemen, noting his consternation, remarked that among reasonable people there was always a way of working things out. "I overflowed with gratitude," he reported. "Marvelous, thanks ever so much. All I ask is that you give me another chance. Bring me together again with the same lady or preferably with another, tear up these humiliating pictures and let me try again, I promise to give a much better performance." After a while the police agents got the point that he was not willing to do anything for them except provide them with pictures that would more adequately document his virility, and the matter blew over.

But back to Charter 77. The affair is of course very embarrassing to the Czech hierarchy and its masters, particularly in view of the forthcoming Belgrade Conference where the implementation of the Act of Helsinki is to be discussed; but there cannot be anyone in a high position in the State Department, certainly not the people who deal with CSCE, who believed at any time that implementation of the Final Act would result in the establishment of an open society in the Communist countries of Eastern Europe. There is every evidence that the State Department, at least under Kissinger, was quite content to see some minor incremental changes in Eastern European behavior—and that position is the only realistic one. (What I had criticized in the strategy that seemed to be emerging was that we lacked priorities among the many things called for in "Basket III" of the document, when it was obvious that we could obtain satisfaction only partially and only on a very few of them.) To my great regret I must record, therefore, that in my opinion the signatories of Charter 77, by asking too much in the name of Helsinki, are actually apt to make it even more difficult to obtain even the modicum of loosening-up that we have every right to seek. If the regime in Czechoslovakia were to grant its people the equivalent of our Bill of Rights, they would be sounding the death knell of Communism there, and that is something that the Russians have already once shown they will not permit.

There is a certain hypocrisy, in my opinion, in the attitude of people in the West who periodically rediscover that Communist regimes are repressive, as if they couldn't have found that out long ago. One of the most pathetic events of that kind was the protest, reported on December 30, by erstwhile opponents of the war in Vietnam, who discovered that the Communist regime there had abridged civil liberties. All the 90 signatories of an appeal handed to the Vietnamese Mission at the United Nations, according to the *Washington Post*, "had been leaders of the anti-war movement of the late 1960s and early 1970s, and their rhetoric against the Socialist Republic of Vietnam was as strongly phrased as their denunciation of U.S. military involvement against the Viet Cong. 'Even those countries that are not democratic must be held accountable for basic human rights,' said Rep. Edward Koch, D., N.Y., one of the most outspoken anti-war members of Congress during the Vietnam era and one of the petition signers."

"I was one of those opposed to our involvement in Vietnam and I was pleased when our involvement ended," Mr. Koch was reported to have declared. "But we now have a new involvement and the United States must bring economic and any other kind of pressure to bear on a new kind of repression over there." But how on earth can the U.S. exert any influence on Communist Vietnam? With $3 billion in aid flowing to that country from other sources and none from the U.S. (from which the Vietnamese demand "reparations"), the expression of disgust at their repressive measures is what the French call *un coup d'épée dans l'eau*, a dagger thrust into water. "The actions of your government," the petition said, "constitute a great disappointment to all those who expected . . . an example of reconciliation built on tolerance." When has a Communist government ever given an example of such a spirit when it came to power anywhere in the world? Asked if there wasn't an inconsistency in their anti-war stand and their present castigation of the Communist regime, one signatory recalled that the peace movement had always been split between those who advocated a military victory by North Vietnam "and those peace demonstrators who opposed an immediate [sic] take-over by the Communists as vociferously as they opposed the presence of U.S. troops in Indochina." But to quote another French saying, "one has to want (also) the consequences of what one wants."

32

Giving the bum's rush to an ambassador to make room for his successor. More comments on ambassadorial appointments. And reflections on the troubles that are bound to be experienced over the nomination of a new SALT negotiator.

February 3. It must now be a month or more since the Carter team announced its first intended ambassadorial appointment— Richard N. Gardner to Rome—and there hasn't been a single nomination since. I think the reason for this must be that Professor Gardner had been considered for a cabinet appointment, so that the security clearances that usually have to run for several weeks before an appointment can be announced, had already been initiated.

I think highly of Professor Gardner, who was one of my predecessors as Deputy Assistant Secretary for International Organization Affairs in the State Department. He left behind a memory of a vigorous if somewhat disorganized executive, an original thinker who was always ready to stand the picture on its head and see if it didn't look better that way, and a true believer in international cooperation through international organization. He is supposed to have functioned essentially as an idea man—who had to be restrained, sometimes, by people who knew why certain things that at first looked like simple ways out of a complicated dilemma, didn't actually work out that way. He is certainly no amateur in foreign policy. While a political appointee, he is in some respects a professional. In short, even though I usually think that a career diplomat will do a better job than an outsider, *ceteris paribus*, Gardner is not a bad appointment for Rome, although he was surely not chosen because he was the best available man for that particular job. At least he has not just dabbled in foreign policy—he has continuously worked on foreign affairs from many different perspectives.

What is not generally known, at least not yet, is that the incumbent ambassador to Italy, John Volpe, a Nixon appointee, was given the bum's rush out of his post—I understand from a letter that he was told to pack up and be out of there before Vice President Mondale got to Rome on his recent trip (when he was accompanied by Ambassador-Designate Gardner). Now, I know nothing about Volpe except that he certainly didn't become ambassador to Italy because he knew much about foreign affairs— perhaps someone had the naive idea that because of his Italian antecedents he would do better there than someone with some other kind of name—but to give an ambassador just a few days to clear out is not exactly evidence for the compassionate and human style of the new administration. It is, in fact, what one might have expected from Nixon or Ehrlichmann.

For the misconception that a particular ethnic background is an asset in representing the United States in a particular country there are other examples—such as Postmaster General Gronouski, who didn't speak Polish but was appointed by John Kennedy as American Ambassador to Poland; or the appointment of a whole gaggle of black bureaucrats or politicians as ambassadors to African countries in the belief that African leaders would thereby be flattered (they usually aren't). And although not exactly an example of presumed ethnic affinity, there is also the case of Kennedy's appointment of General James M. Gavin as ambassador to France, in the pathetically mistaken idea that a general would be better able to communicate with De Gaulle—who gave Gavin, as a "mere" general, the back of his hand; for De Gualle wasn't just a former general, he was "La France" and presumably only the dispatch of General George Washington might just possibly have made him feel that he was in appropriate company. Toward the Soviet Union the opposite approach did sometimes work: Stalin was notoriously suspicious of experts on the Soviet Union. Also he probably did not believe that American diplomats could be more courageous and independent in their reporting and recommendations than were his own ambassadors; so Roosevelt's appointment of a millionaire, Averell Harriman, was a master stroke, though perhaps an inadvertent one. At any rate Stalin must have thought that since Harriman was a millionaire he was obviously speaking for the *real* wire-pullers of American politics. (Perhaps he even thought that Harriman was one of the people who were manipulating Roosevelt, that stooge of Wall Street. . .) The trouble with appointing millionaires is that very few of them have the flair for foreign policy that was displayed by Harriman.

I'm not going to try to comment on many more appointments, but will record my informed opinion that the nomination of Elliot Richardson as U.S. negotiator at the Law of the Sea Conference was just about the best that could have been made. Having been for three years vice chairman of that gigantic floating crap game of the Washington bureaucracy which was called the Law of the Sea Task Force, I know of the complexities and the jungle-like infighting between competing and conflicting vested interests within the American delegation that have attended these negotiations. And to these must of course be added the complexities of negotiating with some 140 other countries. Elliot Richardson, when he was Under Secretary, was one of the few people at the top, probably the only one, who really understood what these vital negotiations were all about; and it was due to his perceptiveness and originality that the American proposal to share the wealth of the deep seabed was developed.

But I am worried by the appointment of Paul Warnke as SALT negotiator and head of the Arms Control and Disarmament Agency. His views on arms control cannot, of course, be as superficial and facile as those he sketched out in the Spring 1975 issue of the magazine *Foreign Policy*; but it is quite appropriate that there are already rumblings in the Senate that the favorable views he then expressed about *unilateral* disarmament do not bode well for his shrewdness as a negotiator. He is undoubtedly much more sophisticated than would appear from the flip manner in which he dealt with life-and-death issues in that article. But a public figure must be held responsible for positions he takes in the public prints, and Warnke ridiculed the whole idea that one is more apt to obtain concessions from the Soviets if one has something to concede than if one doesn't.

In his *Foreign Policy* article Warnke argued that to reduce unilaterally the number of our tactical nuclear weapons in Europe would "improve our security" in addition to improving "the climate for reciprocal Soviet action." But the whole reason of having *tactical* nuclear weapons in Europe is that without them we might be unable to stem a possible Soviet ground attack short of a holocaust created by calling upon *strategic* nuclear weapons. Some of the other things Warnke proposed in his article will now come to haunt him: that we would lose nothing by a unilateral moratorium on further MIRV'ing (equipping with multiple warheads) of our land- and sea-based missiles, because any advantage that the Russians might get during such a test period could be made up easily if the gesture was not reciprocated. But how are we to know whether it is reciprocated? The problem is not only one of how many MIRV'd missiles each side possesses, but much more what perception each side will have of its position vis-a-vis the other. That, and not the alleged desire of Pentagon brass for more and more of everything, is the real issue of the current debate—whether the Russians, through their current faster pace of armament and emphasis on civil defense may some day make an appraisal of the relative power position and conclude that they can face down the United States and its allies on some important international issue. These are matters of vital importance, for it does matter whether the Russians and our own people and our allies see the leaders on our side and their key advisers as pushovers or as tough-minded potential opponents.

Fred Iklé, who has been the head of the Arms Control and Disarmament Agency until now (though not our SALT negotiator) and who is a sensitive and sophisticated analyst of the intricacies of nuclear arms reduction, has put the dilemma of credibility in these remarkably lucid terms: "If a nuclear attack [against us] should ever occur, what purpose would be served by destroying the cities of the nation which launched the attack? What would be accomplished . . . by killing and maiming millions of men, women and children who had no part in the decision to attack? Is such retaliation a rational response to a limited nuclear attack—e.g., an attack against some U.S. military forces overseas? *And if it doesn't seem rational, can we count on it to deter the enemy?*" (My italics.) Put in these terms, there is of course no answer except that we must have a system of graduated response and not only of "massive retaliation"; but Iklé deserves great credit for the way he has pointed out the importance of *credibility* in our nuclear posture. Unfortunately a certain image of toughness is essential if nuclear deterrence is to work.

I have before me the last issue of *The Economist* of London, which was printed well before announcement of the Warnke nomination. That serious magazine defines the problems of the SALT negotiations by setting forth four "guidelines" by which any agreement stemming from those talks must be judged. The two key guidelines, to my mind, were these: "2. Any numerical advantage the Russians retain should not be remotely within range of giving them the power of a disarming first strike. 3. Even short of that, their advantage in numbers—of missiles, throw-weight, megatonnage and maybe eventually multiple warheads—should not be so large that America's allies, or American public opinion, might come to fear that it was tantamount to absolute superiority; because that would paralyze the American president's power to act in the world."

We are, in other words, not dealing only with the old question of "overkill" which leads some facile observers to think that we can reduce our nuclear armaments without fear and even unilaterally "because we will still have enough left over to destroy the enemy" —but also with *perceptions*. What we perceive as unacceptable damage may not always be unacceptable damage to the Union of Soviet Socialist Republics; and indeed the damage we would sustain in a nuclear exchange even today is not directly equivalent to that which they would be sustaining, because they have hardened so many more installations than we have on our side.

Unfortunately, the debate—and I am writing this now on February 6—has involved its own terrible simplifications, with the Neanderthal right, which is opposed to *any* disarmament, joining the more reasonable critics; and the Warnke appointment may thus become a test whether or not one is for early SALT negotiations. Some leading American newspapers have leaped, prematurely I think, to Warnke's defense because they see the issue as liberal versus conservative, and the *Washington Post* has darkly referred to an "anonymous memorandum" that accuses Mr. Warnke of favoring unilateral disarmament. "We find this characterization of his views inaccurate and scurrilous," they editorialized. "And we find the circulating of this sort of anonymous memo a positive disservice to policy debate. This is not the first occasion in which Carter appointment initiatives have been met with this tactic. Are some of the people with reservations about Mr. Warnke so lacking in confidence on the merits that they must resort to sneaky smears?" Sneaky smears are certainly to be regretted, but the issue will not be about subterranean insinuations, it will be about what Mr. Warnke has publicly proclaimed to be his position.

On the other hand, Evans and Novak in the same newspaper wrote: "Critics of Warnke see a distinct possibility that the Carter Administration will experiment with unilateral reduction of the American nuclear deterrent. That chilling prospect was clearly and specifically spelled out in voluminous writings about U.S.-Soviet arms negotiations by Warnke, the latest in a long line of Washington lawyer-statesmen. . . Moreover, Carter's selection of Warnke poses an apparent contradiction between Warnke's highly advertised positions and Congressional perceptions of Carter's own policy. In the second [electoral] debate, Carter pledged that 'in defense' the United States would have a 'capability second to none.' Even a hint of unilateral strategic arms slow-down raises questions about Warnke's devotion to that principle."

With Carter and Vance now strongly backing the appointment, I expect that Warnke will be confirmed, but perhaps the debate and the confirmation hearings will lead to the disavowal of some of his views, which would be salutary. Mr. Vance has already very tactfully disavowed some of them, even while strongly backing Warnke. In his press conference on the 3rd (which I read over the weekend) a reporter asked this question about Warnke: "But you don't agree with him, I gather, on the question of unilateral withdrawal of some nuclear forces from Europe?" And Vance answered: "Well, what I said on that—I think it would be inappropriate at this time to withdraw our tactical nuclear forces or weapons from Europe. That issue is already a subject which is on the table in the MBFR [Mutual and Balanced Force Reduction] discussions, and it doesn't make sense to me to take such a step while it is currently under negotiation."

During the same press conference, incidentally, there occurred an exchange which again shows that Vance is a cool customer and will not say more than he thinks he should even under badgering from reporters. He was asked in several ways when and how the U.S. was going to "normalize" its relations with the Chinese People's Republic and "disengage" itself from its commitment to the security of Taiwan. He answered this prickly question as carefully as he could, and then received this renewed question: "I don't mean to be disrespectful at all, but I don't think you have answered the question. Nick asked you if you really think that the United States can recognize China, and disavow our defense treaty with the Taiwanese." To which Vance simply replied that he had said all he was able to say. In other words, not every question can be answered on the public record. It isn't possible to speak to the American people on a subject of such delicacy without also speaking to the rulers of Peking, and it is better to speak to the rulers of Peking privately on a matter of this kind before doing so in public.

33

More on "divided families," including the sad case of two Czech kids. President Carter nominates the members of an advisory board on ambassadorial nominations. The question is: Why not the best? And a military note.

February 7. During the last week I called on the Deputy Minister for Foreign Trade to discuss possibilities for increased American business and, specifically, the preparations for the forthcoming meeting of the Bulgarian-U.S. Joint Economic Council. The Bulgarians have done their homework; and while the Council is a non-governmental organization (which on the Bulgarian side, of course, is a pure fiction) I wanted to make sure that nothing was being overlooked. Now I shall have to see that nothing is overlooked on the American side.

Also managed to make substantial progress in a very difficult and complex undertaking within our embassy, namely an analysis of all "divided family" cases from the point of view of whether all the relevant documents are available, whether a desire to reunite those families still exists, when or how often certain applications had been turned down by the Bulgarian authorities, what kinds of cases were approved and what the disapproved ones have in common, and where there are things that need to be done on our side and on the Bulgarian side, for instance where approval has been notified to us but actually not carried into effect. We are looking for patterns and trends, and since few cases fit into neat categories this is a difficult and challenging enterprise. Our analytical effort has resulted in our revising downward the number of "real" divided family cases, since we identified cases where the family member in the U.S. has died or is no longer interested in the visit or permanent move of the Bulgarian family member, or the family member in Bulgaria for some reason may no longer wish to apply for permission to leave. The last category is especially delicate since we

241

do not necessarily accept the word of the Bulgarian authorities on whether a particular Bulgarian family member no longer wishes to go to America; but I am satisfied that on the whole we are well informed about who wants to go and who doesn't. In some cases when people find out that others have been allowed to leave they spontaneously renew an interest which had been dormant for a time.

On the basis of this review, which is not yet completed, we can also better identify the "hard" cases and those where failure to receive permission for the family to be reunited may be due to bureaucratic sloppiness—not always necessarily on the Bulgarian side—and not due to any real political obstacle. In fact, we have made quite a bit of progress during the last year in obtaining Bulgarian permission for family members to visit or join permanently their relatives in the U.S. In the last month, there were four more such positive dispositions. It is my guess that by the time of the Belgrade conference over three-quarters of the "real" cases will have been favorably disposed of. When it comes to the residue of hard cases, a political decision will have to be made in each instance on how much pressure should be applied. I proceed from the assumption that we have only a limited amount of influence on the situation and that that influence must be judiciously apportioned where it will do the most good to the most deserving cases.

One tragic case, which isn't really a clear-cut divided family case but all the more poignant, came to our attention the week before last when two Czech children came into the embassy and said they had telephoned their parents in America from Burgas (a Bulgarian city on the Black Sea), and their parents had told them to come in and see us and they would then give them instructions on how to get to America. It turned out that both of the kids had one parent in Czechoslovakia and one parent in America. It also turned out that they had passports—they seem to have joined a group of tourists that brought them to Bulgaria—which were strictly valid only for travel in Communist countries of the Warsaw Pact (which means that they were not valid for traveling to Yugoslavia, which is not a member of the pact and from where they might possibly have managed to go to the West). It also turned out that the kids had gone to the Czechoslovak Embassy here in Sofia and had requested that their passports be amended to authorize travel to Yugoslavia and had been told that this could not be done. We expressed strong doubt that the Bulgarian border control authorities would let them travel to Yugoslavia on their unamended passports. We decided to telegraph Washington instead of putting in a call directly to the two parents in America, and presumably Washington explained the situation to them.

The next day the kids came in to see our consular officer and our press and cultural officer (the latter, as it happens, speaks Slovak and thus acted as interpreter) and reported that they had been accosted on the street by a man who told them that he could help them get to Yugoslavia. The kids were delighted. The man then asked them for their passports, which they gave him. He put the passports in his pocket and told them to come to the Czech Embassy where they would get all the assistance they needed. And of course when they came to the Czech Embassy they were told not to be foolish and that they were going home to Czechoslovakia and would be put on a plane the next morning and that meanwhile the embassy was holding their passports. The kids did make a telephone call from our embassy to their respective parents in America, who told them to do exactly what the Czech authorities asked them to do and that they should keep their heads down and wait for things to change and perhaps sometime in the future they would yet be able to come to America.

—0—

February 8. I'm so disappointed that an excellent idea of President Carter has gone wrong, that I could weep. And while I don't want to burden this diary too much with "in house" concerns of the Foreign Service, it is perhaps natural that the diary of an American ambassador should display concern over the caliber of people appointed to ambassadorships. It has long been a scandal that so many American ambassadorships have been awarded as political payoffs, and not only a scandal but also a danger to the republic—for our embassies are in a way the first line of defense of our country, a kind of distant early warning network. They are also a place where trouble can be headed off by judicious work, by the application of knowledge, tact, and experience, by understanding for American and foreign attitudes, a special empathy for the foreign environment, and a knack for dealing with a multiplicity of problems that do not occur in the everyday experience of other Americans, however meritorious they may be.

When he was campaigning for the presidency, Governor Carter promised to put an end to the practice of appointing unqualified individuals as ambassadors for political reasons. He said such appointments would in future be based strictly on merit. Careful readers of my entry on this report will have noted that I was not yet convinced that he really had thought through the implications of what he had said, for there was still the possibility that "qualified" non-professionals might be appointed on the basis of "merit" of a kind that was not defined; and who was to determine whether a prospective ambassadorial nominee was qualified for the job? I am quite sure that we have put the days behind us when Mr. Maxwell Gluck, a nominee to the post of ambassador to Ceylon, was unable to recall the name of the prime minister of that country (and when Senator Fulbright, either in an effort to be helpful or to get the man still deeper in trouble, asked him to name the Prime Minister of India, the hapless Gluck exclaimed that he did remember it but wasn't able to pronounce it [Nehru] properly). Surely the President will not and cannot appoint *totally* unqualified persons to embassies in light of what he has said.

Then the news came that he intended to appoint an advisory committee on ambassadorial appointments and that he had obtained the willingness of Governor Averell Harriman, former Secretary of State Dean Rusk, and Governor William Scranton to serve on it. More nominations were to come. Harriman, Rusk and Scranton, while not career professionals, know the business, two of them as former ambassadors, and two of them from inside the State Department (Harriman having served in both capacities repeatedly). But today the full list of the twenty-person advisory committee has come out—and it does not contain the name of a single former career diplomat! The committee will be headed by Governor Reuben Askew of Florida. The first few members—the rest are mostly of the same kind—are Anne Clark Martindell, State Senator from New Jersey; Joan Masuck, Unitarian Universal Association Planning Committee, Omaha, Nebraska; Chris Gitlin, Cleveland Council on Human Relations; Nancy Flaherty, Assistant for Special Projects for Pittsburgh History and Landmark

Foundation; and Mary Jean Patterson, Director, Washington Office of the United Presbyterian Church.

What do such people know about diplomacy? How are they going to determine the capacity of a particular nominee to handle very difficult and delicate subjects in a totally alien environment under circumstances that they cannot perhaps even imagine? Why weren't at least a few retired professional Foreign Service officers included on the list? Why can this group be expected to make sophisticated judgments on specialties totally beyond the competence of most of its members? If a committee with such mixed credentials had been appointed to pass on the nominations of generals or admirals or space administration scientists or top disarmament or public health officials, it would have been laughed —or booed—off the stage. The nominees are no doubt all honorable men and women, but being honorable and well-intentioned is not sufficient to make judgments on matters requiring at least prolonged exposure to actual problems of foreign affairs.

Fortunately there are a few members who do bring some experience to the job, in addition to Harriman, Rusk, and Scranton. There is Barbara White, President of Mills College, California, who was a career officer in the U.S. Information Agency and served briefly with ambassadorial rank at the United Nations; there is Professor Stanley Hoffman of Harvard University whose field is foreign affairs; and Professor John Hope Franklin, University of Chicago, who has had some exposure to our problems. But these few qualified people are heavily outnumbered by television producers, lawyers, officials of eleemosynary institutions, and representatives of various ethnic and special interest groups including the redoubtable Leonard Woodcock of the United Auto Workers and Vilma Martinez of the Mexican-American Legal Defense Fund. It is not beyond the bounds of imagination that some log-rolling may take place in a "smoke-filled room."

You can say that the composition of the advisory committee will assure that future nominees for ambassadorial posts will be broadly representative of the country and its multi-faceted interests, ethnic and social groups; but if you say that, you assume that having a broadly representative list of ambassadors also means that you will have the best qualified persons at the right places. No other country in the world, except perhaps Uganda, is placing such handicaps on the quality of its own representation abroad. I am not saying that the only good ambassadors are career people, because I have known too many non-career ambassadors who have been first-rate; but how is a committee with the composition of the one just announced going to be able to identify first-rate non-career ambassadors (or even identify first-rate professionals) from the lists and files submitted to them? Most of them lack the qualifications to make a fair and informed judgment. And although this may not be an absolute requirement, are there any Republicans on the committee? (If Dean Rusk, why not also William Rogers?)

In a deeper sense, of course, we have here the issue of populism against "elitism." I understand the popular demand that our government and its representatives, including those in our diplomatic service, should reflect as much as possible the qualities, the goodness, the shrewdness, the humanitarianism—and the varied interests—of our fine American people. That may sound good but will not get you the best atomic scientist or the best astronaut or the best plant geneticist. Specialist work requires specialized talents, and if you want to get the best—and we cannot afford to get less than the best—then you cannot at the same time erect a bar to selection for excellence; and selection for excellence invariably means that terrible word "elitism." When Carter said, "Why not the best?" he cannot have meant that the best are to be selected by a committee such as he has just appointed. And yet—perhaps that was exactly what he meant. . . We do not know. We will find out.

—0—

A military note: Bulgaria has five combat-ready motorized rifle divisions, and five combat-ready tank brigades which are the equivalent of two armored divisions, for a total of seven combat-ready divisions. The United States has sixteen combat-ready divisions.

According to our Army Attaché, the Bulgarian forces would fight just about as well as the Russians, provided they are deployed against Western forces. How they would fight against, say, the Yugoslavs is a matter of conjecture. My guess is they would fight badly.

But then, much would depend on whether they took part in a winning short war, or in a protracted uncertain one. Any Western psychological warfare expert would be delighted to have the task of inducing East German, Polish, Czech or Hungarian troops to defect or desert.

With the Bulgarians, the task would be a lot more difficult. They would regard the Russians as their traditional comrades in arms, and would find it very difficult to think in terms of giving up to Western opponents—or, for that matter, to any of their Communist neighbors.

Bulgaria has actual or potential issues, or a history of considerable unpleasantness, with every single one of its neighbors. In case of war the Bulgarian army would probably fight with the greatest enthusiasm against the Turks, who are the hereditary enemy.

34

Some dissent rears its head in Bulgaria. An anonymous letter to our Embassy. More black Bulgarian humor. Yet another inning in the complex case of the two "abandoned" Bulgarian children. Some concluding thoughts on Eastern Europe.

February 14. Well, we have the first documented case of recent suppression of dissent in Bulgaria, paralleling what is happening in Czechoslovakia but of a much lower order of magnitude. In fact, the case serves to document the difference between Bulgaria, where the authorities can easily silence such dissent, and countries with an intelligentsia that has a lower boiling point and a tradition of speaking out. A friendly embassy—it is impossible to keep all news away from embassies—came into possession of a report that "something had happened" at the newspaper *Narodna Mladezh* after publication of an article in its January 20 issue. Read the article, the friendly embassy was told by an anonymous informant, and then see what happened to the editorial staff of the paper.

From that point onward it wasn't difficult to piece together what had happened. We first got the article, which was right in our own embassy—our Bulgarian translator, who is no fool, wasn't going to volunteer to translate it until he was asked, but he knew all about it when we got around to asking him. The article, featuring a dialogue between the poet Radoy Ralin and the cartoonist Boris Dimovski, took off from the orthodox theme of attacking "consumerism" among the country's youth, but went on from there to criticize "consumerism" in high places which was furnishing a bad example to the country's youth; and from there went on to speak of the worst kind of "consumerism," namely the *consumption of people.*

Nothing, it seems, was sacred to the pair, and especially to Ralin who has a record of speaking unpopular truths for which he apparently has been disciplined before. He criticized the system of

248

higher education in Bulgaria which was producing "learned fools" because of its narrow focus on producing experts and technicians rather than educated and cultured citizens. Nowhere in contemporary education in Bulgaria, said Radin and Dimovski, is there any fostering of creativity or imagination; indeed, nowhere is there any recognition that such qualities exist and are important.

Having gone this far, the article then concluded with a fusillade which most literate Bulgarians must have understood as directed against the inner sanctum of the BCP, particularly its Politburo: Why, asked the authors, in the wake of the July Plenum of the Central Committee, has no important figure come forward and said, "Comrades, in the interest of a most just division of wages throughout society, in the interest of streamlining government, of improving quality and efficiency, I am going to give up my second or third or fourth title and position, and just concentrate on doing one job well and drawing one salary"?

Bulgarian sources told us that strenuous efforts were made to recall all copies of the offending issue. (*Narodna Mladezh* is the official organ of the Dimitrov Communist Youth Union, which is the Bulgarian equivalent of the Soviet Union's youth organization, the Komsomol.) A look at the 1977 directory of government positions, which has just come out, discloses that there is an "amendment sheet" which indicates that the editor of *Narodna Mladezh*, Gencho Arabadzhiev, was dismissed from his position sometime between the printing of the directory (apparently in late 1976) and its issuance earlier this month. Radoy Ralin, who is about 52, reportedly was already once before expelled from the BCP, forbidden to publish, and placed under house arrest in Northern Bulgaria. He probably has been consigned there again— if he is lucky.

There are no resident foreign journalists in Sofia, and so it took a few days before this item, and other news about alleged dissidence in Bulgaria, made its first appearance in the newspaper *Die Presse* in Vienna. They had the story about the Ralin-Dimovski episode wrong, but they also had something that was news to us—that some forty Bulgarians had been interrogated in January after a translation of Charter 77 had begun to circulate here, and that fourteen of them had been arrested and were being held by the authorities. This took us a little longer to run down, and as of February 17 it does not appear that any of those interrogated were actually placed in detention. It probably isn't necessary: the interrogations suffice to discourage further dissident activity.

Exile organizations outside of Bulgaria have used the report about the detained intellectuals as a "peg" on which to hang their claims of widespread repression and large numbers of political prisoners in Bulgaria. For instance, the leader of the Bulgarian Social Democratic Party in exile declared in Vienna that there are 28,000 people in prison or in concentration camps (one other report includes, not implausibly, psychiatric clinics) in Bulgaria. An estimate of the true number of political prisoners is of course very difficult for any foreign embassy to come by; but I am inclined to give greater credence to a recent BBC report which read as follows:

"According to unconfirmed estimates from former prisoners in Bulgaria, there were in 1975 something like one thousand political prisoners in the country, including about 500 classed by the authorities as 'Maoists,' which could mean various kinds of supporters of the Trotskyist or anarchist 'New Left'. If this figure is approximately correct it would mean that, compared to its population, Bulgaria has more political prisoners than the Soviet Union."

There is no doubt that the Soviet Union regards Bulgaria as a model of the relationship that it would like to have with the other Eastern European countries and of the internal situation that it would like to see prevailing there. It is, in a sense, an early version of the shape of things to come if the Soviet Union can have its way for a generation or two in the rest of Eastern Europe. Therefore it is well worthwhile to study how the government here deals with dissent before it has a chance to snowball, before any real cohesion can grow up among potential and actual dissidents, and how it tries to motivate the people and to deal with their discontents. Most recently it was announced that the government has set up a special unit to study public opinion, as part of its campaign to encourage criticism of shortcomings of the economy and other aspects of contemporary life.

But how does one take the pulse of public opinion in a country where people know the penalties for speaking their mind to strangers as well as, sometimes, even to their friends? This is an age-old problem of all police states, and it is partly solved by police agents posing as members of the populace and cocking a sharp ear for what is being said around them. But one way for the government to learn what is going on among the younger members of the intelligentsia is surely for it to pick up comment on the *Narodna Mladezh* affair. In our own circle of acquaintances we have found very few people willing to talk about it; but there is no doubt that among wide circles of the younger intelligentsia the lesson has sunk in—that criticism is fine if it doesn't "go too far," if it doesn't involve the system itself, and above all if it doesn't involve the ruling class.

—0—

February 16. What I predicted has happened during the Warnke nomination hearings—he has set aside and disavowed his earlier pronouncements on unilateral disarmament. And a good thing, too. *Time* magazine has featured an interview with him in which he says that in the SALT negotiations he would seek to "reduce the nuclear armaments on both sides in a fashion which preserves stability rather than adding any element of instability. It requires that you do not allow a situation to develop in which the Soviets acquire any sort of superiority over us." In the Senate Foreign Relations Committee hearings he said that he did not have "any preconceived positions with respect to the arms control field." Confronted with what he had written on various occasions, he said: "I reject any concept of unilateral disarmament on the part of the United States," and in answer to another question: "I don't think it is sufficient for the United States merely to have the capacity to respond after a Soviet first strike and kill some substantial number of Soviet citizens, because I think you have to look at deterrence from the standpoint both of military capacity and also from the standpoint of perceptions."

I have a letter from a colleague in Washington which speculates that the Carter Administration is pushing the issue of human rights in order to demonstrate its anti-Communist credentials to people on its right flank, for the purpose of neutralizing the attacks from that flank on its disarmament policies. In this view the President's letter to Sakharov and the various statements made by Vance and others about the violation of human rights in the Soviet Union are designed to give the Administration more running room with respect to SALT, and of course the nomination of Warnke cannot be seen as evidence of "softness" toward the Russians as long as a drumfire is kept up gainst them on the human rights front. The only trouble is that looking out for the welfare and safety of Sakharov and Ginsberg and Orlov is a matter totally incommensurable with looking out for the continued existence of the United States. I refuse to be pessimistic about SALT. It seems that the Warnke after the confirmation hearings is a different man than the Warnke before; and in any case during the debate the Senate will have learned more about the realities of arms control.

—0—

Excerpts from letters that come to us by various means—never through the mails, which presumably are screened by the authorities.

"Peace?" writes one of the letter-writers, "If any country conquered half of Europe it would certainly want peace thereafter. Thus one can take an oath that Russia sincerely wants peace now, in order to maintain the situation. As far as the Universal Declaration of Human Rights is concerned, here in Bulgaria we know only that such a document exists, we know nothing about its contents. We have heard of Charter 77, but know little about its contents.

"I do not wish to live here any longer. I would flee, if I could follow my emotions . . . to escape from this enslaved country. If you will not hear my plea, why are you going to Belgrade? In order to guarantee Russia's feudal rights here? In order to allow them to continue to torment us freely? To leave them with their conquests undisturbed, now and for all time? I protest against such discussions with Russia. They are vile compromises against man's basic freedoms."

I record this letter in my diary not because I agree with its contents—the Belgrade conference does not dignify the Soviet regime any more than any of the other conferences in which we negotiate with it, and it certainly doesn't have the purpose of "guaranteeing Russia's feudal rights here." The letter was anonymous. It is impossible to know whether its anti-Russian tenor is at all reflective of any significant stratum of the population here. My guess is that it is not.

—0—

A joke, a rather bad one, but one is grateful for any note of levity here. Impossible to tell whether this joke really circulates in Bulgaria or is just a version of jokes that circulate in other Eastern European countries.

The scene is the Paris automobile show. Two Bulgarians find themselves standing in front of the General Motors exhibit.

"Ah," says one of them, admiring a Cadillac, "what a wonderful car, how solid, how powerful, how elegant."

"Well," says the other Bulgarian, "the Russian Chaika isn't bad either."

Next they encounter each other again in front of the Mercedes stand, and the first Bulgarian admires the sleek lines of the Model 280 SL.

"What an elegant sports car, and so powerful, too."

"Well, the Russian Moskvitch isn't any less elegant," ventured the second Bulgarian.

And so it goes. The first Bulgarian admires the new Peugeot, and the second Bulgarian, while agreeing that it is a fine car, points out that the Russian Zhiguli is really just as good. Finally, in exasperation, the first Bulgarian turns on the second:

"My God, man, don't you know anything about cars?"

"Well, yes, I do," replies the other, "but you see, I don't know much about *you*."

—0—

February 17. I've had another inning in the long-running battle over "divided families" with Stoyan Zhelenski, the head of the Consular Relations Department of the Foreign Ministry. Actually, the Bulgarian record is quite good, and Mr. Zhelenski claimed that his government had either approved the exit, or didn't oppose it, in a total of 88 out of 98 cases. What struck me during our conversation was the gap between our two cultures, when he commented on the case of the Bulgarian in Washington who is demonstrating in front of the State Department.

Those demonstrations, he said, were trying to blacken Bulgaria's image in the world, they were (therefore) a violation of the Final Act of Helsinki, they were in violation of international law, and should not be tolerated by the U.S. authorities. When I explained to him that the Bulgarian in question had a perfect right under our law to demonstrate in front of the State Department, Zhelenski expressed disbelief.

His disbelief seemed to deepen when I told him that at the very moment when we were talking, there were probably people in front of our White House demonstrating against something the President had done or was thought to have done or to be planning. I said our police had authority to keep demonstrators a certain distance from a foreign embassy, but under our Constitution the government has no right to prohibit someone from protesting publicly against it.

The disbelief of Mr. Zhelenski reminded me of another instance, when I had called on Ambassador Lyuben Avramov, the head of the fourth department of the Foreign Ministry, to discuss the issue of Puerto Rico in the United Nations. When I told him that the people of Puerto Rico were free to chose independence any time they wish to do so, but that in every election they had voted against independence, by a large majority, there came from him a little involuntary gasp of disbelief, as if he were saying to me "Come now, Mr. Ambassador, we know how free elections are conducted, and don't try to kid me that the Puerto Ricans don't want to be independent. Who, given a chance, wouldn't want to be independent?" (He did not say this in so many words, because he is a diplomat, but that little involuntary gasp of disbelief spoke volumes.)

When Mr. Zhelenski noted that demonstrations against the American Embassy here could take place at any time if it weren't for the vigilance of the Bulgarian authorities (presumably said to encourage American authorities to show similar "vigilance" in Washington), I had to explain to him that while people are free to demonstrate in the United States, the same is not true in Bulgaria so that if a demonstration were to occur in front of our embassy we would have to hold the Bulgarian government responsible. We again went over the case of the Bulgarian children whose parents wanted them to come to the United States, and I believe we made a certain amount of progress, though such progress must be measured in fractions of inches.

Four days later I learned that on the same day the Deputy Secretary of State had called in the Bulgarian Ambassador and made representations in the same matter—but because the State Department had not thought of coordinating that demarche with this embassy he had some of his facts wrong and was corrected by the Bulgarian Ambassador, which isn't very helpful in such situations. At any rate the Bulgarians are in no doubt that we aren't going to let go of this matter, although it is clear to me that now the next step must be to ascertain what the wishes of the two little girls really are. Will this be possible if they are intimidated into saying that they do not wish to go? We shall have to find a way to ascertain their true desires, and in my opinion that is not impossible if it is done the right way.

In the light of this latest review, and of the internal review that we had made in the embassy, we shall now be able to send to Washington a better estimate of the extent of Bulgarian compliance with the Final Act of Helsinki in the matter of family reunifications. The record, despite the blow-up over two evidently political cases, is better than I had estimated up to now—and than the Deputy Secretary of State had estimated in his conversation with the Bulgarian Ambassador. It is clear that the Bulgarians are making a major effort to pull up their socks prior to the across-the-board review of performance which will take place at Belgrade.

—0—

The 215 days that I had given myself to record the trials and tribulations, the successes and failures, the joys and disappointments, and the passing thoughts and broader judgments of an ambassador in Sofia during this period of transition, are now over; and since there was no logical point for me to begin and I arbitrarily set myself this period for my informal record, it is time to close.

I have already noted why I think the view from here in Bulgaria to be significant. Not because the country is important but because it furnishes a front-line seat from which to observe the Soviet Union and the other Eastern European countries, and perhaps the "shape of things to come" in Eastern Europe if the Russians continue to occupy and control it. I have little doubt that they will indeed continue to control this part of the European continent in the foreseeable future.

That we have an interest in what is going on in those countries, quite aside from the way their official actions have an impact on the rest of Europe and on other parts of the world, is being demonstrated right now by President Carter's declarations regarding the human rights situation in the Soviet Union and Czechoslovakia. Here I would like to record more clearly what I have already mentioned in passing, that I believe the expression of that interest to be entirely legitimate. However, I also believe it to be essentially futile.

The reason why we are not going to be able to change the human rights situation in the Soviet Union or elsewhere in Eastern Europe is, in my opinion, that the granting of extensive human rights to the people of those countries would result in the collapse of their Communist system of government; and the existence of that system in the Eastern European countries is a matter of vital national security concern to the Soviet Union. Stalin expressed this at Potsdam in 1945 when Secretary of State Byrnes rather sanctimoniously declared that "The United States sincerely desires Russia to have friendly countries on her borders, but we believe they should seek the friendship of the people rather than of any particular government" and went on to plead for free elections in those countries.

"A freely elected government in any of those countries," Stalin replied according to Professor Philip E. Mosely, "would be anti-Soviet, and that we cannot allow." It might not have been true then, and it may not be true even today in Bulgaria, but it was a self-fulfilling prophecy in the rest of Eastern Europe. If the lids are taken off now, the cauldrons could too easily boil over. But with the lids tightly clamped on, the steam can be contained by judiciously moderating the temperature. We would have an interest in seeing the lids come off, but since that isn't going to happen we have no interest in fiddling with the temperature to make it go up;

for as long as those lids are tightly clamped on, an explosion would bring untold suffering to millions.

Therefore, while I am hopeful about détente, while I support serious and energetic but hard-nosed arms control negotiations, and while I am delighted that our President is standing up for human rights, I do not look for fundamental changes in Eastern Europe during the lifetime of any of the readers of this journal, and recommend to them a skeptical attitude toward all those who promise to bring about such fundamental changes, well-intentioned though some of them may be. Does this make me an advocate of spheres of influence, of leaving this part of the world alone, of recognizing the regimes as permanent and legitimate and perhaps even in our interest?

Absolutely not. I think there is ample reason to abhor the system of government in these Eastern European countries, and it is a pity that more young people from my own country cannot come here and see what Communism really looks like in practice. One can be for peace and what the Russians call "co-existence between different social systems" as a matter of realistic appreciation of its necessity, without closing one's eyes to the reality of the ugliness of those systems and of the danger that they might expand to engulf the rest of the world.

But recognition that the status quo is the best we can hope for doesn't mean that we think it ethical and right. Our own values are not involved when we have to make a hard judgment of what is the most reasonable way to assure our security. My heart goes out to the people who live in this part of the world, but my mind tells me that we cannot affect their fate, even though we should continue to let them know about our own beliefs, about our own system, and about our hopes for a better world sometime in the future when all people everywhere should be able to enjoy their essential dignity as human beings.

And so concludes my diary, two hundred fifteen days after it began, as I had promised.

35

Try to stop me from making still more comments on ambassadorial nominations! A poignant case, in microcosm, of how kindness goes unacknowledged despite one's best intentions. And some absolutely final observations on a career in diplomacy and what it means, in retrospect, to have been an ambassador.

Postscript, May 3, 1977. It is now more than two months since I finished my "215 Days," and for quite a time the urge to keep on writing continued, somewhat like the phantom pain or itch in an amputated limb. One reason why I am adding this postscript is that something happened to the second part of the manuscript which also illustrates, in a way, the life of an American ambassador to such an out-of-the-way country. The simple fact is that the second part of the typescript, which I had sent in early March to my friend Mrs. Rhoda Weyr in New York, got lost in the mails. (Of course, I didn't use the Bulgarian mails but entrusted the envelope to someone who had gone to Athens in March.)

In the meantime I showed the copy that I have here to three people. One of them immediately exclaimed that I could no longer say, as I did in the introduction, that "nothing earthshaking" is apt to happen here in Sofia, since we experienced a rather strong earthquake at the time of the much more damaging tremors in Romania. Well, that is a minor matter. Nobody was injured in Sofia. Our residence shook pretty badly, and our chandeliers swung wildly, but there was no damage.

(Even the earthquake had a political aftermath for us in Bulgaria. After we had—*at Bulgarian request*—provided the government here with scientific data from our earthquake research center which suggested that another severe quake might occur in the same general area within weeks or months of the first one, the Bulgarian press agency carried a vitriolic piece charging the U.S. with trying to "foment panic among the Bulgarian and Rumanian

258

populations" with such reports, which were characterized as a "flagrant, inhumane provocation . . . directed against the public order of socialist countries." It was of course unfortunate that our warning had been made public before the scientific information had been handed in officially. But I felt I had to lodge a protest against the slanderous accusation—which probably was due to the well-known bureaucratic phenomenon of the right hand not being aware of what the left hand had been doing.)

A more important observation on the manuscript was made by my friend George von Peterffy who said that while *he* found the reading pretty interesting, he was quite certain that the general public would find little of interest in it. (No doubt, he is right.) He urged me to write more about how an American embassy helps American business, perhaps with the idea that after my retirement the documentation of such activities would help to raise my stock if I try to make some connection with an American business firm. But his suggestion would make the book even less interesting to the general reading public.

He also commented that I have devoted too much space to my concerns about particular appointments of the new Administration, and he thought those concerns would be regarded as "parochial." Well, perhaps they are, but they also involve something pretty important to our country. So rather than take out those comments, I would like to add more of them on how things have actually worked out in practice after the misgivings that I voiced in January and February. Alas, I hadn't been wrong in worrying whether the new Administration really meant what it had said about future diplomatic appointments being made strictly on the basis of merit.

On November 9, 1976 President-elect Jimmy Carter had said in the course of a press interview: "Second, I plan to appoint diplomatic officials who have superb credentials, strictly on the basis of merit, not reward people for political favors. And that's a commitment that I've made on my word of honor. I'm not going to break it."

And speaking to Cyrus Sulzberger of the *New York Times*, he had said (in a column that appeared in the *International Herald Tribune* on August 23, 1976): "The Secretary of State must be the President's number one adviser on foreign policy. I would like to help him out by improving the quality of our major diplomatic appointments. I want these to depend firmly on merit. I am not under obligation to anyone, and I don't believe people should be paid off for helping to elect a president by getting embassies."

Now let us look at the record. To Australia, which had protested once before that it wanted professional diplomats to represent the United States and not unqualified political appointees, he appointed Mr. Philip H. Alston, Jr., a lawyer from Atlanta, Georgia. To Belgium he appointed Anne Cox Chambers, chairman of Atlanta Newspapers and director of the Cox Broadcasting Corporation. To Mexico he appointed Governor Patrick J. Lucey of Wisconsin. The press has reported that he intends to nominate a former governor of South Carolina to be ambassador to Saudi Arabia, and that to Austria he will nominate Mr. Milton Wolf, described only as a prominent Democratic Party fund-raiser from Cleveland, Ohio. The only thing that seems to have held up some of these appointments is the need for security clearances before they are made public.

Now, I am not, contrary to appearances, against well-selected non-professionals in diplomatic assignments. I've seen some that were excellent, and have served under some that were superb, but they all had backgrounds relevant to their new duties. It is not churlish to suggest that our ambassador to Mexico should speak fluent Spanish and know a lot about our relations with Latin America, or that our relations with Saudi Arabia are sufficiently important that it would make sense to send there someone who speaks Arabic, who knows the Middle East, and who knows something about the intricacies of oil diplomacy. The President has also made some less controversial non-career appointments, such as that of Robert F. Goheen, president emeritus of Princeton University, who knows India intimately, as ambassador to that country. That's fine, but a good appointment doesn't reduce the odor of a bad one.

I am even suspicious about some of the career appointments that came out in the first batch, which presumably had been the result of deliberations of the newly appointed advisory board (of which Mrs. Chambers had been a member, as well as Leonard Woodcock, whom the President reportedly plans to send to Peking). Two of those career officers, extraordinarily able men, are W. Tapley

Bennett who goes to NATO and William H. Sullivan to Iran. Could it be a coincidence that Bennett, like Mr. Alston and Mrs. Chambers, hails from Georgia? And could it be a coincidence that Sullivan, who doesn't hail from Georgia, has long been a protégé of Governor Harriman, who is a member of the advisory board? And the only assignment to Africa so far goes to Mr. Lemelle of the Ford Foundation, who has been connected with its Africa program—but why does he have to go to Nairobi, the only *agreeable* post in tropical Africa, instead of one of the 21 hardship posts on that continent?

If diplomatic assignments are to be strictly on the basis of merit, and if this is a principle to which the President has pledged himself on his word of honor, then they should not be made on any other basis. It isn't good for the country, it isn't good for the President, and it isn't good for those in the Foreign Service who have devoted a lifetime to the pursuit of diplomacy as a profession and who have acquired knowledge and experience and skills which are precious to the country and who, in every such case, are set aside in favor of less qualified people who are less useful to the country in those positions, though perhaps more useful to the President from the point of view of internal politics.

I have it on good authority that Budapest is going to go to a political appointee who knows nothing about Eastern Europe, but it must be said in his favor that he is not inexperienced, he has held several diplomatic assignments before. The man who should have gone to Budapest, and who would have gone there but for this political appointment, is a highly skilled professional who has followed our relations with Hungary and other Eastern European countries for decades. All right, after some rumors that Sargent Shriver might be sent to Moscow, the President has decided to leave Malcolm Toon, a Soviet specialist, at his post. Toon was left dangling for two months while the administration was considering sending Shriver in his place—Shriver who doesn't know one percent of what Toon knows about the Soviet Union.

Or take Senator Mike Mansfield who is going to Tokyo. No one can say that he doesn't know something about the Far East, or that he lacks any qualifications for the post of ambassador. He is a distinguished retired Senator. But I happen to know Marshall Green, a career diplomat who has served with distinction in Tokyo,

Seoul, Djakarta and Canberra, who speaks Japanese, has been intimately involved with our diplomacy toward Japan since the days of Ambassador Grew before World War II, and is generally regarded as the best qualified man in America to represent our country in Tokyo. My heart goes out to him. He will soon reach mandatory retirement age, while Senator (now Ambassador) Mansfield, who at 74 is entitled to an honorable retirement, adds Tokyo to his already distinguished record.

Well, at my age of 60 I am also entitled to an honorable retirement and this was made clear to me in a flurry of telegrams and telephone calls on February 28, just before the new raise in retirement pay went into effect. I had told the Department that I wasn't eager to quit in a hurry just for the sake of 5.4% more in retirement pay, and had received in reply a tactfully worded telegram asking if I had considered the full extent of the financial advantage that I would forego. It is now May, and I fully expect to receive the usual telegram telling me to request *agrément* for my successor and to get the hell out of this post to make room for him as soon as possible; and I on my part have told Washington that even if this doesn't happen I intend to leave here no later than August. We aren't disappointed, we aren't disgruntled, we have had a good career and an interesting life in the public service, so my remarks about diplomatic appointments are neither self-seeking nor inspired by any disappointment of my own aspirations.

I once remarked to a visiting friend that the President certainly wouldn't appoint admirals and generals to command carrier task forces or army corps the way he is appointing ambassadors—a few good, experienced professionals here and there and the rest political friends—but Elisabeth pointed out that I really cannot compare my own "command" in Sofia with a carrier task force or an army corps. It is more like a minesweeper or a company or battalion in an advanced position. But even minesweepers and companies in advanced positions are better commanded by professionals than by amateurs.

There is nothing important or even very interesting to report about Bulgaria during the intervening period except that we have been battling the divided families battle again; that the expected Bulgarian "preemptive offensive" about the Final Act of Helsinki has begun; that there has been a flurry of excitement in the

Bulgarian press about exile activities (which in my opinion must have just aroused interest in them which didn't exist before); and that we have had our share of frustrations, visitors, petty bureaucratic harassments, debates with Washington about next steps and about administrative matters, preparations for the Plovdiv Fair, argum nts about the reception of some Bulgarian visitors to the U.S., and gaps in our staffing which have made more work for everybody. But I do want to record one little non-event which somehow seemed more poignant precisely because it was little.

One day, about two months ago, there arrived at our embassy a large package addressed to the American Ambassador. The package was delivered by a man who seemed to be Bulgarian. In accordance with standing regulations, it was subjected to certain tests to see that it didn't perhaps contain some explosives. It contained some gifts for me, Bulgarian handicrafts, a bottle of wine—and a lot of writing, which needed to be first scanned by one of our language officers and then either sent to our Bulgarian translators or, if it contained something politically sensitive, for more careful deciphering by an American. As it turned out, the writing was mostly poetry. It also contained some vague political sentiments having to do with peace and brotherhood and friendliness toward the United States. Since the address of the sender appeared only on the wrapping of the package, we laid that wrapping aside on top of an empty desk while the material was being evaluated. It was my intention, if it could be done without harming the writer of those lines, to acknowledge his gift and to thank him for the expression of his (innocuous) friendly sentiments.

The next morning the wrapping of the parcel was gone. The char force of elderly Bulgarian ladies who come to clean up our offices every morning under the supervision of a stern-faced Marine, had just taken it off the empty desk and put it with the garbage; and by the time we noticed that it was missing it had left the building on a Bulgarian garbage truck. Asked why he had allowed this to happen, the Marine said he thought the torn wrapping paper had served its purpose and could be thrown away. (The Marines were instructed that henceforth "nothing, but absolutely nothing"— except the ashes from the ashtrays—is to be removed from the top of any desk.) So that nice man from somewhere out in the provinces who had gone to all that trouble to let us know about his feelings for peace and for the United States will never learn that I had received his gifts and appreciated his writing to us. I suppose every organization has foul-ups of this sort, but this one seemed to me more heartbreakingly irretrievable than the usual run of such occurrences. Perhaps I'm getting too sentimental.

What will I do next? I don't know. John Kenneth Galbraith, in one of his characteristically puckish articles (this one in *Esquire* some years ago), has written: "An American ambassador to a country of more than marginal consequence is accorded considerable deference by most people, including himself, until the day he retires. Then he disappears into a Stygian and often well-merited darkness; unless he lends his name to some offshore fund of a peculiarly fraudulent sort he will never be heard of until his obituary, which will be brief." I seem to qualify for that kind of future, except that the country of my assignment was not of "*more* than marginal consequence." It is, or was by the time this is read, of strictly marginal consequence to the United States.

The third person who read the manuscript remarked that he thought something was missing at the end, namely an assessment of what a lifetime in the diplomatic career has meant to me. That would seem to call for a catalogue of accomplishments—most of them, of course, in other places of assignment—which would embarrass me. I have had the privilege of being at much more exciting posts than Sofia at much more exciting times, but not as ambassador—in Vienna during the Russian occupation, when I was able to help in the fashioning of the American policy that eventually resulted in removal of all foreign occupation troops; in Paris, where I was associated in a very small way with the birth of European integration; in Phnom Penh where I learned, among other things, that "good judgment comes from experience, and experience comes from bad judgment"; in Tokyo where I was privileged to help in the negotiation of a new and mutually beneficial security treaty; in African affairs in Washington at a time when the African nations burst upon the world scene; in Tehran where I was able to observe (and, in a small way, affect) the interaction of American and Russian power and influence in a manner that eventually resulted in a surprisingly stable equilibrium; in Saigon where my most useful contribution was in preventing some awful things from being done; and in Washington, working on the United Nations, where I helped to fight useful rearguard actions as we learned to accomodate ourselves to no longer having our way; and now in Bulgaria.

Perhaps I will be forgiven if I end with a bit of plagiarism from a book published in 1938 by an Italian diplomat, Daniele Varè, who was able to describe much better than I possibly could what it means to be an ambassador.

"It is usual to envy diplomats," wrote Varè, "because they travel about the world and meet 'the best people' in foreign lands. Admitting this to be an advantage, it has to be paid for, like everything else. Not all posts abroad are pleasant and healthy, nor are all governments and colleagues agreeable to deal with. The circles in which we move are not always brilliant or smart.

"When a diplomat comes home, he finds that he is out of touch with his own country. His friends have got used to doing without him. The women he might have loved (and who might have loved him) have found other husbands and lovers.

"The supreme moment of a diplomat's life may come in a closed room, when he is alone, (working at) a telegram, and that moment passes all unbeknown to the world. . . A diplomat's vanity must be satisfied with a passing mundane success; with the first place at table, a private car . . . and the national flag over his coffin, when he dies. . ."

He said it so well, but perhaps Elisabeth has put it somewhat more realistically. "You still believe in serving your country," she said to me the other day, "but you have really been serving a faceless and insensitive bureaucracy. You have never been really free. The satisfactions you derived from serving have been at the expense of many other things. The ideal of service has gone out of fashion. I'm not trying to depreciate the usefulness of what you've done, but now you should put all this behind you. It's something you can't really communicate to other people, least of all when you write about our service in Bulgaria. You yourself have said that while it's the highest post you've held in your thirty-six years of government service, it's also in many ways the least important one. Are you trying to show people what it is like to be an American ambassador in a place that is *unimportant?*"

Yes, yes, yes, I said, that's exactly what I've tried to do.

Index of Personalities

FOI CASE NO. 8102985

SEP 8 1981

Ambassador Martin F. Herz
Director of Studies
Institute for the Study of Diplomacy
School of Foreign Service
Georgetown University
Washington, D.C. 20057

Dear Ambassador Herz:

I refer to your letter of August 10, 1981, submitting to the Department of State the final galley proofs of your forthcoming book "215 Days in the Life of an American Ambassador."

After careful review, we have determined that the Department has no objection to publication on grounds of classification.

Sincerely,

For the Deputy Assistant Secretary for Classification/Declassification

Thomas W. Ainsworth
Director, Mandatory Review
Bureau of Administration